SCENES FROM THE PAST : 50

THE 'BUXTON LINE' - PAF

STOCKPO

DAVENPORT AND HAZEL GROVE

TO

DISLEY, NEW MILLS (NEWTOWN) AND

WHALEY BRIDGE

Davenport station was home ground to Wallace Sutherland. There appears to be very little that happened here that didn't get to his ears, or in his note book, and the train seen here was no exception. The Manchester Exchange to Ashbourne excursion of Sunday 29th May 1960 had been advertised both in the press and the handbills to be found as usual at all the local stations. The organised rambles in association with these trains were extremely popular, generating good business for the railways. As a result, not many weeks went by without there being a similar event. Scheduling of this excursion however managed to exclude Davenport and Hazel Grove, but the omission did not escape Wallace, who promptly wrote to the District Passenger Manager for Manchester (Mr T W Polding). The details of his letter are unknown but the response was positive and so Davenport and Hazel Grove got their Special Excursion to Ashbourne. (Above) Arriving alongside the Up platform on the outward journey with a 10 coach train is Stockport (9B) 'Crab' No **42932** with Stanier Class 4 No **42439** (26F). The excursion was reported to have been crowded. This book is dedicated to the memory and work of Wallace Sutherland and his passion for the 'Buxton Line'. ***J W Sutherland***

GREGORY K FOX

ISBN 1 870119 85 1

PRINTED BY
THE AMADEUS PRESS
CLECKHEATON
WEST YORKSHIRE

PUBLISHED BY
FOXLINE LIMITED
P O BOX 84 BREDBURY
STOCKPORT SK6 3YD

CONTENTS

DEDICATION............................ COVER
FOREWORD............................ 3
HISTORICAL SUMMARY............ 5
EDGELEY JUNCTION TO CHEADLE VILLAGE JUNCTION 13
DAVENPORT JUNCTION........... 25
DAVENPORT GOODS................ 33
WOODSMOOR.......................... 45
HAZEL GROVE......................... 49
NORBURY CROSSING.............. 59
MIDDLEWOOD......................... 62
DISLEY.......................... 78
DISLEY GOODS.............. 85
TURNERS SIDING........... 91
NEW MILLS (NEWTOWN) 92
FURNESS VALE.............. 108
WHALEY BRIDGE........... 113
SHALLCROSS GOODS..... 120
DIESEL MULTIPLE UNITS - THE EARLY YEARS..... 125
DIARY EXTRACTS - 1956 TO 1962.......... 131

Manchester Piccadilly, c. June 1966. Regulars on the Buxton line will remember views such as this with some nostalgia. The crisp well tended bodywork of the diesel sets in attractive dark loco-green livery, still with just less than a decade of service behind them, were the mainstay of services for almost thirty years. The Birmingham Railway Carriage & Wagon units, later designated Class 104 under the British Rail T.O.P.S renumbering system, carried the green livery well, the only changes being the addition, initially, of the 'speed whiskers' which were soon replaced by the half yellow warning panels seen here. Ultimately, the ends were completely transformed by the all-over yellow covering, a identity more familiar with the 'standard' BR blue livery adopted in the late 1960's. The view here is thought to have been taken on a Sunday afternoon, the train possibly being the 14.20 departure for Buxton. It was not scheduled to call at Middlewood Lower, Furness Vale or Dove Holes on the 55 minute journey, a time comparable with the weekday 'off-peak' frequency which missed out Levenshulme North and Heaton Chapel. Surprisingly, the suffixes applied to both Middlewood and Levenshulme stations were being retained despite the fact that Levenshulme 'South' had closed some eight years previously and Middlewood had lost its 'Higher' contemporary in 1960. To the left, on the 'eastern' side of Piccadilly, is one of the 1500V dc 3-car sets - the Driving trailer standard (DTS) vehicle of these sets was also a BRCW vehicle - produced to operate the Manchester to Glossop/Hadfield service. This train is possibly the 2.15pm to Glossop and Hadfield; there was of course still a Sunday service to Sheffield via Woodhead. *Authors collection*

One of the first photographs taken by Wallace Sutherland after arriving from New Zealand was this wintry scene of **Davenport** on 14th February 1953. Fowler 2-6-4T No **42315,** at the head of the 2.25pm Manchester London Road to Buxton train, was to remain a Buxton (9D) engine for another three years, leaving at the time Wallace started to keep his Buxton Line diaries, one page of which is reproduced on page 4. ***J W Sutherland***

FOREWORD - ACKNOWLEDGEMENTS

I am deeply indebted to the Sutherland family, in particular Wallace's wife Tril, son Graham and daughter Cara for entrusting and having the faith in me to produce a work which will hopefully go some way to commemorating a period of the 'Buxton Line' as seen and portrayed through the eyes of Wallace Sutherland. If any one person had a passion and understanding of this particular piece of railway, it was Wallace.

The importance of the records kept by Wallace of the line, particularly between 1956 and 1980, are unique and there can arguably be very few railway lines/services that have been chronicled in such detail by one person. There were few occasions throughout that period that did not include a sighting of something on the line, or a visit to one location or another to describe particular or everyday happenings. As his local station, there can be no doubt that Davenport received the lions share of his attention, with trips to Buxton and the numerous shed visits coming a very close second.

Within those considerable and very comprehensive records - which include the notes (or diaries), handbills, tickets, local and national timetables, press cuttings, etc; - was a not inconsiderable number of black and white photographs, all taken with the skill of a man who new his camera and subject well.

Almost from the beginning of sifting through and analysing the gathered information, it was soon apparent that the records were categorised in two ways, the 'Buxton Line' and the 'non-Buxton Line'. Simply translated, the latter category covered the rest of the world !

The term 'Buxton Line' belongs to Wallace, it has been chosen for the title of this work not out of historical correctness, for as far as the LNWR, LMS, British Railways and the most recent of custodians, Railtrack and Network Rail are concerned, it was and remains the LNW Buxton Branch, to distinguish it from the Buxton Branch of the Midland Railway which ran between Millers Dale and Buxton. Generations of railwaymen and individuals have fondly referred to it as the 'Wessy', again to distinguish the line from its Midland neighbour. The 'Buxton Line' was (and is) a community railway long before the term became popular. Wallace soon found that out as he regularly visited stations, signal boxes, goods yards, engine sheds, etc; meeting with individuals and characters who were completely loyal to 'their' line.

Son Graham, a constant partner on many trips, was occasionally, but politely, told by his father that it would be unwise to accompany him *because dad was going trespassing !* Having had a lineside permit, the thoroughness with which he composed and compiled the range of photographs from virtually every vantage point between Edgeley Junction and Buxton will hopefully show up within the pages of this and any subsequent work.

Broadly speaking, the period covered is that as recorded in both diary and photographic form between 1953 and 1968. I have drawn on other photographers work where appropriate and would like to take the opportunity to thank the following contributors :- Derek Ashworth, Mike Bentley, A H Bryant, H D Bowtell, N Fields, R E Gee, N K Harrop, L Hobdey *courtesy J M Bentley*, Eddie Johnson, R Hughes, D Ibbotson, Norman Jones, E R Morten *courtesy J R Morten,* Trevor Moseley, A Moyes, Graham Neve, R D Pollard, H B Priestley, Stephen Shaw, Harry Townley *courtesy J M Bentley,* C H A Townley, Graham Whitehead.

Although mentioned above, both Mike Bentley and Derek Ashworth, railwaymen with a very close affinity for the line, have helped freely, particularly with their memories, both factual and anecdotal.

A special mention must also be made of the contribution by good friend and fellow Foxline author Norman Jones, late of Warrington. Having finally decided to retire from writing, Norman very kindly offered to word process the contents of Wallace's Buxton Line diaries, having completed a similar task with the Cromford & High Peak diaries of Dr J R Hollick for his own books. The result was an incredible 180 pages (A4) of typescript which would prove to be his final project before becoming ill, passing away after a short illness on 13th March 2003, barely one month before his 85th birthday. He is greatly missed but it is hoped that his contribution to this work will also provide a testament to Norman's immeasurable qualities.

As a consequence of the amount of material available, it became obvious that more than one volume would be required to do justice to the Buxton line. Fortunately, the historical and chronological development of the line, firstly as the Stockport, Disley & Whaley Bridge Railway, made this a practical solution.

Therefore, this first volume provides a summary of the historical development of the line together with an illustrated review of the route between Stockport (Edgeley Junction) and Whaley Bridge. The line also took on something of a pioneering role in 1956 at the onset of British Railways modernisation when it was used to enable different manufacturers of the new diesel multiple units to test their equipment. The final section in the first volume concentrates on the diary extracts during the period 1956-1962, complimented with captioned photographs adjacent to the appropriate entry.

On a personal note, I have gained a great deal of pleasure and satisfaction in compiling and writing much of the text and captions and generally designing the book. It is now twenty-one years since I set out to produce *Railways in and around Stockport*, a book that was the first of three planned. The 'Buxton Line' will be my third and last solo work. My gratitude is also due in no small way to my wife Jacqueline, Catherine and Neil (not forgetting granddaugter Emma) Andrew and Judith. Last but not least the Cardiac teams at both Manchester Royal Infirmary and Stepping Hill (Stockport) Hospital.

To you all, my heartfelt thanks.

Greg Fox
Romiley ***January 2006***

if it still gets some use. [illegible] is still open, I am told - [illegible] still intact. But noted former siding on down side at [illegible], north of station has gone (perhaps months or years ago!)

16-4-65 Good Friday. Went to Hayfield via N. Mills Newtown and Central with [illegible] at Gorton. Noted no changes on Buxton line since last up. One service wagon was in siding adjoining up platform at N. Mills Newtown. The train home, 5.47 from Newtown, was a very crowded 6 car train.

11-5-65 Tuesday. 44867 was on the up parcels, consisting of a bogie parcels van and blue fish van.

26-5-65 Wednesday. 42942 was [illegible] Edgeley on the down parcels. The same evening spoke to Ron. Gee on the platform and he told me the early morning goods to Buxton ("mail") did in fact continue to run daily till cancelled entirely about the beginning of March. This contradicts [illegible]

The Railway and Public Transport User's Association

President: J. B. PRIESTLEY, Esq., M.A., LL.D., D.Litt.

Please reply to:

21, Kingsleigh Road,
Heaton Mersey,
Stockport,
Cheshire.
10th May 1963

Dear Mr. Sutherland,

You recently assisted in collecting signatures for the petition organised to express opposition to the possible closure of the Manchester-Buxton railway line and of Davenport station. You will no doubt be pleased to learn that some 2,090 signatures were collected in all.

The petition has now been delivered to the Town Clerk of Stockport, who has stated that it will be submitted to the appropriate committee of the Council at their next meeting. It is to be hoped that this expression of opinion will achieve its aim, but this is by no means certain, and all those interested will need to continue to press their views as strongly as possible.

Meanwhile the thanks of all are due to you for your great help in gaining support for the petition.

Yours sincerely,

A.C.Bubb
Area Representative

(Left and above) Page extracts from Wallace's diaries and the letter acknowledging his contribution in the campaign to save the Buxton line following the Beeching proposals.

Stockport Edgeley, 20th April 1957. Just under one hundred years before this picture was taken, the finishing touches to the Stockport, Disley and Whaley Bridge Railway were taking place. The 'Buxton line' as it was to become known, was still six years away. From the outset, trains commenced their outward journey from what is now Manchester's Piccadilly station although between Manchester and Stockport, all traffic to and from the city shared an increasingly congested run through the southern suburbs. Stockport Viaduct was still only half of its present width (two running lines) and the station would have to undergo further intermediate enlargements before becoming (in 1890) the four (through) platformed station of recent years. In a scene very different from that of a century before, Stanier 2-cylinder Class 4 2-6-4T No **42594** (9A) stands alongside platform 2 with the ex-12.50pm(SO) London Road to Buxton service.

HISTORICAL SUMMARY BY J W SUTHERLAND

The historical summary commencing below was from notes prepared in 1962 for an article in the Railway Magazine and reproduced with the permission of Graham Sutherland. The contents of the article are as appropriate now as they were then, but were produced at a time when the future of the Buxton line was very much in the balance. Its survival was in no small way due to the efforts, persistance and continual use by individuals, supporting groups such as the High Peak Rail Users (of which Wallace was an active member) and railway enthusiasts such as Wallace himself.

On 30th May 1863, completion of the Buxton Extension from Whaley Bridge resulted in the line from Edgeley Junction (Stockport) becoming known as the Buxton branch of the erstwhile London & North Western Railway. The line (in 1963) seems to have received little attention from railway historians, being perhaps overshadowed in the vicinity by the more glamorous Cromford & High Peak Railway and the Midland main line through the Peak District. The story, nevertheless is not without interest.

There had been several abortive early schemes for railways in the Stockport- Buxton area, perhaps the first serious one being that put forward at a meeting in the Warren Bulkeley Arms Hotel, Stockport, in 1828. Mr Thomas Legh, of the well-known Lyme Hall family was in the chair, and a line was proposed to connect the Liverpool and Manchester Railway with the Cromford & High Peak Line at Whaley Bridge. Both these railways were then under construction. Later the Manchester, Buxton, Matlock and Midlands Junction Railway was intended to serve the district but only the Ambergate-Rowsley section, opened in 1849 was ever built.

The present story begins at the Swann Inn, Disley, on November 25, 1853, when the first meeting of the Committee of Management of the Stockport, Disley & Whaley Bridge Railway Company. The aforementioned Thomas Legh, together with other local landowners and some London capitalists was responsible for this development. Mr Legh was appointed Chairman, John Lowe, Secretary and Joseph Locke and J E Errington, Engineers.

A Bill was submitted to Parliament but it met with considerable opposition, while alternative schemes were discussed with the Manchester, Sheffield & Lincolnshire and the London & North Western Railways. These came to nought, but a decision was made as early as April 1854, to promote jointly with the Cromford & High Peak Railway, a Bill for a short junction line to the latter railway. In spite of opposition from the MS&LR., the Warrington & Stockport and the Midland Railway Companies, the Duke of Devonshire and land-owners on the line, the Act of incorporation was passed on July 31, 1854. The company's capital was fixed at £150,000, with borrowing powers for a further £50,000.

The contract for the construction was let to John R. Davidson & Company of London, for the sum of £100,000. An agreement had been made with the L&NWR that the latter would work the line, paying all working and maintenance expenses and retaining 50 per cent of the takings. The ceremony of turning the first sod was performed at Disley on September 30, 1854, by Mrs Legh, the Chairman's wife, after the Act of Parliament had been read by the company's solicitor, J. B. Townsend.

Provision was made in the original Act for the MS&LR; the C&HPR; or any other local railway, to make a junction with the Whaley Bridge line between 6 miles 4 furlongs and the end of the line at Whaley Bridge. However, the company's own proposals were included in the second SD&WBR Act of July 16, 1855, which enabled it to construct a Junction Railway of approximately a quarter of a mile from its own line to join the Cromford & High Peak Railway at Whaley Bridge. The L&NWR was empowered to subscribe up to £85,000 in the SD&WBR, while the C&HPR was required to subscribe £3,750. The original railway was not to be opened to traffic until the Junction Railway was completed - a requirement that was not carried out.

Construction of the line from Stockport seems to have proceeded fairly uneventfully, the major operation being the filling for the large embankment between Hazel Grove and Norbury Hollow. In September 1856, the company decided to make the Junction line double track instead of the single line originally proposed, and a contract was let to Davidsons to carry out the work for the sum of £8,000 inclusive of *"an iron bridge over the turnpike road"*.

In February, 1857, it was reported that 1,400 men, 80 horses, and two locomotives were employed on the line. By April 7, the line was sufficiently completed for a special engine to run over it, taking the directors on an inspection trip.

The official opening ceremony took place on Thursday, May 28, 1857, when a train of ten First - and Third - Class carriages left Stockport station at noon for Whaley Bridge, returning to Disley where a dinner was held in the schoolroom. Thomas Legh had died a few weeks earlier and the new Chairman, John Chapman presided. The workmen were regaled the same evening with a bountiful supper at the company's expense.

Work was not quite sufficiently completed, however, and the passenger train service did not commence until Tuesday June 9. Intermediate stations were provided at Hazel Grove, Disley and New Mills. Goods sidings and warehouses were also included at these points, as well as at Whaley Bridge, but initially these facilities were incomplete and practically the only revenue was that obtained from passenger traffic. Connecting coaches to and from Buxton with through fares, were provided from the beginning. A coach also ran to and from Chapel-en-le-Frith and was described by a writer in 1862 as *"a very unpretending vehicle, certainly a rickety tumble down sort of affair"*.

A joint Traffic Committee was set up with the L&NWR and at its first meeting on June 3, 1857, the requirements at the various stations were laid down. It is interesting to note that these included an *"engine house at Whaley Bridge to be furnished with lamps, ash pit, and hose for washing out"*. Very little is known of this engine shed, which Mr J. Ramsbottom stated at the next meeting on July 10 was *"in progress"*. It has been stated that the brick structure supporting the present water tank at Whaley Bridge was part of the original building.

Initially goods traffic seems to have been virtually confined to limestone, and so on from the C&HPR line, which commenced in mid-August, 1857, although, as the viaduct over the River Goyt was not finished wagons had to be moved across by the contractor, using his own horses. It was reported that on September 11 that *"on an average three trucks had been*

An old picture postcard view (c.1900) of Davenport station long before the days of Wallace Sutherland. The original building on the Down (Manchester bound) platform has been adorned by the standardised signs and platform furniture and fittings of the London & North Western Railway. A train approaches on the Up line although it is unclear whether it is a passenger or freight working. The time on the clock at 11.15 suggests perhaps the latter as passenger trains were still of an irregular/infrequent pattern outside the peak periods.

despatched by every passenger train". However the Minutes show that from the beginning of November engines were able to use one line of rails of the Junction Railway, and the second line was completed about a month later. In addition a regular daily goods train began running on November 1 and from then on a moderate amount of general goods traffic seems to have developed in addition to a healthy quantity of minerals, more than 6,000 tons a month by 1860.

The pleasant and fashionable spa of Buxton was a logical and desirable terminus for which the new railway should aim and the SD&WBR Extension Act, authorising the construction of nine miles of railway beyond Whaley Bridge was passed on July 27 1857. This was no doubt facilitated by a previous agreement which had been made with the Duke of Devonshire and by discussions with the MSL and Midland Railways. The Extension for which additional capital of £200,000 could be raised, was to form a separate undertaking from the original line and the company was required to keep separate accounts of its receipts and payments. The L&NWR was empowered to subscribe an additional £16,000 in the original SD&WBR undertaking, together with £105,000 in the Buxton Extension. The MS&LR was also empowered to subscribe up to £5,000 and £35,000 respectively in the two undertakings. An interesting clause in the Act allowed a charge as for three-quarters of a mile to be made for traffic over the 1/4 mile Junction Railway at Whaley Bridge, as this vital section had proved more costly than anticipated.

On March 1, 1858, as a result of a complaint from Colonel William Davenport, a local landowner, that the company had not honoured its original promise to provide a station at Bramhall Lane (then just outside the Stockport Borough boundary), a small passenger station was opened there and named Davenport. But the traffic seems to have negligible and, in spite of the colonel's protests it had been closed by October, 1859. The date of the re-opening of what is now probably the line's busiest station has been given as January 1, 1862, but this has not been confirmed.

Although the Buxton Extension Act had been passed in 1857, no action was taken to build the line until early 1859. Mr Knight's tender to construct the railway for £110,845 was accepted in July of that year. Work proceeded generally in accordance with the original plans, but the one intended tunnel became 440 yd. long instead of 300 yd. and a second tunnel of 120yd. Replaced a cutting 87 ft deep. An unusual constructional feature was that no less than four working shafts were provided for the longer tunnel.

Joseph Locke died suddenly on September 10, 1860. He was evidently actively concerned with the line, until very nearly the end as, in June, 1860, he had expressed dissatisfaction with the contractor's's rate of progress and had urged him to put more men on the line. Relations between the directors and the contractor apparently deteriorated, and at the end of the year Knight was replaced by Thomas Stone, of Newton, but with a new comple-

The Stockport Co-op sidings at Adswood hosted the daily trip working, popularly known as the 'Divi-shunt', for approximately one hour each morning between eight and nine o'clock. To the left is the bi-directional 'Khyber Pass' line connecting Davenport Junction with Cheadle Village Junction. The brake van is standing on what was a through siding, used also by goods trains - from the Liverpool direction - which would quite literally crawl along the rails given the low level of maintenance. Crews were given the option of this somewhat risky manouvre but expected to keep quiet about it because of local authority rating. In contrast, the shiny rails indicate the 'official' route. The siding closed to traffic in 1969 but the yard continued to be served by road transport from the entrance on Adswood Road. This Saturday view of 1st May 1965 shows 8F 2-8-0 No **48182** prior to re-commencing its journey towards Buxton. On Saturdays if necessary, the train stopped over at Whaley Bridge for a longer spell than on weekdays, including the short trip down to Shallcross Yard.

J W Sutherland

tion date of June 1, 1862, instead of June 1, 1861.

After a satisfactory initial period, Stone in his turn failed to satisfy both Mr Errington and the directors, with the result that in January, 1862, he was relieved of his post and his duties were taken over by the company's resident engineer, Mr Crosse. Only six months later the sudden death of Errington resulted in Crosse being given complete charge of the engineering works. By this time half the permanent way (nine miles of track had been laid and the two tunnels completed. 100,000 cu.yd. of excavation remained to be done, five bridges to be built, and ten others completed; nevertheless, Crosse expected the line to be finished by the end of the year.

But Nemesis was at hand and by October Crosse was having trouble from subsidence in the high embankment where the line curves round past the Combs. It was found impossible to establish firm foundations for a road underbridge and eventually he decided that the only solution would be to divert the road so that it passed under the railway at a shallower part of the embankment where the ground was firmer. No further difficulties were experienced but several months' delay had in the meantime been caused to the completion of the line.

The original intention was to provide an intermediate station at Chapel-en-le-Frith only but, as a result of a petition from a Mr Bibbington, it was decided in February 1863, to have a station at Dove Holes also. It would be only half a mile north of a lime works siding which Bibbington had been authorised to put in at his own expense and with true L&NWR style economy it was decided that one railway agent should attend to traffic at both places.

As early as February, 1861, it was resolved to co-operate with the Midland Railway regarding the siting of the stations and yards at Buxton - it being understood that the Duke of Devonshire would make a free grant of land for both station approaches. It was agreed that the two stations should be of similar design, but subsequent discussions between the SD&WBR and L&NWR companies with a view to reducing the cost of the former's station necessitated a reminder from the Midland company of the desirability of uniform structures. The result was a meeting with Sir Joseph Paxton to discuss the subject - an uneventful one apparently, but of interest as indicating that the famous designer of the Crystal Palace also had some say in the design of both Buxton stations.

The company was by now very much in the hands of the L&NWR which was directly helping to finance the building of the Extension line. In November 1859, C E Stewart, Secretary of the L&NWR had been appointed Secretary of the SD&WBR also, because of the L&NWR's large interest in the latter.

A firm known as Stevens & Sons was mentioned in connection with the supply of signals for the original section to Whaley Bridge, but those for the Buxton Extension were provided by Saxby & Farmer, in line with the latter's agreement with the L&NWR. Similarly the Electric & International Telegraph Company had been instructed to erect a telegraph to the SD&WBR office at Buxton on the same terms and conditions as under its agreement with the L&NWR. The Buxton line telegraph was complete by August, 1860, being perhaps one of the earliest-ever applications of the telegraph to a branch railway. In June 1862, it was agreed that the L&NWR would work the Extension line on the same terms as those already operating on the SD&WBR.

By May 1863, the line was almost complete and Saturday, the 30th of that month was a red-letter day for the town of Buxton. At 2pm a luncheon was given by the directors of the Midland Railway in the Assembly Rooms in the Crescent to celebrate the completion of their line from Rowsley. Mr S. Beale, MP., presided, and among those present were the Duke of Devonshire and Sir Joseph Paxton. To quote the Stockport Advertiser, *"Congratulatory speeches were made and it was especially remarked that the line was opened on the day originally fixed[!]*. After the luncheon the party returned by special train to Derby.

Shortly after 1 pm on the same afternoon a special train of directors and guests had arrived at Buxton from London Road Station, Manchester, and two hours later the party sat down to dine at the St. Ann's Hotel. The chair was taken by R R Notman, one of the original directors and now Chairman of the SD&WBR Company; once again Sir Joseph Paxton was among the diners. When the Chairman proposed the health of the Duke of Devonshire who he said, had greatly aided the construction of the line, Paxton replied and, after apologising for the Duke's absence because of a previous engagement, expounded on the Duke's sincerity in wishing for the prosperity of railways as evidenced by his promotion of both lines into Buxton, although he would lose virtually the whole of his revenue from the turnpike road through the country south of Buxton. Paxton hoped that peace would always prevail between the two great companies which had now entered the town. Later, Mr Bancroft of the L&NWR. spoke of the desire of that company for peace and co-operation with all other railway companies - but not peace at any price!.

In its description of the new line the *Stockport Advertiser* related the difficulties experienced at the Combs and then went on : *"It is not often that any romance, and much more a ghost story, is associated with a railway, but there is one in this case. In the window of a neighbouring farmhouse is the skull of a man who there met with a untimely end. His ghost, as the story goes, has unpleasantly resisted several attempts to deposit the skull in a churchyard and has forced the restoration of the relic to the window of Tunstead Farm. The railway company were so unfortunate as to incur the hatred of Dickie, as the ghost is called by removing a portion of what had been his land. It is the steadfast belief in the district that every night the ghost would undo at the Combs embankment the work which had occupied many men during the day, and that Dickie was only propitiated at last by an interview with the engineer at which he was promised a free pass over the line for ever."*

"Dickie of Tunstead" is a well-documented local notability still reputed to frequent the remains of the skull at Tunstead which, however, are not open to inspection. The re-positioned underbridge is known to some as 'Dickie's bridge' and the way in which the road was re-aligned is evident both on the site and on the Ordnance Survey Map.

The interesting point about the activities at Buxton on May 30, 1863, was that although the Midland Railway began a

Davenport, 22nd May 1959. Regular diagramming of Edge Hill (8A) based engines on the 7.50am ex-Buxton to Manchester London Road sees 'Patriot' Class 6P 4-6-0 No **45539** *E C Trench* bringing its train alongside the Down platform. Fifty-five minutes were allowed for the service which excluded Dove Holes, Furness Vale and New Mills Newtown, reflecting the use of such big engines on the working. ***J W Sutherland***

regular passenger service to Buxton on the following Monday, June 1, the SD&WBR line was not really ready for traffic and the service did not commence until a fortnight later, June 15, when, in the language of the period, *"there was a fair number of passengers to and fro, the carriages being decorated with flags on the occasion, and the station at Buxton displaying manifestations of welcome on the appearance of the iron horse amongst the Peak scenery of Derbyshire"*. The obvious deduction is that the rather premature L&NWR and SD&WBR function was timed with the idea of ensuring that their arrival was not unduly overshadowed by that of the Midland Railway.

Thus, by the middle of 1863, there was a completed double-track railway between Stockport and Buxton, virtually in the same form as it remains today. The need for the original promoters no longer existed and in fact the Stockport, Disley & Whaley Bridge Railway Company disappeared into history when the line, including the Buxton Extension, was transferred to the L&NWR on agreed terms on November 16, 1866.

The Buxton branch leaves the electrified Manchester-Crewe line at Edgeley Junction No 1 signal box, half a mile south of Stockport Edgeley Station and six miles from Manchester Piccadilly (formerly London Road) ; overhead wires for electric traction are provided for about 100 yard along the branch as an overlap. The branch curves sharply to the left, climbing steadily. The double-track connecting spur line from Cheadle Village Junction, on the Stockport-Northenden line, trails in from the right at Davenport Junction. This spur was opened to goods on December 12 1883, and to passengers on July 1, 1884, but is now normally worked as a single goods line on the staff system and very rarely sees a passenger train.

There is a small coal siding on the Down (right) side just before **Davenport** Station which, like all intermediate stations on the line, has separate Up and Down platforms. The buildings here are of plain red-brick construction, somewhat enlarged in more recent times, the platforms also having been extended.

The line flattens out and after passing Up and Down goods loops beyond **Woodsmoor** Level Crossing reaches **Hazel Grove** Station, also built of brick. There are Up and Down sidings, often used to hold diesel trains terminating or starting there, and also a tiny goods siding. But the goods shed is relegated to non-railway purposes and other sidings, including those of a former coal yard, have disappeared. A short distance beyond the station the line is crossed by the New Mills-Heaton Mersey section of the former Midland Railway, opened in 1902. In 1933 the LM&SR planned to connect the two lines by a loop but the scheme lapsed.

At this point, 2½ miles from Edgeley Junction, the Cheshire Plain is left behind as the line commences a continuous 3¼ mile climb at 1 in 60. **Norbury** Level Crossing with its two co-acting Down signals on opposite side of the track (see The Railway Magazine May 1952, page 359), is passed, after which **Middlewood** Lower Station with its wooden buildings, in a pretty setting of trees is reached. Directly above is Middlewood Higher Station, closed on November 7, 1960, on the Great Central-North Staffordshire Joint Railway, which dates from 1869.

One of the intermediate stations on the Buxton line, albeit unrecognisable from its early days, Disley became one of the busiest, getting preferential treatment by virtue of morning and evening 'express' services to and from Manchester. Even as recent as 1983, additional crossover arrangements were sponsored by the GMPTE to allow two morning and two evening trains to start/terminate their journeys at Disley. This 1962 view from the Down side approach looking in the direction of Stockport shows the station not much different as it would have been in 1919 when the new buildings replaced fire damaged structures. It remained a tidy and well kept station until the rationalisation policies of the mid-1970's. ***Authors collection***

The two routes were connected by a curve opened on May 26, 1885, which permitted through running between Macclesfield and Buxton. The points at the Macclesfield end were removed in 1954, but the curve and interchange sidings remain, in a simplified form, with a connection from the Down Buxton line, although a flyover which formerly brought traffic on to the Up line has been removed.

The embankment of the Macclesfield Canal, a one-time adjunct of the MS&LR, is pierced by a very short tunnel and the line continues past Lyme Park on the right, to **Disley** - a more modern looking wood and brick station with verandah shelters, rebuilt just after the first world war. There are short Up and Down sidings here. After traversing a cutting and a short tunnel (originally intended as a deep cutting by Joseph Locke - who was no lover of tunnels) the railway reaches the valley of the River Goyt, which it shares almost to Whaley Bridge with the former Midland Railway as well as the main A6 road and the Peak Forest Canal. From Disley Summit there is a gradual descent as far as Furness Vale. **Disley Goods** station, just beyond the tunnel, has two short sidings which are usually full, with perhaps one or two coal wagons, but mainly with vans for transporting cardboard drums and similar products from Bowater's nearby factory. Between 100 and 150 wagons a week are despatched to places as far afield as Kittybrewster and Bridgewater, with occasional traffic to Cornwall. **New Mills (Newtown)** Station has the small, austere blackened stone and wooden buildings typical of the remainder of the line. The large warehouse still handles a miscellany of merchandise and small consignments of goods traffic with the aid of a fleet of collection and delivery lorries, which also cater for the nearby goods depot on the Midland Line. **Furness Vale** Station handles passenger traffic only, an adjacent private siding having been closed in recent years. At **Whaley Bridge** there is still some coal traffic but, as has been the case since 1863, most of the goods traffic (though now little more than coal) is handled at Shallcross Yard. This yard, a remnant of the Cromford & High Peak Railway, is reached by half a mile of single track which leaves the main line just past Whaley Bridge Station. Vans for Bowater's Disley traffic are often stored both at New Mills and at Shallcross and occasionally are even loaded there from the firm's road vehicles.

After leaving Whaley Bridge and crossing the River Goyt and the route of the C&HPR line down to the wharf at the terminus of the Park Forest Canal, the Buxton Extension line commences an almost unbroken 1 in 60-58 climb for six miles which ends at Dove Holes. En route there is first a series of deep cuttings followed by the long left-hand curve past the Combs, and over *"Dickie's Bridge"*, to **Chapel-en-le-Frith South** Station -

The Buxton line as we know was built in two stages, although the independent Stockport Disley & Whaley Bridge Railway provided the first section of the route to Whaley, opening in 1857. Just over a hundred years after the SD&WBR had commenced operations, we see another veteran in the form of Class G2a 0-8-0 No **49391** (9D-Stockport), popularly referred to as a 'Super D', standing alongside Whaley Bridge goods yard prior to its departure for Buxton with a freight from Stockport. The engine had just returned to the main line after shunting Shallcross Yard. To the right is a water tank mounted above the remains of a brick structure, formerly part of an engine shed from SD&WBR days in the period that Whaley Bridge was terminus of the line. ***J W Sutherland***

less convenient but better served with trains than the Central Station on the Midland line. Here, at the South Station, a new signalbox and reconstructed platform bear silent witness to the fact that this was the site of the fearful accident on February 9, 1957, when a runaway freight train crashed into the back of another freight train, killing the driver of the former and the guard of the latter. The driver, John Axon of Stockport, was posthumously awarded the George Cross for staying on his engine in a vain attempt to regain control and his deed was uniquely celebrated in a BBC radio programme *"The Ballad of John Axon"*.

There is practically no goods traffic at Chapel-en-le-Frith South now, but two short sidings and the shed remain. Just beyond the station, the Midland line, before it enters the northern portal of the Dove Holes Tunnel, passes under the Buxton line, which continues to climb while making a big swing north-eastwards and round to Barmoor Clough. It then passes through two tunnels and skirts the still well defined route of the adjoining Peak Forest Tramroad. At **Dove Holes** there is an oil-fuel depot with rail sidings which, however, has not produced any traffic in the last two years or so. The station sidings still deal with a few wagon loads of scrap. Half a mile further on, after a gentle rise provided with Up and Down goods loops, the line reaches a large mound of lime ash, remnants of lime kilns and the associated sidings and buildings, a tiny siding and a signalbox still bearing the legend **Bibbington's Sidings**. This is all that is left of the lime-works established by Mr Bibbington at the opening of the line.

"Bibbington's" is more than 1,100 ft above sea level and the railway has climbed 900 ft. from Edgeley Junction, leaving in the process the soft Cheshire countryside for the bleak, stone-walled and almost treeless uplands of the High Peak of Derbyshire. A two mile descent, mainly at 1 in 66, completes the 19 mile line into Buxton. Half a mile from the terminus is the site of Fairfield Halt, an alighting platform on the Up side only and adjacent to the golf links which was closed in September, 1939. In Buxton, the handsome twin terminal station buildings make a fitting end to an interesting journey and stand as worthy memorials to the pioneers who brought the railways to the town. How long they will continue to stand it is impossible to say, for both the Stockport-Buxton line and the Midland line between Millers Dale and Buxton were listed for withdrawal of passenger services in the recent Beeching Report.

Authors note; Fortunately, the line to Stockport, populaly known as the 'Wessy', survived, although the era of the steam hauled freight would end in 1965. It still sees use for occasinal stone-trains diverted from the truncated Midland routebut remains a basic regional railway, invaluable to the communities it serves.

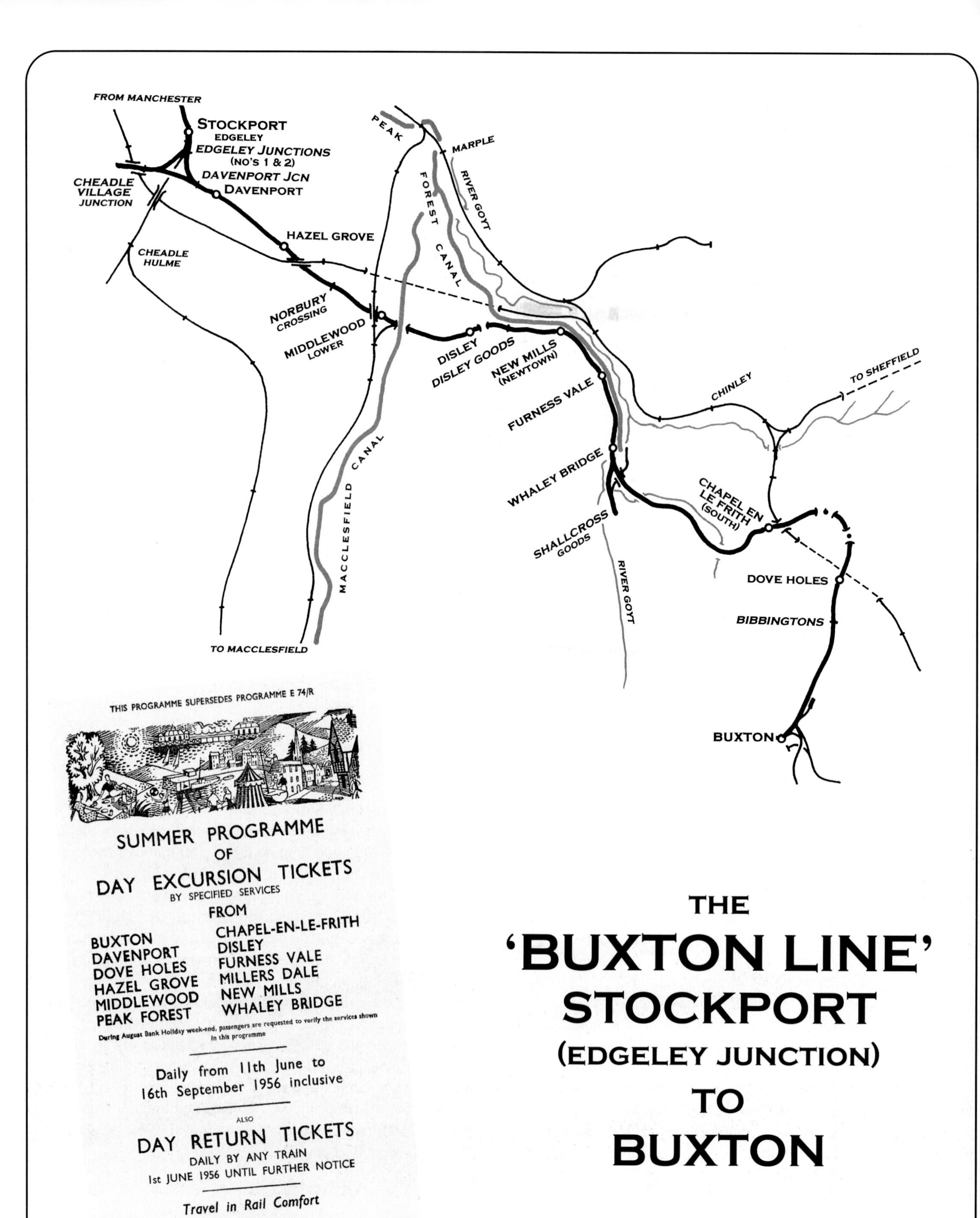

THE 'BUXTON LINE' STOCKPORT (EDGELEY JUNCTION) TO BUXTON

EDGELEY JUNCTION TO DAVENPORT JUNCTION

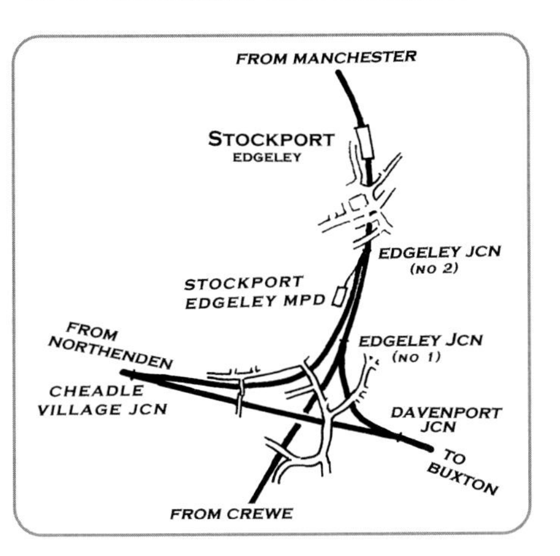

(Above-right) Edgeley Junction, 13th June 1959. A vantage point unchanged for over half a century as 3-car Birmingham RC&W diesel multiple unit enters the branch at the start of its 19 1/2 mile journey to Buxton. Edgeley Junction No. 1 signal box is to the rear left of the train, controlling a generation of signalling equipment that would soon disappear with the onset of the Main Line Electrification scheme. The track layout however, would not change dramatically, even allowing for electrification, and it would be 1976 before any thought was given to rationalisation. Edgeley Junction No 1 signal box, originally with a 90 lever frame, then had its number of working levers reduced to a modest 29. As a result, one effect on the Buxton branch was that it lost the connection from the Up Fast, the line seen in this view to the left of the diesel train. ***J W Sutherland***

Edgeley Junction, 21st August 1956. Fowler 2-6-4T No **42365** (9D - Buxton) passes the Edgeley Junction Down branch home signal with the 9.10am Buxton to Manchester train in readiness to take the fast line into Stockport Edgeley station, where it will call before running express to London Road. This was one of the principle morning trains on the branch, making just one intermediate stop, at Chapel en le Frith, before the Stockport call. Arrival in Manchester was scheduled for 9.53, giving an overall journey time of 43 minutes. **42365** was transferred to Longsight the following year as passenger work became the domain of the diesel multiple units. ***J W Sutherland collection***

Edgeley Junction, 13th June 1959 (Saturday) 'Crab' No **42930** (9A - Longsight) heads cautiously along the first few yards of the branch before encountering its first real obstacle, a half mile 1 in 106 adverse gradient as far as Davenport. In the *Working Timetable of Freight Trains, 2nd November 1959 to 12th June 1960, inclusive or until further notice,* this Saturdays Only working departed Longsight at 3.5pm comprising a train of empty mineral wagons and a brake. After a train crew change at Edgeley Junction (3.26), the train proceeded to the Goods Loop at Woodsmoor where it would be passed by the 3.20pm Manchester London Road to Buxton passenger train. Some thirty minutes would now be allowed for the eight miles to Whaley Bridge where a water stop of five minutes was allowed in order to tackle the seven miles, mostly at 1 in 58/60, as far as Bibbingtons Sidings. A further eight minutes were then allowed for brakes on the wagons to be pinned down, a period which also allowed for the passage, if necessary, of another passenger train, the 4.20pm (SO) London Road to Buxton. Scheduled arrival time in Buxton was 5.19, giving an average journey time for the $23^{1}/_{2}$ miles from Longsight of $10^{1}/_{2}$ mph.

J W Sutherland

Edgeley Junction, 27th August 1959. First bridge on the branch was a brick structure (comprising cast iron girders and brick jack arches) carrying Adswood Road. The bridge had a weight restriction - note the diamond shaped sign above the parapet - which remained until it was reconstructed in 1980. Approaching the bridge is 8F No **48465**, recently transferred to Longsight after many years at Buxton, and pressed into service on this occasion with the 5.50pm London Road to Buxton train. This fifteen chain radius, commencing at the junction, continued for almost half a mile to Davenport Junction. Latterly, a catch point was located on this side of the bridge to arrest any would be errant vehicles, although prior to May 1937, a short siding/sand drag had existed alongside the Up line.

J W Sutherland

Stockport (Adswood Road), 25th March 1958. This view through the bridge 'hole' in the direction of Davenport shows the elevation of bridge No 1 (Buxton branch) from the Edgeley side. The structure carries Adswood Road through the Shaw Heath / Cale Green / Edgeley districts of Stockport to Adswood, chiefly the Bridge Hall area. To the right is the complex that developed on a site aquired in about 1913, the main feature being the multi-storey building known as the 'Bakery Warehouse'. The single storey building immediately to the right of the bridge housed the offices for the coal yard, alongside which was an entrance with weighbridge.

(Centre) Looking across bridge No 1 along Adswood Road in the direction of Adswood. Although not visible in this view, just beyond the right hand parapet was the access road to a whole range of buildings needed by the Co-op to maintain its services, such as:- joinery, boots and shoes, wheelright and repair shops for milk and coal carts as well as lorries. An abbatoir with offices, together with a holding field for livestock abutted the fence alongside the Crewe line.

(Right) The Co-op coal yard office is on the immediate right of the picture in this view across bridge No 1 looking along Adswood Road, this time in the direction of Shaw Heath.

(Left) Viewed from the bridge (No 1 on the Stockport Junction Railway), which took the name of 'Bakery bridge', we see the other side of the bakery warehouse which faced the 'Khyber' line. The Warehouse was, quite typically, used for all manner of business undertaken by the Co-op. Tea chests, butter barrels, sacks of coffee, biscuits and ranges of goods from the docks and other suppliers. You name it, the Co-op stocked it. From under the same roof, food batching and processing together with the making up and delivery of consignments was undertaken in order to keep the branches within the Stockport area supplied. The road in the left foreground was the original route of Adswood Road before the coming of the Khyber line in 1882 and latterly known as Adswood Old Road.

(Centre) Following closure of the rail connection in 1969, all coal was dealt with by road vehicles, the entrance here providing access. For many years, this once attractive range of buildings to the right served as stables for the Co-op's horses. At the bottom of the yard, lorries now occupy the site formerly containing railway sidings some three years after the facility was withdrawn. the 'Khyber' line ran parallel with and to the rear of these buildings (see page19).

(Below) At track level we see the elevation of bridge No 1 looking in the direction of Edgeley Junction (see page oppositer-top photo). The tall chimney, with letters SCS emblazoned in yellow brick, served the needs of the adjacent Co-op operation.

The approach to Edgeley Junction from Davenport Junction had long provided signal sighting difficulties for Down trains. With the modernisation of the Crewe line and the introduction in 1960 of colour light signalling on to the branch as far as Davenport, the home signal for Edgeley Junction No 1 was relocated to the south side of Adswood Road bridge. In this June 1960 (Sunday 19th) view, the calm of Vicarage Road is no doubt being shattered as **44741** (9A - Longsight) waits impatiently at a signal check with a Hazel Grove to Blackpool Central (via the Marton Line) excursion. A typical return fare for the seaside trip was 9/- (45p). Evidence of the main line electrification can be seen through the bridge 'hole' in the form of catenary supports.

Davenport Junction, 21st December 1957 (Saturday). With a fairly light load of four carriages, 'Crab' No **42935**, a Longsight based engine, crosses the junction on its way to Buxton with the 12.30pm (SO) train from Manchester Mayfield. Davenport Junction, a London & North Western Railway 'type 5' signal box to a design introduced in 1904, controlled movements between Edgeley Junction and Woodsmoor and to and from Cheadle Village Junction. The box was a replacement for an earlier structure dating back to 1884 with the opening of the 'Khyber', the line to Cheadle Village Junction and seen here trailing away to the left of the train. Davenport Junction survived as a block post until 4th January 1970 when, following closure of the nearby Stockport Co-op coal sidings, it became redundant. It was demolished during February of that year. Both; ***J W Sutherland***

Davenport Junction, 1st May 1965 (Saturday). A low-level view along the bi-directional line towards Cheadle Village Junction, locally known as the 'Khyber', gives a clear indication of how straight the line was. In the distance is the overbridge carrying Adswood Road and for a few hundred yards from Davenport Junction, the 'Khyber' was built on the level. However, when passing over the Crewe line, the formation fell away rapidly towards Cheadle Village Junction at 1 in 68. This useful link, opened in 1883 (12th December) to goods and 1884 (1st July) to passengers, was double track throughout, although it is thought that the siding connection requirement for Stockport Co-op (c.1911) saw a modification to the arrangement between Davenport and Cheadle Village Junctions which resulted in bi-directional operation. In the *Sectional Appendix to the Working Timetable for January 1st, 1931 (Local Instructions)* 'the line between Davenport Junction and Cheadle Village Junction must be used for freight trains, empty coaches, ballast trains, and light engines only, and no loaded passenger trains must be allowed to travel over the branch'. The view here also shows **48182** shunting the Co-op siding after travelling from Cheadle Village Junction. Last day of operation came on 30th April 1966 with the passing of the 'shunt' behind 8F No 48428. ***J W Sutherland***

Davenport Junction, 24th June 1964. Given the 'all-clear' to proceed, the driver of Austerity No **90620** (56A - Wakefield) will move his train forward in readiness to hand over the single line token which had been collected at Cheadle Village Junction. In the distance, the signalman (relief) from Davenport Junction box is making his way into the 'six-foot' to collect the token. This daily (Mondays excepted) working, reporting number 7H66, was the 4.30pm from Arpley (Warrington), due at Davenport Junction at approximately 5.45pm after taking water at Cheadle Village Junction. With a train comprising empty mineral wagons bound for Kirkby (Notts), only twenty five minutes ensued before another water stop was scheduled at Whaley Bridge. Another testing climb for the next 6¾ miles would end at Dove Holes where the train would seek the relief of the Down Goods Loop whilst the 5.57pm Manchester Piccadilly to Buxton passenger train passed by. Arrival in Buxton was due at 7.11pm where wagons would be arranged for forwarding over the Midland lines. ***J W Sutherland***

STOCKPORT
INDUSTRIAL & EQUITABLE CO-OPERATIVE SOCIETY

Adswood, 1st September 1961. The 'triangle' of land between the 'Khyber', Buxton and Crewe lines contained an 'ad-hoc' range of buildings from which, to give it its full name, the Stockport Industrial & Equitable Co-operative Society provided many of its customer services. Retired joiner and St Petersberg Road resident Geoff Holt recalls his time here in the late 1940s/early 1950s when it was a hive of industry. Between Adswood Road and the Crewe line were buildings containing Garage, Joinery/Boot & Shoe/Morgue facilities. Across the road was the main building, seen in this view to the right of the engine, and which was the 'Bakery' warehouse. Behind the engine were the stables, the inhabitants of which produced a familiar pungent bi-product which was transported by the bucket load to the residents of St Petersberg Road. Geoff recalls that the reward for his efforts was sufficient to enhance his Dinky Toy collection. To the right of the picture is the Paint Store and Maintenance Depot. On this occasion, **48165** (9D) gets ready to continue on its journey to Buxton after shunting the Co-op coal sidings. Following the removal of any remaining coal wagons, the Co-op Siding was closed from Monday 3rd December 1969. ***J W Sutherland***

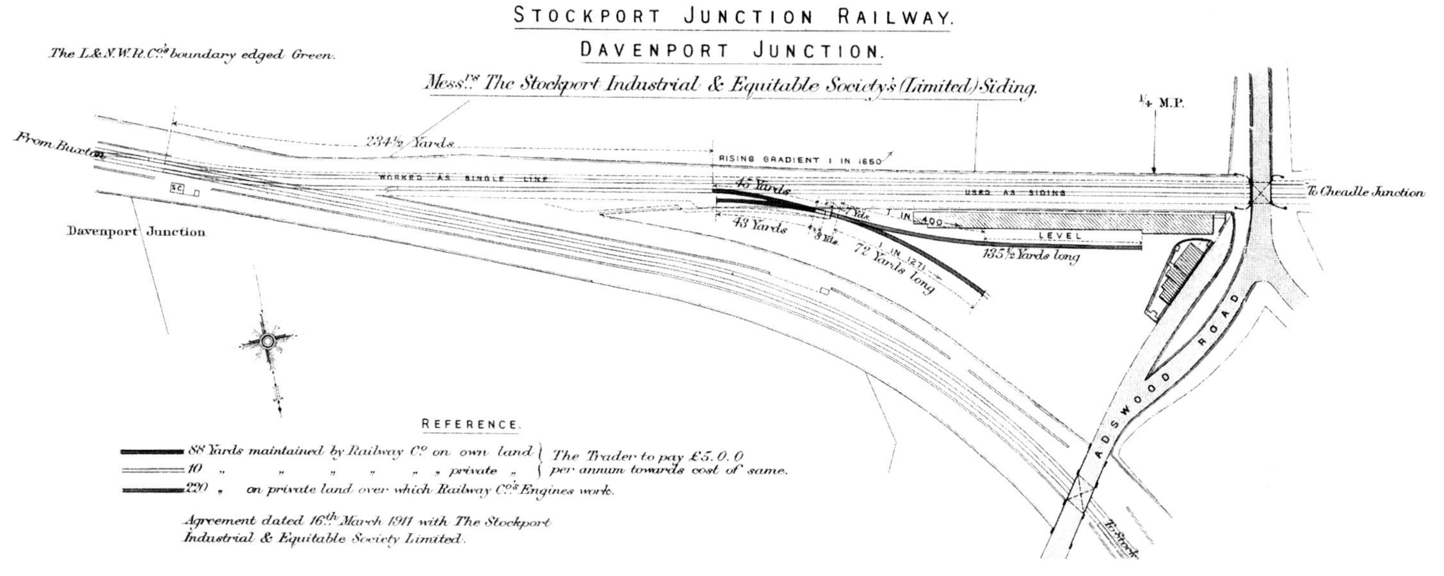

Adswood, 6th March 1960. Due to engineering work (permanent way) at Edgeley Junction, Down Buxton trains were, throughout the day, up to and including the 5.07pm from Davenport, routed via Cheadle Village Junction. The single line token was carried between Davenport Junction and Cheadle Village Junction and the points clipped at the latter. Here we see the 2.30pm Buxton to London Road approaching Adswood Road bridge. The lower of the signal arms is the Cheadle Village Junction distant (fixed). Apparently this was the first occasion diesel trains had operated over the line - carrying passengers at any rate - although some years previously the morning Down passenger trains had been diverted due to a derailment at Edgeley Junction. The view also illustrates once again the extent to which Stockport Co-op had developed the site. The buildings extending as far as the rear of the train housed the stables, whilst behind the single storey section were the coal sidings. ***J W Sutherland***

Adswood, 23rd June 1963. Once again, owing to permanent way work at Edgeley Junction, the 'Khyber' was utilised for re-routing Down Buxton line trains. This Sunday afternoon working crosses the Crewe line at Adswood on its way to Cheadle Village Junction where it will link up with the Cheadle-Northenden line before 'reversing' to Edgeley Junction (No 2) and rejoining its normal route into Edgeley station. Following reconstruction in 1960 of the Crewe line bridge it had been necessary to increase the headroom by some eighteen inches to accommodate the overhead wiring. The subsequent 'lifting' of the bridge affected the gradients from both Davenport and Cheadle Village Junctions resulting in a short section from 'Bakery bridge' becoming 1 in 218 and the 1 in 68 climb from Cheadle becoming 1 in 64. Whilst the line was in use, this area of Stockport remained largely unchanged. Even after closure, the abandoned route remained intact until the intersection bridge was removed in 1976. However, the picture has another story to tell commencing with reference to the building in the upper left of the picture, Bridge Hall School on a site previously occupied by Savage's Farm. Development of the housing estate had put an end to such scenes as the periodic shepherding of sheep between Edgeley Station and Adswood. Petersburg Road, forming the skyline to the right, is dominated by Sykes chimney. The larger houses seen beneath the base of the chimney had bathrooms, whilst the smaller semi's were of the two-up, two down variety; no bathrooms. Geoff Holt, by the way, lived at No 41, his grandfather at No 99. The large houses to the right, in Adswood Grove, were owned by a railway company official and members of the Woodrow (hat manufacturers) family respectively. The Cheadle end of Petersburg Road was a 1930's development. Locally, the Edgeley Park area became popularly known as 'Siberia' as a result of some of some of the street names which included Moscow (Road), Berlin (Road), Finland (Road) and of course Petersburg (Road), etc., Residents of that era also knew it as 'over Sykes', indicating that they lived the other side of Sykes's reservoir. ***J W Sutherland***

Adswood, 23rd June 1963 (Saturday). Earlier in the day, another of the diverted Down Buxton line trains is seen passing the Cheadle Village Junction outer home signal on its way down the 1 in 68 gradient. The overgrown sidings to the left had not seen use for the best part of three years. ***J W Sutherland***

Adswood, 25th June 1960 (Saturday). A regular working over the years had been the morning Birkenhead to Buxton train, frequently with motive power well away from its natural habitat. The *Working Time Table for Freight trains, 9th June to 14th September, 1960*, informs us that the 3.20am from Birkenhead made a water stop at Cheadle Village Junction between 9.23 and 9.31am. It was then allowed a further eighteen minutes to clear Davenport Junction, by which time the 8.00am 'empties' from Garston to Rowsley was on its heels. Although it can hardly be described as a procession, the 'Khyber, during the 'summer' of 1958 was scheduled to witness the passage of some twelve Up trains and eight in the Down direction during a twenty-four hour period. By 1960, the number had reduced to to ten and five respectively and the pattern of decline would continue through 1961 and 1962. However, 1963 would see the bubble burst with only two Up trains, the 12.30am ex-Birkenhead and the 7.5pm empties Latchford Old Line to Rowsley scheduled to pass between Cheadle Village Junction and Davenport Junction. The Birkenhead was cut back to Arpley (dep 4.30am) from September 1963 with a progressively diminishing payload. On 5th November 1964, 8F No 48668 (8H - Birkenhead, still carrying a 1E shed plate) was recorded passing through Disley with just eleven tank wagons and brake. Ordinary freight traffic over the Buxton line ceased from Monday 4th January 1965 with the exception of one trip, which found its way from Heaton Norris Junction via Cheadle Village and Davenport Junctions to Hazel Grove, before returning to Adswood Sidings. **(Above)** At the head of Birkenhead to Buxton train is **90369** (6C - Birkenhead) on its way up the 1 in 68 gradient with thirty three wagons and brake in tow. **(Below)** Assisting at the rear is **48210** (41B - Staveley). The sidings alongside the 'Khyber' were at the time being used to store condemned wagons although it is perhaps a little strange that the 16-ton minerals wagons adjacent to the footbridge were possibly of a more recent construction than the wooden-bodied vehicles in the train. ***J W Sutherland***

Cheadle Village Junction was the point west of Stockport that the 'Khyber' and the Cheadle branch came together. **(Above)**, 8F 2-8-0 No **48210** (41E-Staveley) times its run up to the brake van of the Birkenhead to Buxton freight, which it will assist as far as Buxton, 25th June 1960.

(Centre) Summer Saturdays saw a something of a variety when a number of cross-country passenger trains were routed via Stockport. Jubilee Class 5XP No **45694** *Bellerophon* (55A-Leeds Holbeck) heads past Cheadle Village Junction signal box with the ex-9.15am Llandudno to Newcastle train, consisting of ten carriges.

(Below) Working in the opposite direction, **44687** (6G-Llandudno Junction), again with a load of ten carriages, approaches Cheadle Village Junction the ex-9.3am Leeds City to Llandudno train. To the right on the Khyber line is 4F No **44284** (9G) on a local goods service, Broadheath to Edgeley. This and the picture above (centre) were taken on Saturday 21st July 1962. All (3): ***J W Sutherland***

Stockport, 23rd June 1963 (Sunday)**.** During to Main Line Electrification period of the early 1960's, the 'triangle' formed by Davenport Jcn-Cheadle Village Jcn-Edgeley Jcn (No2) proved invaluable in allowing weekend work to take place in the Edgeley Junction area. The Buxton line retained its service throughout these engineering possessions without much disruption by simply diverting trains over the 'Khyber'. The diversion added some 9-10 minutes to the journey in the Down (to Manchester) but enabled the somewhat rare opportunity of travelling over a line normally opened only to freight trains. In the view to the right, a Buxton BRC&W 6-car set, having reversed at Cheadle Village Junction, heads back towards Stockport along the Cheadle Branch, which at the time did not carry regular passenger services apart from summer holiday trains and occasional excursions. The houses of St Petersburg Road provide the backdrop. ***J W Sutherland***

Stockport, 25th March 1958. The view from rail level of Bridge No1 on the Cheadle Branch. The lines from Edgeley Junction (No 2) to and from Cheadle (LNW) and Northenden were designated the 'Liverpool' lines. The view above shows the west face of the structure that carried Stockholm Road over the railway. Although the 'wires' never reached the bridge, official BR pictures were taken of structures which might possibly be affected by the MLE scheme. **(Left)** The road provided a main thoroughfare between the Edgeley and Adswood districts of Stockport, the right hand parapet affording a view of Edgeley sidings and Edgeley Junction No 1 signal box. ***British Railways***

(Above) Stockport, 25th March 1958. The Edgeley Sidings face of Bridge No 1 of the Cheadle Branch in this view towards Cheadle Village Junction and Northenden. The houses to the right of the picture are at the corner of the junction between Stockholm Road and St Petersburg Road. The diverted trains seen below and on the previous page will have traversed this route, coming towards us from the confines of a shallow cutting and forty-chain radius curve. Sighting for both signalling and safety at this location has always been problematic, a point perhaps supported by the signals which have 'sightboards' mounted behind them. **(Below)** Edgeley Junction, 23rd June 1963 (Sunday). An afternoon Buxton to Manchester Piccadilly 6-car DMU approaching Edgeley Junction after being diverted via Cheadle village Junction. The coal sidings have by now fallen into disuse although the rusting hulks of Stanier 'Crab' 2-6-0 No **42921**, withdrawn some three months before whilst at Stockport (9B), and 'Jubilee' **45678** *De Robeck,* await there last journey to the breakers yard. ***J W Sutherland***

Davenport Junction, 7th June 1960 (Monday). After our detour via the 'Khyber', we rejoin the branch again at Davenport Junction and the sight of Stockport (9B) 'Crab' 2-6-0 No **42886** at the head of the 12.29pm Longsight to Buxton freight which also included a pair of passenger coaches off the morning trains being worked back to Buxton. Scheduled to pass Davenport Junction at 12.53, a stop to change trainmen was allowed for before the 9½ mile climb to Whaley Bridge (arr 1.25) commenced. Once again we see the familiar outline of the Co-op bakery to the rear of the train. The tall LNWR signal post continues to share the elevated views of with Vicarage Road rooftops and will do so for another few years until officialdom decreed the shortening (by 19ft).

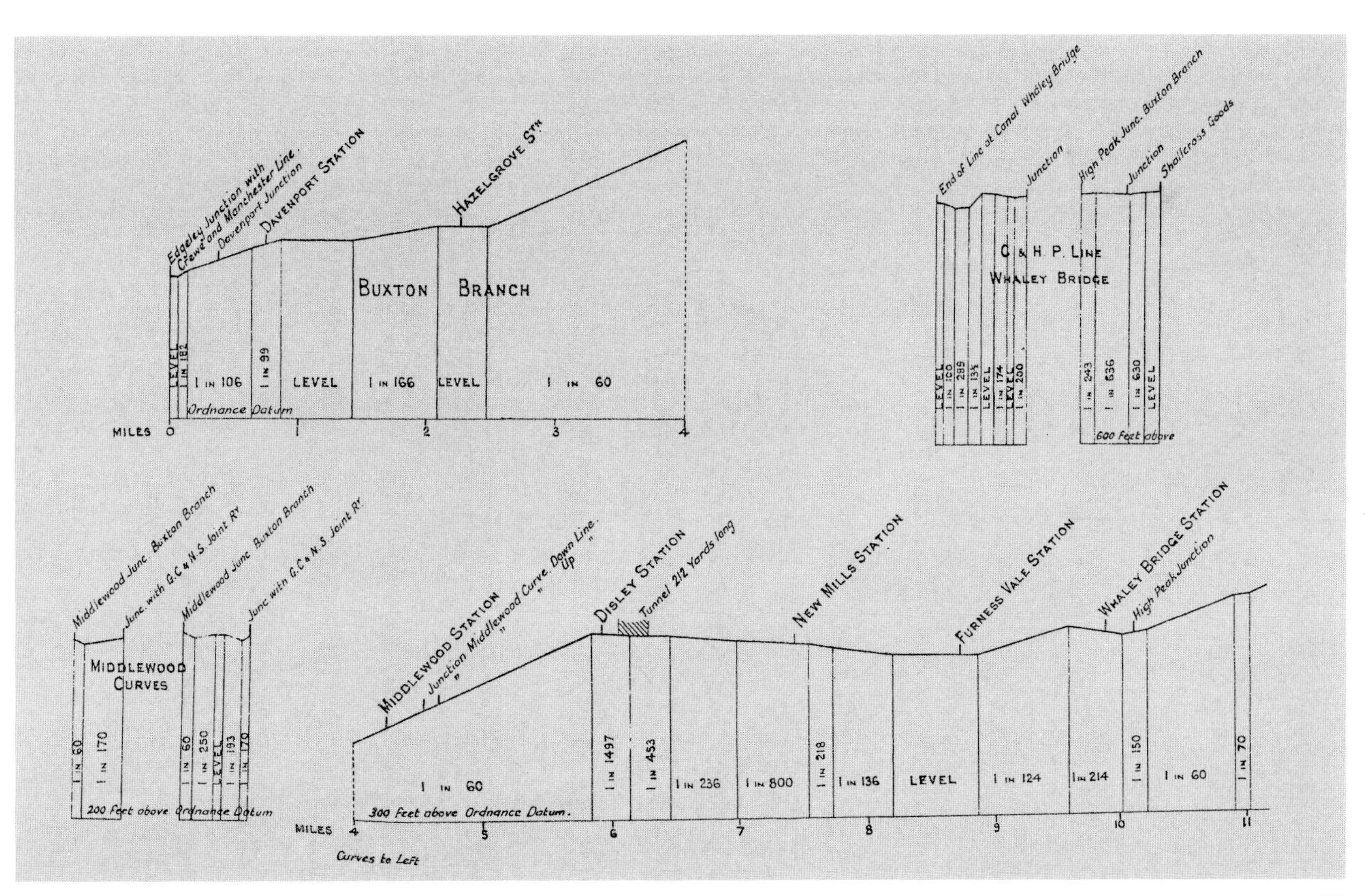

46252

46252

The effects of British Railways Main Line Electrification programme could be seen far and wide. Unusual although not entirely unexpected were the scenes created on this and the page opposite whereby large passenger engines found themselves negotiating a 'backwater' of the network. The 'triangle' formed by the four junctions at Stockport Edgeley No's 1 & 2, Davenport and Cheadle Village came into its own with the removal of the turntable at London Road for electrification work during 1958. To complicate matters, Longsight was unable, with its 60ft turntable, to accommodate such large engines as the 'Duchesses' so for a couple of years sightings of numerous of the Class could be had negotiating the 'triangle' to the south of Stockport. The three views seen here, all taken on June 21st, illustrate 'Coronation' Class Pacific No **46252** *City of Leicester* being turned in the 'clockwise' direction, entered the Buxton line first and proceeding tender first to Davenport Junction (Opposite-top). Crossing over to the Down line (Opposite-lower), she then moved forward on to the Stockport Junction Railway - to give its proper title - for the short run over the 'Khyber' to Cheadle Village Junction. Above, *City of Leicester* moves forward steadily towards the rear of houses of Aintree Grove, where it was not unkown for the residents to occasionally provide refreshments. A routine reversal at Cheadle Village Junction saw 46252 the 'right-way round' for when she arrived back at London Road. The other option was to 'turn' the engines by first of all sending them tender first from Edgeley Junction (No 2) to Cheadle Village Junction, thus completing the movement in the opposite direction. There were also occasions when the turntable at the nearby Edgeley MPD failed so the operators were quick to take advantage of the 'triangle'. All; ***J W Suherland***

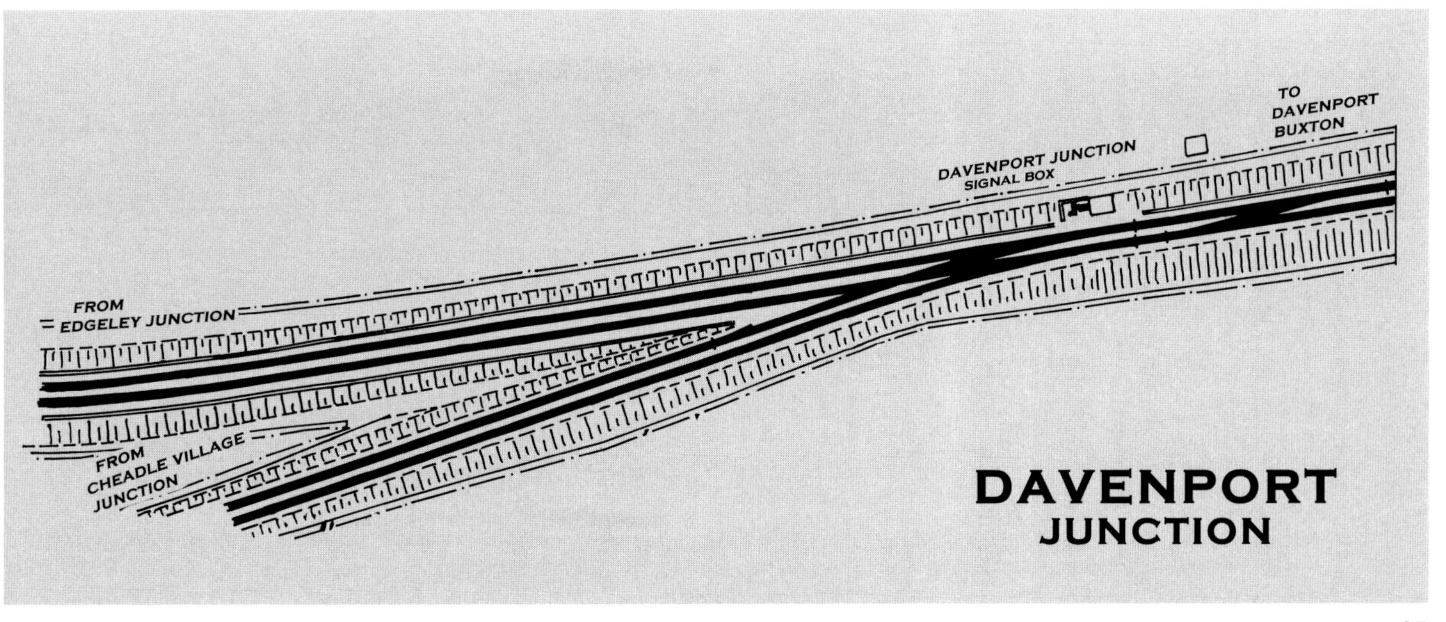

DIARY EXTRACTS FOR......
DAVENPORT JUNCTION, CHEADLE VILLAGE JUNCTION, EDGELEY JUNCTION

DAVENPORT JUNCTION TO CHEADLE VILLAGE JUNCTION

6 3 60 (Sun). Owing to track work at Edgeley Junction, the Down diesel today up to and including the 5.07 from Davenport are routed via Cheadle Village Junction between Davenport and Edgeley and the points were clipped at the latter place. This may be the first time diesel (dmu) trains have operated between Davenport Junction and Cheadle Village Junction, carrying passengers, out at any rate. I was told that a few years ago, morning Down passenger trains were routed that way owing, apparently, to a derailment at Edgeley Junction. I took photographs of some of the earlier trains and spoke to the signalman at Cheadle Village Junction. He said that the wagon repair and demolition work there had stopped two or three months ago and the yard now looked rather derelict. He said that for a time he frequently saw 2-10-0s on the Buxton line trains.

13 3 60 (Sun) Diesels (dmu's) in both directions today ran via Cheadle Village Junction.

3 4 60 (Sun) Almost all of the Buxton trains were diverted via Cheadle Village Jcn. today.

27 4 60 A J39 seemed to be out on a train of mineral empties going up from Cheadle Village Junction at about 3.15pm.

5 5 60 The Birkenhead comprised forty-six wagons and brake and an LNW 0-8-0 was banked from Cheadle Village Junction. A 'Crab' and 47 vans, one flat wagon and brake went up from Cheadle Village Junction between 2 and 3pm. About 5.45pm noted an 8F shunting Davenport coal siding; from a Down train 42930 was on the express to Buxton.

25 6 60 (Sat) Went to Cheadle Village Junction where I saw 48558 (9 on the train to Hooton. 48210 (41E Staveley) banked the Birkenhead train from Cheadle Village Junction, 90369 (6C) being in front of the 33 wagons and brake.

26 6 60 (Sun) Was told that several special goods trains were diverted off the Midland line today (due to repairs to Disley and Dove Holes Tunnels) and ran on the LNW line. Mainly or all ICI Hopper trains, about two each way.

21 7 60 (Tuesday evening). At Davenport Junction. 42778 (6C Birkenhead) was on 4.10 am Rowsley - Adswood. 48519 (9D) was on the 7.5pm Latchford - Rowsley. 42966 (5A) was on the Buxton - Arpley (running much earlier than shown in my last winter timetable but trains should be correctly described as they were given by R. Platt the signalman. 42355 came right behind the Arpley train on the parcels.

1 9 61 (Fri) While waiting at Davenport Junction, noticed a Down train at about 8.20am was only a two-car set (Metro Cammell). With the present interval service most rush hour trains are 3-car sets.

DAVENPORT JUNCTION

14 4 62 In the afternoon I went down to Davenport signal box thinking to get a colour photo of the Up mid-afternoon goods but it did not appear. However 48679 (9D) brought down a train to Arpley - apparently a timetable revision. 'Joe', the signalman, told me that a lot of goods are being re-scheduled because of the non-co-operation of train drivers with regard to crew crossing: e.g. the Hooton is going to be much earlier. A 'Pacific' *City of Leeds* had brought a train from London so it was a pleasant surprise to have it come to turn on the triangle.

EDGELEY JUNCTION

27 3 60 Noticed from a main line train that some or all of the overhead for the first 200 yards or so of the Buxton line, i.e; from the junction of the Adswood Road Bridge (No.1)

9 4 60 Confirmed that wiring beyond the junction had been completed. A colour light signal on the down line is also installed, but not in use, as well as new signal wiring to and beyond Davenport Junction box.

10 6 60 The colour light signalling at Edgeley Junction was brought into use recently. (Probably 30.5.60). Including all Down signals on Buxton line as far as distant for Davenport Junction, which is now a three position colour light, incorporating 2 yellow and 1 green light. The line is track circuited.

18 6 60 (Sat). Went up to Dove Holes on 7.50 am from Davenport.

Adswood, 13th June 1959. Having first reversed from London Road to Cheadle Village Junction via Edgeley Junction (No 2), 'Coronation' Pacific No **46233** *Duchess of Sutherland* was captured on camera heading east across the 'Khyber' towards Davenport Junction, having just passed over the Crewe line south of Stockport. Reversal at Davenport Junction would be followed by a tender first trip back to Manchester. ***J W Sutherland***

Davenport Junction, 6th March 1960. One of the numerous occasions when Down Buxton trains were diverted over the 'Khyber Pass' as a result of Sunday engineering work at Edgeley Junction sees the first morning service of the day (dep. Buxton 8.30) head off towards Cheadle Village Junction.

(Below) Davenport, 13th May 1961. Activity on the branch frequently increased with movement of ECS (Empty Coaching Stock) to and from nearby Woodsmoor. This Saturday operation sees Fowler Class 4 No **42391** (9B-Stockport) passing Davenport coal sidings with a nine coach train. The coal siding closed to traffic on 15th June 1964 and was removed during the early months of 1965 following a January Redundant Assets meeting at which Mr Nicholson - Station Master, Davenport - was in attendance. All this page; ***J W Sutherland***

(Right) Davenport, 6th October, 1962. On its return trip, the New Mills 'shunt', having just worked the coal siding, heads off on the last stage of its journey to Adswood. Over the last few years, the scheduling of the 'shunt' had seen a regular 'slot' at Disley Goods around ten o'clock to deal with Bowaters traffic, allowing sufficient time for the run down to Woodsmoor where the train would be put inside the Down Loop there whilst the 10.15 ex-Buxton passenger train passed. Here we see 'Jubilee' Class No **45632** *Tonga*, a Stockport (9B) engine from 12/62 until 8/65, re-commencing its work - a 'Bowaters' van leading the train - in the direction of Davenport Junction.

(Above) Giving the appearance of the main line rather than a secondary route, Black Five No **45439** (21C-Bromsgrove) pulls its train of twelve empty carriages past Davenport Junction on the short trip to Hazel Grove where the stock, from an ex-Aberystwth working, will be stabled. The overlap in technology is evident with the cantilevered bracket (colour light) signals, commissioned in June 1960, for Davenport Junction (home) and Edgeley Junction (distant) , whist beyond the signal box is the tall LNWR signal post with the Davenport Junction home 'board'which still had a few more years life in it. **(Below)** The headlamp code (lamp positioned above left hand buffer-facing) was carried on Freight, Mineral or Ballast Trains stopping at intermediate stations. Of all the Down freight trains, this, the 3.30pm ex-Buxton to Stockport was arguably the slowest. It was scheduled to pass Davenport Junction at about 7.30 in the evening, having stopped on three occasions en-route at Bibbingtons/Dove Holes, Disley and Woodsmoor to allow for the passage of passenger trains. Add to that shunting requirements at Whaley Bridge and wagon brake adjustments (as required) in the usual places, it was not difficult to see how fours hours was consumed. An Edge Hill (8A) Class 5 No **45398** approaches Davenport Junction on 24th August 1961.

Both: ***J W Sutherland***

The popular perception that LNWR 'Super D's' were the only form of freight motive power on the 'Wessy', as the line was frequently known, can be given credence by the three views here at Davenport. They were certainly regular performers over the line and both Buxton and Stockport Edgeley depots had modest allocations, particularly in the last years that the class remained in operation.

Above is **49210** (9D) approaching Davenport Junction with a Down Class J goods from Buxton on 9th July 1958. The coal siding would remain in use for another six years. 49210 was built in 1913 as LNWR No 767 (Crewe Works No 5152) and renumbered 9210 in 1927. It was originally built as a Class G1. ***J W Sutherland***

(Centre) Long time Stockport Edgeley (9B) engine No **49010** was into the last twelve months of its life when photographed at Davenport with the returning 'New Mills shunt' on 5th July 1958 (Saturday). Surprisingly, the crew of the engine on this particular morning did not enjoy the protection of a tender cab. ***J W Sutherland***

(Right-lower) Having left the bulk of its train - mainly vans from Disley Goods and New Mills Newtown - on the main line, **49453** (9B-Stockport) stands alongside the coal siding, 'buffering-up' to the loaded wagons to enable the shunter to uncouple them. ***J W Sutherland***

(Right) Davenport, 9th October 1954. Tidy under-foot conditions are notable in the foreground alongside the coal siding in this view of Buxton's stalwart Fowler 2-6-4 tank No **42368** with a modest load of three carriages which form the 2.25 (SO) Mayfield to Buxton train. It is worth reflecting here that the Buxton line services were still two years away from the regular interval pattern accepted as standard by today's travellers. During the week, there was a gap approaching four hours after the 12.10pm departure from London Road. Four additional trains softened the blow on Saturdays, the 2.25 being the last before one at 4pm which called at Longsight en-route, no doubt to pick up returning visitors sampling the attractions of Belle Vue Gardens. ***J W Sutherland***

(Left) Davenport, 9th October, 1954. Described by the photographer as an 'Up Goods', Stanier 8F No **48726** (6C-Birkenhead) will have no problem 'hauling' this short train of two cattle wagons and brake van. There is every likelyhood that the train was bound for Chapel-en-le Frith South which, along with Chapel Central station on the Midland line, catered for a particular variety of French 'Charolais' cattle which were being brought into the area for 'fattening-up' by local farmers. Derek Ashworth, at the time *'box lad at Chinley*, remembers opening the wagon doors with a certain amount of trepidation to water the newly arrived beasts and then making a hasty retreat as the they sought their freedom.

J W Sutherland

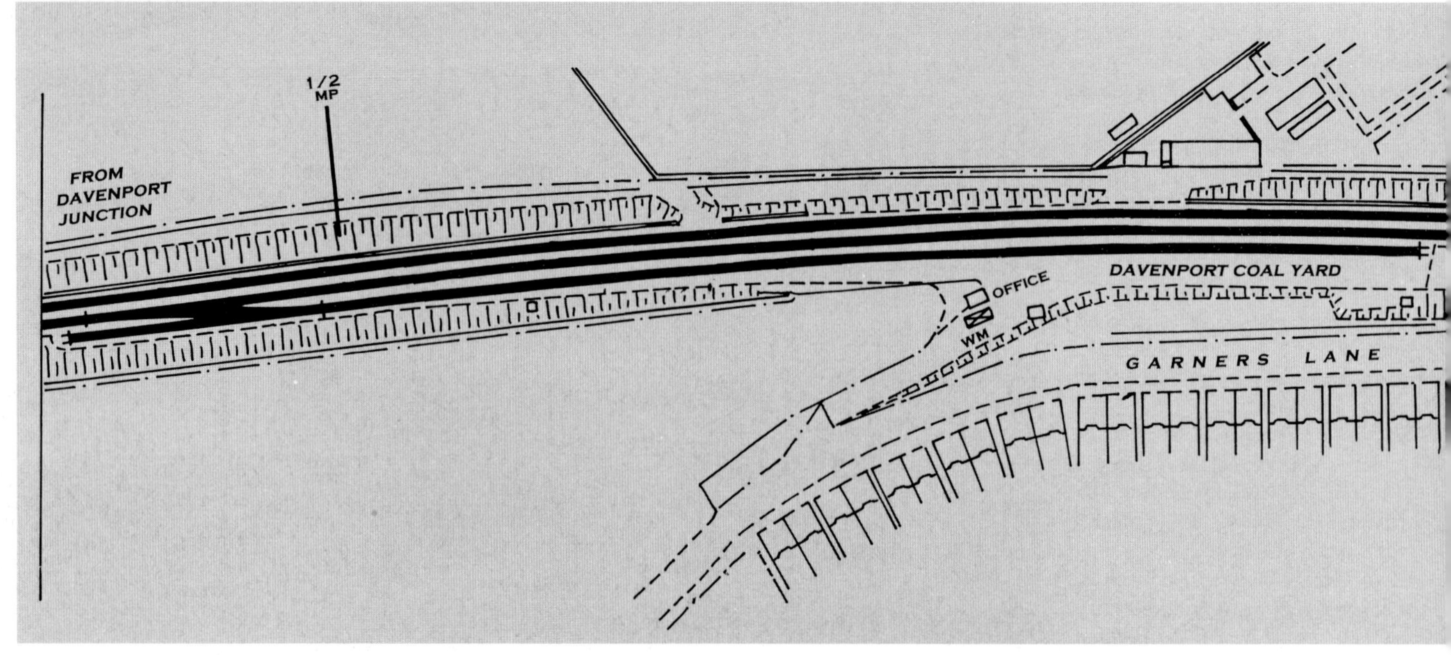

Davenport, 8th September 1956. In the weeks before the introduction of the diesel railcars, 8F No **48425** (9A-Longsight) pulls its train, the 2.25pm ex-Buxton to Manchester, away from Davenport station. On Saturdays, the service terminated at Mayfield. The engine is likely to have been used in emergency due to non-availability for whatever reason of other motive power, normally the 2-6-4 tank engines. Although nowadays the facility would be regarded as 'useful', a perhaps tenuous connection with this train was possible at Middlewood where passengers for Higher Poynton or Bollington could have alighted to catch the 4.30 ex-London Road to Macclesfield via Reddish service. ***J W Sutherland***

(Left) Davenport, 9th September 1958. The 5.50pm 'commuter' train from London Road to Buxton casts an early evening shadow across the embankment of the shallow cutting on the approach to Davenport station. This Monday to Friday working ran non-stop to Stockport (Slow Line), being allowed 11 minutes for the six mile first stage of the journey to Buxton. A Class Five was a booked regular on this turn, **45111** (9A-Longsight) being the representative on this occasion. The gradient post to the right of the engine marks the end of a 1 in 106 climb stretching back to a point just after Edgeley Junction. The change to 1 in 99 indicated here continues through the platforms of Davenport station. ***J W Sutherland***

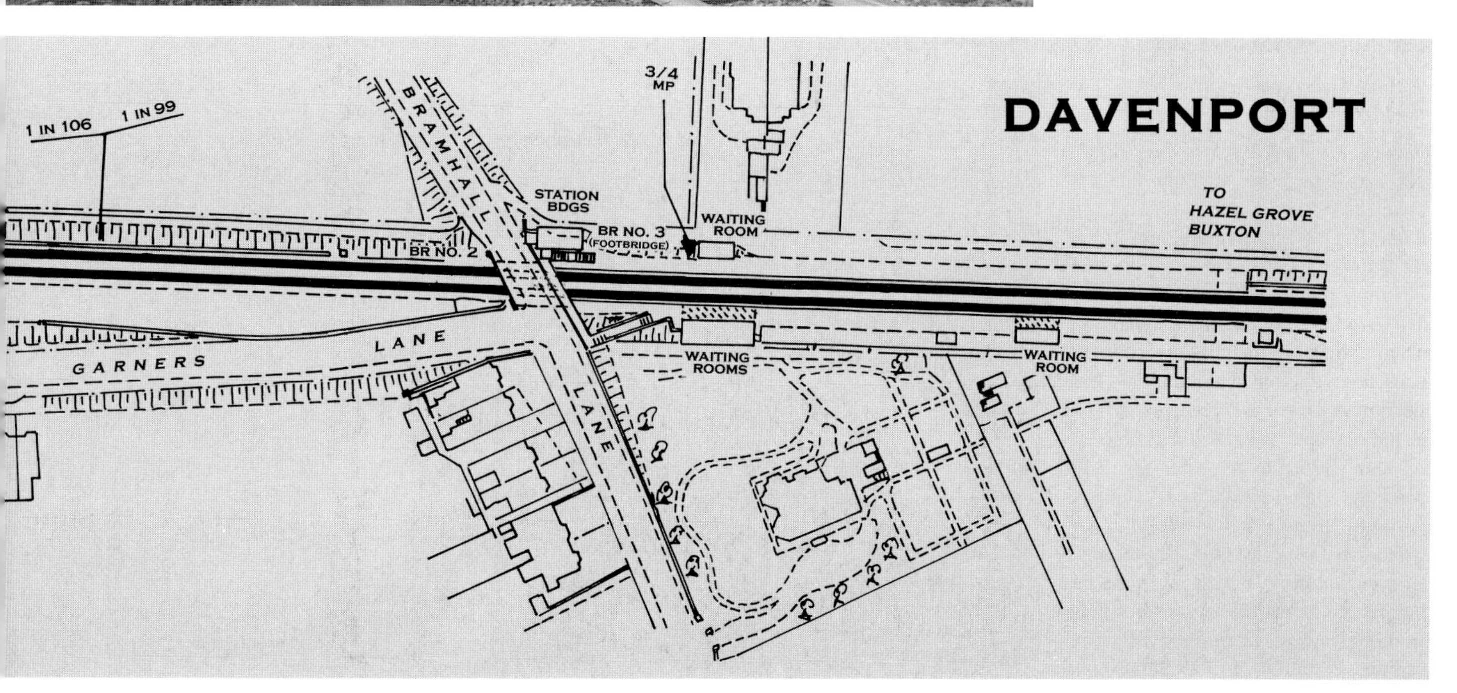

(Left) Davenport, 24th September 1960. The main entrance to Davenport station was, and still is, at road level on the Buxton side of Bramhall Lane. Small timber canopies protected the passengers from the weather over both the entrance and access to the footbridge (to the Down platform) and stairway serving the Up (to Buxton) platform. Thought to date from around 1880, the booking office building was, broadly speeaking, an above average two-storey block, highlighted by traditional London & North Western Railway features. Notwithstanding the close proximity of the 'Belisha beacon' (flashing orange globe on a striped post, marking a pedestrian crossing) and street lamps, the station lighting was by gas; note the mantle beneath the station sign. Davenport, although only four minutes travelling time by rail to Stockport's Edgeley station, was more of a commuter facility for Manchester, best times in the region of 14/15 minutes. Competition, if there was ever any doubt, came from the buses of the North Western Road Car Company and Stockport Corporation (No's 23 and 25) which, with tuppence halfpenny (1p) single fare to Mersey Square (Stockport), was more than a match for British Railways sixpence ($2^1/2$p), which included an unprotected walk up or down Edgeley station's approach! Not so subtly placed is the bus timetable notice case affixed to the bridge parapet. ***Graham Whitehead*** **(Below)** The leafy suburb of Davenport Park looking in the direction of Cale Green (and Stockport) is seen in this immediate post WW2 period view of Bramhall Lane. The road rises just beyond the parked car to cross the Buxton line at Davenport station. Centre to the skyline is the spire of St Georges Church, Stockport

(Right) Davenport, 5th July 1961. The retaining wall abutting Garners Lane (right) and parapet of Bramhall Lane (Br. No 2) provide the backdrop to 'Jubilee' Class 4-6-0 No **45700** *Amethyst* (26A-Newton Heath) as she leaves with the Buxton to Stockport parcels train. This almost nocturnal view is remarkable in that the train was scheduled to leave Davenport at 9.44 in the evening. Having left Buxton at 8.20pm, five minutes after the 8.15 passenger train to Manchester, calls of varying times were scheduled at stations en-route prior to arrival around 9.48 in Stockport, a mere $7^1/2$ minutes before the 9.15 passenger departure from Buxton was due to enter Edgeley station. ***J W Sutherland***

(Right) Davenport, 15th October 1958. Schoolboys take note of the 'big-wheeled' visitor alongside the opposite (Down) platform about to depart with the 8.26am service to Manchester. This, the 7.50am train from Buxton was a longstanding regular in the timetables and was still diagrammed for steam working. A clean looking member of the 'Patriot' Class, No **45521** *Rhyl* (8A-Edge Hill) prepares to leave for Stockport, confirming the regular use of engines based at the Liverpool shed for this turn. By the beginning of 1960, the train, which had long enjoyed 'express' status between Stockport and Manchester, was scheduled additionally to call at Heaton Chapel and Levenshulme, albeit with only an increase of four minutes to the journey time. Although publicly advertised as the 8.26 train, it was not authorised to depart before 8.29 according to the Working Timetable. ***J W Sutherland***

Davenport, 1st March 1958. Despite the introduction of an hourly interval diesel service, steam managed to retain a foothold. However, this Saturdays Only service, the 12.10pm ex-London Road had managed to keep the old traditions alive and was given a schedule of 56 minutes for the journey to Buxton, calling all stations after Stockport. With the introduction of the summer timetable in June, the working was placed in the hands of a dmu. 'Crab' No **42942** (9D) departs with an Up train, leaving behind a deserted Down platform. The platforms at this end of the station incidentally were extended in the early 1920's. The waiting shelter on the left was part of the improvements to accommodate longer trains, which included a requirement -by affected residents - for the railway company to provide high close-boarded fencing at the rear of the platform to retain privacy. The presence of sleepers on the platform suggests some spot replacement, carried out no doubt between trains. The gas lamp once again reigns supreme. ***J W Sutherland***

(Right) Davenport, 24th September 1960. The 'busy' end of Davenport's Down platform had a substantial awning to the buildings which when first built comprised two waiting rooms, Ladies and Gentleman, the former which included toilet facilities - note the roof ventilators at the far end - Gents urinals were later added externally on the Buxton end of the building. It is not totally clear if the refinements (such as the canopy) included modifications to the previous structure. The window arrangements/layout certainly appear to be the same as the original. It was replaced in the 1970's as part of a GMPTE station improvement scheme. ***Graham Whitehead***

(Centre) Davenport, c. 1915. An earlier era but a scene instantly recognisable. The waiting room on the Up platform (for Buxton) was built as just that, a large, single room; one can imagine a large coal fire during the winter months. The tended gardens would be kept in similar good order for the best part of the next five decades, the cast iron letters of Davenport's 'running-in' (name) board only succumbing to the maroon enamel sign of British Railways some forty years later. The spacious end walls of the building, advantageously facing incoming trains, advertise local businesses such as Finnigans (then of Deansgate, Manchester) long before they transferred to Wilmslow (later becoming Hoopers), and Ellis Sykes, long established owners of a much missed hardware store in Princes Street, Stockport. The L&NWR was advertising excursions to Belle Vue. The view here, taken from the footbridge, shows the station before the platforms had been extended in the early 1920's.

(Left) Davenport, 19th August 1961 Stockport and District 'Wakes' brought alive many local stations during August. The second Saturday of the fortnight sees holidaymakers lining the Down platform as the 9.45am Whaley Bridge to Blackpool North special runs alongside, comprising Class Five No **45218** (27C-Southport) and eight non-corridor coaches. Programmes of special and excursion trains were advertised locally throughout the fortnight's duration. ***J W Sutherland***

Excursions provided for and promoted by the Ramblers Association were extremely popular, particularly for locations along the freight only Buxton to Ashbourne serving Dovedale. The occasions brought double-headed trains to the Buxton line, regularly consisting of ten coaches. Both views on this page show Stockport (9B) based locomotives providing pilot duties and the obvious need for additional motive power. **(Above)** Leisure attire of varying degrees is in evidence although two items follow the common theme, walking boots and walking stick. Both engines, Fowler 2-6-4T No **42379** and Class 5MT No **45133** (5B-Crewe South), have steam to spare as an Ashbourne excursion (from Manchester Exchange) pulls alongside Davenport's Up platform on Sunday 10th May 1959. **(Below)** Another Fowler 2-6-4 tank, No **42372**, in its last months before withdrawal, pilots **45382** (8B-Warrington) at the head of eight carriages forming the Manchester Piccadilly to Ashbourne Ramblers Association excursion (27th May 1962). ***J W Sutherland***

DIARY EXTRACTS FOR......

DAVENPORT

2.6.57. We travelled on a half-day excursion (to Ashbourne) as far as Alsop-en-le-Dale. It was a train from Bolton via Manchester Victoria and was headed both ways by **42859** and **42655** (9 bogies). Another train from London Road was hauled by **42322** and **42382**. Other excursions were run from Nottingham and, I believe, Kidsgrove and Stoke. In the evening a 'Crab' was seen on a 3 total train and, I think an 0-6-0 4F and a BR 4MT - or 5MT 4-6-0 on another.

4.6.57. After visit to Hayfield I travelled back from New Mills Newtown to Davenport on the 8.54pm Buxton to Manchester train which consisted of diesel units Sc50341 and Sc56096. At Disley we passed a Down goods hauled by **49153** which had been shunted on to the Up line, while just beyond the station (Manchester end) another goods (Up) hauled by **48479** was waiting. On the 7.59am departure from Davenport that same morning were Gloucester RC&W set Sc50339 and Sc56094.

17.6.57. From today the 7.59am departure from Davenport has usually, if not always, been a 4-car set or, if a Birmingham RC&W 3-car set is included in a 5-car set.

On **2.7.57.** the 6.24pm Down departure from Davenport consisted of dmu's E56077/E50225 (running about 8 - 9 minutes late). The 6.20pm from London Road was M50433/M59141/ 50485 + 50434/59142/50486. Fitters in the cab and obvious engine trouble. On time at Davenport but time lost immediately train got on to the long grade beyond Hazel Grove. On the 8.54pm from Buxton we had Sc50339/ Sc56094. It was running about 5 minutes late probably due to the antics of the over cautious driver who approached the stations as if we didn't have any brakes.

29.6.57. The 9.02am departure from Davenport (Saturday) consisted of M50134 /M56030 (Metro-Cammell) 50429/59137 and 50481 (Birmingham RC&W).

23.7.57. The 7.20 London Road to Buxton train comprised M50135/M56091 (Metro-Cammell).

26.7.57. 9.02am departure from Davenport to London Road (ex Whaley Bridge) consisted of Metro-Cammell No's. M50390/M56145 coupled to Birmingham RC&W M50430/ M59138/ M50482.

26.8.57. M56148 (Metro-Cammell) was noted, presumably on the 7.59am departure from Davenport to London Road.

On **30.8.57** Sc56102/Sc50347 was noted, apparently on the 7.59am departure from Davenport to London Road (ex Hazel Grove).

On **20.9.57** the 3.20 pm London Road - Buxton consisted of BRC&W new set M50446, M59154, M50498.

On **12.10.57** Went into Manchester from Davenport in set M50501/ M59157/ M50449.

On **14.10.57** 7.56am from Hazel Grove to London Road. Train included M56109 (Gloucester RC&W).

On **23.10.57**. Same train consisted of M56090 and M50134 (Metro-Cammell with Rolls Royce engines).

On **9.11.57** 50498/59154/50446 + 50453/ 59161 and 50505, made up the 10.20am London Road to Buxton train.

Note on **16.11.57**. It can now be said that practically all Buxton diesels are probably worked by Birmingham RC&W 3-car sets (or multiples thereof).

Davenport station is being repainted. The station won prizes for tidiness and gardens this year.

19.5.59. Saw a taper boilered 2-6-2T running light at about 3pm between Hazel Grove and Davenport - possibly it had brought up to Bramhall Moor Lane some of the 15 to 20 coaches that are stored up the goods line there.

26.9 59. We all went to Blackpool on a cheap day excursion to see the illuminations - and had the afternoon on the beach. The 9 carriage train which started at Buxton was headed by **42943** for both the outward and return journeys.

28.9.59 **42839** was on the 5.50pm London Road - Buxton train.

3.10.59 (Sat) Caught the 8.38am departure from Davenport for Dove Holes.

17 10 59 Shunted Davenport Siding, (put off one wagon-coal) On way back from Adswood saw **42888** on the train to Hooton.

25 10 59 (Sun) A Manchester Exchange and Stockport rambler's excursion to Hartington and Ashbourne was hauled by **42583** and **42494.**

28 10 59 (Wed) Saw the Up Buxton parcels train running late on my way to work this morning, **42874** and a bogie parcels van.

29 10 59 (Thurs) **46114** was on the 8.26am departure from Davenport (to Manchester).

3.11.59 (Tues) Parcels train to Buxton again late, consisted of 42792, two fish vans and a goods brake.

18.11.59 (Wed) For the first time that I can recall, noted the Birkenhead - Buxton train leaving Cheadle Village Junction behind a LNW 0-8-0, 36 wagons and brake, no banker.

19.11.59 (Thurs) The Birkenhead - Buxton train consisted of 51 wagons and brake with 8F back and front.

27.11.59 (Fri) A Class 5 on the Birkenhead - Buxton train (8F banking).

28.11.59 (Sat) Just after arrival (back from Middlewood) at 11.54, 49554 came through on an Up mixed goods, probably a special.

10.12.59 (At Cheadle Heath) Saw an LNW 0-8-0 banking the Birkenhead - Buxton train.

29.12.59 Birkenhead train was banked by a 4F 0-6-0.

3.2.60.(Weds) An unrebuilt Patriot on the Birkenhead train today, 47 wagons and brake van, with an 8F banking in rear. Have noted some weeks now that the Stockport - Buxton morning 'Shunter' runs via Cheadle Village Junction, There is a brake van on each end of the train and the engine runs round the train by leaving it at Cheadle Village Junction and going off west to the nearest cross-over probably at Cheadle Goods Station.

9.2.60. 48406 on Stockport - Buxton 'shunter'.

12.2.60 An LNW 0-8-0 with tender cab, was on the Birkenhead train. A Crab was banking.

13.2.60 49277 (9D) on special Buxton - Arpley.

16.2.60 Birkenhead train, 8F - 54 wagons, brake 'Crab'

23.2.60 73139 was on the Up parcels, which consisted of 3- 4 Sheet vans and a goods brake.

7.3.60 An 0-8-0 on the Stockport - Buxton shunter, probably 49277, which I had seen earlier in Adswood Yard, from which the train was started.

Davenport, c 1965. A Manchester bound train prepares to leave amidst a scene, probably one of the last, of well cared for station gardens which had been a proud part of railway tradition for generations of railwaymen. Rationalisation of the railway system following Dr Beeching's tenure was in its infancy although the waiting shelter at the Hazel Grove end of the Down platform had been removed, possibly as a result of shorter trains and the withdrawal of First Class facilities which tended to segregate intending passengers to particular parts of the platform.

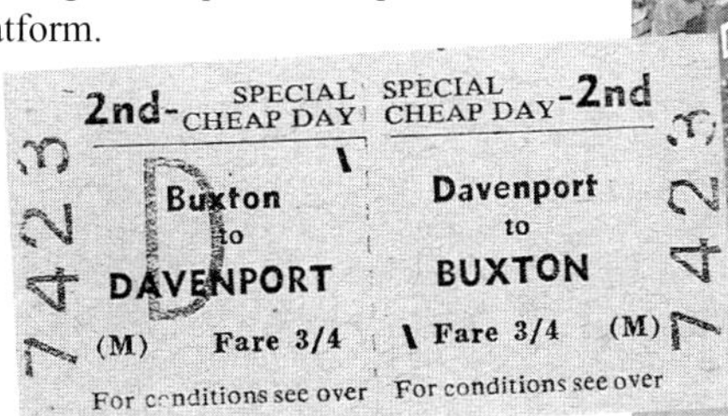

14.3.60 (Mon) Noted following en-route to and from Buxton 42935, 42937, 48679, and 48728.

6.4.60 2-10-0 noted banking the Birkenhead train on these days. On the 7th, 42925 was noted on the 5.40pm train from London Road.

15.4.60 42886 was on a 10 total excursion Hazel Grove etc., to Blackpool North (Good Friday).

18.4.60 (Easter Monday) The one Down steam train in the morning was hauled by 42786.

21.4.60 LNW 0-8-0 on Birkenhead train.

11.5.60 Birkenhead train, 59 wagons and brake 8F back and front from Cheadle Village Junction.

13.5.60 (Fri) LNW 0-8-0 apparently up from Cheadle Village Junction about 10.30 am with vans and open wagons.

2.5.60 (Fri) A Jubilee on the Birkenhead train (8F banking)

26.5.60 (Thurs) 42369 on 5.37pm Up train.

28.5.60 (Sat) By 7.47am departure from Davenport to Dove Holes, and walked to Buxton by degrees.

29.5.60 (Sun) We travelled on the Ashbourne excursion as far as Tissington (somebody lying in luggage rack as no seats left by time 10 coach train got to Davenport. Took water at Whaley Bridge on outward journey. Engines both ways 42932 (9B) and 42439 (26F). At Parsley Hay we passed 42605 and 44394 on a train from Nottingham and at Alsop a 6-car DMU (Cravens I think) from Hinckley, Loughborough and Leicester. During the early afternoon saw (I think!) 42932 and 42439 going north again with only 4 coaches and another DMU (If I remember correctly). There is now no loop or siding at Tissington while some of the second (Up) track north of Parsley Hay has just recently been lifted.

4.6.60 (Sat) Caught the 8.38am departure from Davenport as far as New Mills. For some reason it consisted of 2 power cars only No's M50422 and M50426.

7.6.60 (Tues) 42886 (9B) plus 4 on 7.26am ex Buxton, 5.37 am 42923 (9A) and 5 on 5.50 train. 49401 (9B) was on the return shunt from New Mills. 42886 was on the mid-day Longsight - Buxton (with two coaches) off the morning passenger trains as usual.

8.6.60 48308 (8D-Widnes) on Rowsley - Adswood 48280 on special of sand for Whaley Bridge, 42943 Longsight - Buxton (with two coaches).

19.6.60 (Sun) We went to Blackpool Central (direct route) not via St. Annes on an excursion from Hazel Grove but calling at Davenport, Stockport etc., 10 total hauled by 44741 (Caprotti)

9.6.60 (Tue) 42892 (9B) Was on 8.26am from Davenport 48715 (8B) on the Down goods - possibly Arpley. 48326 (8D) on later Down goods 8.45 Rowsley - Adswood. 48504 (2B Nuneaton) was on the Birkenhead backed by 92009: 42943 was on the goods from Longsight (with usual coaches).

10.6.60 (Whit Friday) 42772 + 4 on 5.50pm Mayfield - Buxton 92008 (17C) on 4.10pm Rowsley - Adswood.

22.6.60 (Weds) 42381 (9A) was on 5.37 express. 42848 (9B) was on 5.50 train.

1.7.60 Evening at Davenport.48451 was on the train to Briggs Sidings. 48088 (17C) was on the train from Rowsley consisting of ballast hoppers only. 42355 (9C Macclesfield) was on the Down parcels which consisted of about 5 vans and the brake.

12.7.60 MLS visit to Buxton Yard. Went up to Buxton from Davenport on 5.37pm from Mayfield - Buxton express, stopped at Davenport, Disley and Whaley Bridge only. 8.55pm 48558 (9D) passed Davenport with an Up load of empties (probably 7.5pm Latchford Old Line to Rowsley).

6.8.60 (Sat) 44941 was on the ECS Edgeley - Buxton 9 coaches as usual.

10.8.60 (Wed) 42570 + 4 on 5.37pm express. 42854 (9B)+ 5 on 5.50pm passenger. 42942 (9D) on Up goods to Briggs - all empty mineral wagons.

1.9.60 42938 (9A) on 5.37 express (4 total). 45190 on 5.50pm slow (5 total). All trains running to and from London Road since last Saturday i.e. none to be from Mayfield which was closed on Saturday 27th August.

............continued on page 41

(Above) Davenport, 23rd November 1963. A sight which greeted so many passengers in the early 1960's following publication of the 'Beeching Report' for the 'Reshaping of British Railways'. The green notices announcing the withdrawal of railway passenger services were systematically part-covered by an announcement that 'objections had been received'. What followed was a bitter and protracted struggle by groups and individuals (in which Wallace Sutherland played a prominent part) to keep the line open. Needless to say, the campaign was won, but more of that elsewhere. **(Right)** The entrance on Bramhall Lane provided access via the Booking Hall to the footbridge and a staircase serving the Up (to Buxton) platform. Features such as the sash windows and cast iron staircase ballustrade highlighted the LNWR policy of component standardisation.

Davenport, 15th February 1969. Will someone shut those doors! We have all been in trains when some thoughtful individual jumps from the carriage door and leaves the doors open to the elements. A wintry scene at Davenport station which clearly indicates the work that has been put in to keep the platforms functional as a 6-car diesel train waits pending departure for Buxton. ***J W Sutherland***

Davenport, 8th August 1954 (Sunday). Until the end of 1956, the 10.20am had been one of those trains which had operated every Sunday on the Buxton line throughout the year for many years. It was one of the four trains which made up the winter timetable, increasing to six each way during the summer months. Following introduction of the diesel units, the Sunday service was initially increased to seven trains in each direction, a three-hour gap in the morning reverting to a two-hourly basic interval for the rest of the day. By 1958, this too had given way to an hourly interval service which continues to this day. Returning to our picture, the 10.20am ex-London Road, comprising Fowler tank No **42350** (9A-Longsight) and seven coaches, darkens the atmosphere on its arrival at Davenport.
J W Sutherland

.....continued from page 39
5.9.60 42658 on 5.3pm express. 44834 on 5.50pm train.

8.9.60 Went to Derby via Buxton. 42943 was on the 7 bogies 7.26am Buxton to London Road and 44940 on the 7.50.

26.9.60 (Mon)Was told tonight that the last regular steam passenger train ran last Friday

23.9.60 The timetable is unchanged for the present! Tonight the 5.40, 5.45, and 5.50 trains all consisted of 6 cars (2 x 3)

1.10.60 (Sat) We went up to Whaley Bridge on the 9.35 am departure from Davenport (6-car)

3.10.60 (Wed) 5.17pm Piccadilly - Disley train extended to New Mills, Furness Vale and Whaley Bridge from today.

15.10.60 (Sat) To Whaley Bridge.

29.10.60. Visit to Middlewood to take photos in view of Middlewood Higher pending closure (on 7th November).

18.11.60 (Fri) 44556 was on the Up parcels - one bogie and one 4 wheel van.

24.11.60 44413 was noted running up light past Davenport at about 8am.

6.4.61 (Thur) 48519 was on Up 'shunter'.

8.4.61 Visit to Middlewood.

13.4.61 (Th) 42947 noted passing Davenport about 8am with a short Up goods, presumably a special.

15.4.61 (Sat) Visit to Davenport coal siding. 42931 (9B) on return New Mills shunt: 92047 (probably 8C) and 48182 (17B) banking, on Birkenhead. 48428 (9D) on train to Hooton 48322 (9D) - 40 wagons and brake - to Widnes. 42889 (9D) from Rowsley which arrived at 12.45 and went onto the Cheadle Village line.

9.5.61 (Tues) Evening. Went to Buxton Shed ex 5.28pm; 5 Birmingham Cars. Noticed we went up the bank after Hazel Grove at steady 30 - 31mph. The train was very full at Davenport where a lot got off. At Disley I got off and later caught the express (dep Piccadilly 5.40pm).

14.5.61 (Sun) 42849 pulled a well filled 8 total Ashbourne excursion from Piccadilly only.

23.5.61 (Tues) 48062 was on the Up 'shunter ' to Buxton.

26.5.61 (Whit Friday) Went up to Disley.

30.5.61 'D' was on the Birkenhead train today; 45198 (5B) was on the evening Down parcels.

31.5.61 45074 was on the Down parcels.

13.6.61 (Tu) 92033 was noted at Davenport on an Up mixed goods at 7.55pm.

30.6.61 (Fri) 42947 passed Davenport at 9pm on a Down mixed goods; 45299 was on the Down goods.

5.7.61 (Wed) 45700 (26A) very dirty, was on the Down parcels (2 bogie parcels vans and 2 four-wheeled goods vans - one at least a 'fish').

8.7.61 (Sat) 42849 (9B) was on 12 total empty stock to Hazel Grove about 5.40pm, probably ex SO train from Aberystwyth.

22.7.61 (Sat-pm) 45439 (21C) was on the 12 coach empty coaches to Hazel Grove ex the Aberystwyth train and 42849 (9B) on the 6 coaches of the Paignton train.

Davenport, 9th June 1960 (Thursday) A regular occurance for the period took the form of carriages marshalled within the 12.29pm Longsight to Buxton freight. This operation was carried out to balance the working of vehicles used during the peak periods. The leisurely progress of the train was only interrupted at Bibbingtons Sidings where the Up Loop provided refuge whilst the 1.20pm ex-Manchester London Road passenger diesel passed on its way to Buxton. ***J W Sutherland***

2nd - SINGLE SINGLE - 2nd
Davenport to
Davenport Middlewood (Lower) Middlewood (Lower) Davenport
MIDDLEWOOD
(LOWER)
(M) 0/8 Fare 0/8 (M)
For conditions see over For conditions see over
9695 9695

29.7.61 (Sat) 45291 (9B) was on 12 empty coaches to Hazel Grove ex-Aberystwyth.

8.8.61 (Tues) 48677 (9F) was on a Down mixed goods (largely coal) passing Davenport at 8.15 and running onto the branch towards Cheadle Village Junction.

9.8.61 (Weds) 48322 (9D) was on a Down goods at Davenport about 6.35pm, 3 wagons only, of which one of coke, was shunted off at Davenport Siding. 49391 was on the Up Briggs and 45129 took 15 empty coaches up towards Hazel Grove.

12.8.61 (Saturday-Stockport Wakes). With Graham at Davenport before breakfast, saw 45132 on the 9 non-corridor of the 6.45am Whaley Bridge - Fleetwood (IOM boat connection). Train 1Z82. After breakfast we went up to Hazel Grove on the 8.14 diesel. Here, 45426 (5A) and 42943 (9B) came up coupled together and went back on the Down line. 45553 *Canada* (5B) was on the 9 non-corridor of the 8.25 Whaley Bridge - Birkenhead Central train (1Z84). The Buxton 'shunter' although a long train, came through at a fast clip headed by 48502 (5B); 42316 (9B) came through light engine. After the 9.8 diesel departure, 45426 shortly backed in - with 10 coaches, which had been lying in the Woodsmoor Down Loop when we went up (was told that the 'Crab' had been sent up to assist this manoeuvre but had been sent back when it was realised that it was quite unnecessary. 45426's train was 1Z79 (1X79) according to the sign on the engine, the 9.15 to Bridlington, Filey and Scarborough. The first Wakes train was 1P89, the 10am Whaley Bridge - Morecambe, which consisted of two Buxton 3-car sets and I gather an ordinary Summer Saturday Buxton - Morecambe working which is usually ECS to Edgeley. Before going home we saw 90147 (6B) on the Hooton train which, according to Graham was 49 wagons and brake. The Birkenhead train was cancelled through lack of staff and I don't think the Widnes train ran either. In the evening noted 42931 at 5.45pm with 6 coaches ex-Paignton.

19.8.61 (Sat) 45218 (27C-Southport) was on the 9.45 Whaley Bridge - Blackpool Wakes train (8 non-corridor).

23.8.61 (Wed) 48373 (8B) was on the evening train to Briggs.

24.8.61 (Thursday) 45398 (8A) came through Davenport at 6.40pm with a few vans, presumably on the 3.30pm from Buxton; 48262 was on the train to Briggs. 90678 (56D) Mansfield was on an Up empty stock train at 7.10pm(8 corridor bogies).

26.8.61 (Sat) 48448 (6C-Birkenhead) was on an 8 total Up empty stock past Davenport at 6pm.

1.9.61 (Fri) In the morning photographed 48165 (9D) on the Buxton shunter, shunting the Co-op Coal yard - two loads left. 13 empties picked up; this is the daily duty of the train.

6.9.61 (Wed) 49281 (9D) was on the evening train to Briggs which I saw passing Davenport in fine style and had observed at 6pm waiting in the coal yard (Up Side) at Edgeley.

16.9.61(Sat) Morning visit to Middlewood. Back at Davenport at 12 o'clock, the Birkenhead was still 'held' at Davenport Junction. It was headed by 90686 (8F-Springs Branch) and banked by 44134 (17C); Several wagons in the train were way billed to *"Private Siding, Ladmanlow"*

28.2.62 The 6.26pm departure from Davenport to Manchester was a 2-car Metro Cammell set. stencilled 9A on the buffer beam.

12.3.62 (Mon) 48165 noted at Davenport on Down goods (mixed) at 5.20pm.

24.3.62 (Sat) 45431 noted on shunter.

13.4.62 (Friday) 49141 seen on the Birkenhead - Buxton goods.

20.4.62 (Good Friday) Went down to Davenport Station and saw; 45385 (9A) and 12 bogies on the excursion to Llandudno; 44747 (9A) + 10 bogies on the excursion to Blackpool. Both trains consisted of modern express stock, the first being a kitchen car and the latter a restaurant / buffet car. There might have been a total of over 120 passengers from Davenport for the two trains, in spite of the uncertain weather prospects. A 5-car diesel to Buxton consisted of a 3-car Birmingham and 2 car 'Stalybridge' type sets was packed.

27.5.62 (Sunday) The Manchester (Piccadilly) to Ashbourne ramblers excursion consisted of 8 bogies headed (at Davenport) by 42372 (9D) and 45382. The train was well patronised but only about three-quarters full, the day being dry but dull and for the time of the year, cold.

23.5.62 (Wed) 49447 noted on Birkenhead train.

3.6.62 (Sunday) Went on Ashbourne, etc, excursion. Warm day though slightly overcast most of the time. The train was a diesel, 8 cars made up of four Derby type train sets, our car in one direction was 79669. There are one or two other diesel excursions on the line during the day. (Tissington Well Dressing was the

Davenport, 14th December 1957 (Sat) Longsight 'Crab' 2-6-0 No **42925** takes its train, the 12.50 (SO) ex-Manchester London Road to Buxton, away from the station and through the prestigious surroundings of Davenport Park. This service will soon be given over to diesel railcars which will perform to the same schedule despite being given the advantage of Fast Line running between Manchester and Stockport. The impressive housing of the Davenport area was spread out on both sides of the line and mirrored the aspirations of the business community during the latter part of the nineteenth-century. The 'striped' signal post to the left, painted in such a way as to ease sighting, carried the Davenport Junction distant signal.

J W Sutherland

main attraction). Also I noted one steam excursion which we crossed at Alsop (not officially a crossing place) in both directions. It was from Nottingham to Buxton and headed by 42896 (16A-Nottingham).

6.6.62 (Wed) 45369 was on the evening Down parcels, consisting of 2 four-wheel vans, 2 bogie vans, and a white fish van bringing up the rear.

8.6.62 At Davenport, 49381 noted on the Birkenhead.

14.6.62 (Thursday). 49438 on Birkenhead.

11.8.62 (Sat) Stockport Wakes. Noted the Liverpool (for Isle of Man) train at Davenport. 44911 (9B) + 73125 + seven coaches. Very few passengers, only about 3 joined at Davenport and none I was told at the starting station, Whaley Bridge.

18.8.62 (Sat) Went up to New Mills on the 8.35 am from Davenport. The only departing Wakes train was an 8 total from Whaley Bridge to Blackpool, which was hauled by 45291 (6B). 42892 (3B) was at New Mills on the 'shunt'. 48389 was on the Birkenhead - Buxton (no banker) and 48062 (9D) on the 'shunter'. While walking back from a look at New Mills Midland goods, saw a train go up with a 2-6-4T moving backwards, piloting a Class 5 or perhaps a return Wakes period train.

4.10.62 (Thurs) Davenport. A fine day, mostly sunny, so took many colour photos. Left Davenport on the 8.35am departure for New Mills.

26.11.62 90566 noted at Davenport at 10.5pm. On Class F Up empties.

19.1.63 (Sat) There being some snow about, went up to Middlewood in the morning. However, was too late for the Up goods trains and only saw 90197 on the return New Mills shunt and 48420 on the Rowsley-Adswood goods, now the only Down goods from Buxton on Saturday morning. Returning home passed 44497 running up light between Davenport and Woodsmoor. Spent most of my time in a permanent way hut talking to the men and keeping warm by their fire. Then was in the signal box for a while with Mr Ford. The latter said he understood the Hooton was now running over the Midland route.

25.1.63 (Friday) Arthur at Davenport told me that the 8.12am from Hazel Grove this morning had ordinary coaches hauled by a diesel loco - possibly due to a shortage of serviceable diesel units owing to the cold weather. Roads have been terrible in the Ashbourne - Dovedale district.

26.5.63 (Sun) Family all went on Ashbourne excursion. 6-car diesel set. We got off at Tissington to see Well Dressing, then walked same route as last year to Ashbourne where we got the return train. There were other excursions from Alsager (via Stoke) to Buxton, Nottingham to Buxton and Colne to Alsop-en-le-Dale. I think, 6-car diesels. Was told the speed limit now 15mph on the branch. Of course we exceeded this as track really quite good and spent much time standing at stations. June SLS Journal stated this was last day passenger trains would appear on the line. A lot of condemned open goods wagons are now stored in the sidings at Middlewood. The new Up distant signal post at Disley is still not ready for use.

24.3.64 (Tues) 46401 was on the Up goods (one bogie van and one 4-wheel van) near Davenport this morning. Noticed yesterday that a stop block appears to have been placed on the 'block' Up line between Cheadle Village Junction and Davenport Junction, fairly near the Cheadle Village end.

21.1.64 (Tues) 48275 noted passing Davenport at 9.50pm with Up train of 42 mixed empties and brake.

26.5.64 (Tuesday) 44916 noted running late on the morning Up parcels.

29.6.64 (Friday) 42920 was noted passing Davenport with an Up load of vans - no doubt for Buxton. All trains are 6-car but not particularly full. Davenport Coal Yard appears to have been closed to traffic from about August Bank Holiday. At any rate has retained no wagons on the siding since the previous week. Greenwood is still using the Up yard.

21.8.64 (Friday) C&HP Brake Van Trip. Graham and I joined the party on the 7.51am departure from Davenport to Buxton.

3.9.64 (Thurs) Caught 8.35am departure from Davenport and I travelled to Disley.

Woodsmoor, 1st January 1964. The signal box and crossing keepers cottage make a fitting frame to 'Caprotti' Class 5 No **44748** (9A-Longsight), a well known engine in and around Manchester. No New Years Day hang-over here as the engine and crew strive to take the 12.35pm ex-Longsight to Buxton freight away from Davenport. Line occupancy was maximised to allow for the passage of this train, being set inside at Whaley Bridge (37 minutes) to allow for the 1.20pm ex-Piccadilly Dmu to pass. Ten minutes were also allowed at Bibbingtons to pin down wagon brakes as required for the descent to Buxton (arr. 3.5pm). Woodsmoor signal box was an LNWR type 4 structure of 1879 with a 20-lever frame. The box closed as a Block Post in 1973 but was retained during the construction of the 'infamous' footbridge intended to replace the crossing. Final 'closure' took place on 4th November 1974. ***J W Sutherland***

Woodsmoor, 16th February 1957. The open fields surrounding Woodsmoor Crossing give a unique view of the signal box and crossing keepers cottage. With diesel multiple units still in their infancy, the railcars here are represented by Derby 'Lightweight' sets **M79681** (Driving Trailer Composite) and **M79188** (Motor Brake Second) on the 11.54am ex-Buxton to Manchester London Road train. This was an all stations service which included calls at the now long gone Heaton Norris and Longsight (for Belle Vue). Its schedule was a very creditable 58 minutes, especially for a unit with only one power car. However, uphill to Buxton, these units struggled somewhat requiring eight minutes over the hour. ***J W Sutherland***

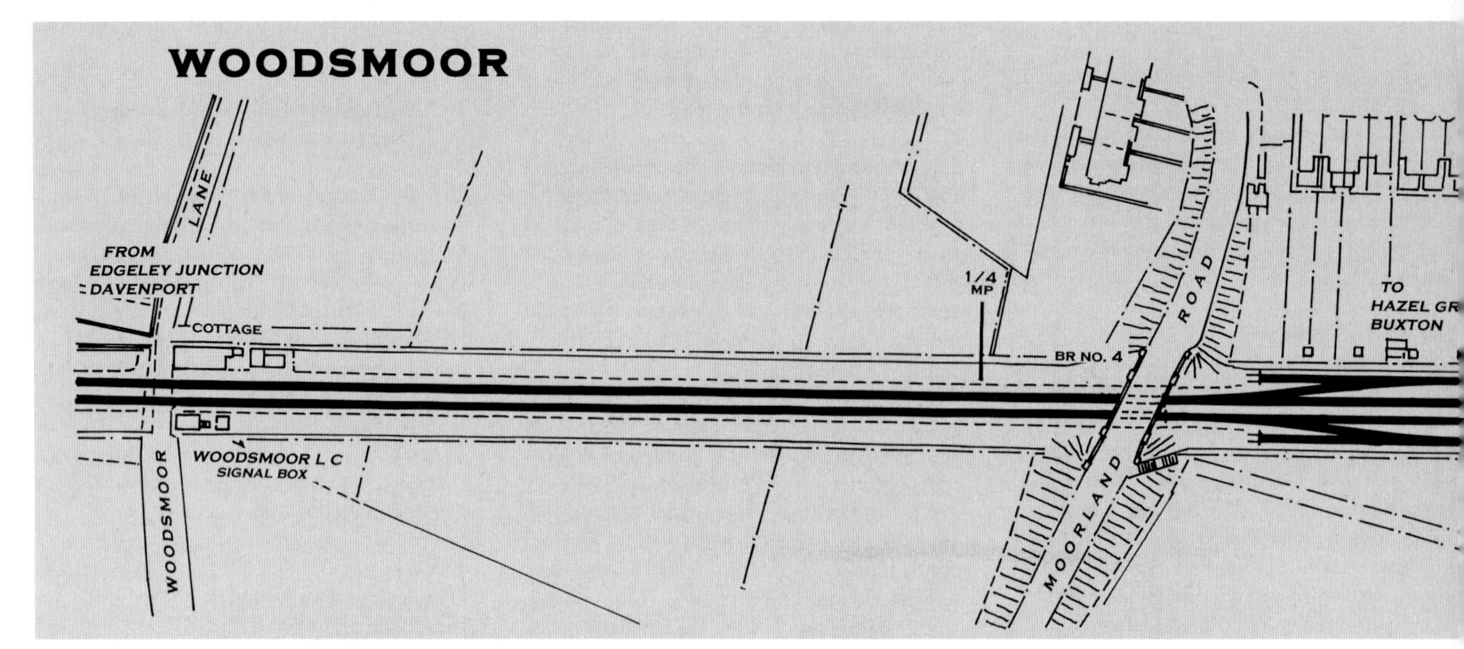

(Above) Woodsmoor, 21st May 1959. In the distance, the bridge over Moorland Road marks the starting point of the Woodsmoor Loops and site of the current Woodsmoor station. 'Jubilee' Class No **45678** *De Robeck*, at the time allocated to Edge Hill (8A), heads towards Davenport with the 7.50am ex-Buxton to Manchester train. Still capable of express passenger workings, the fortunes of *De Robeck* would change some three years later following transfer to Stockport Edgeley depot in September 1962. Relegated to 'shunt' duties on the Buxton line, the engine was withdrawn by the end of the year due to a cracked frame. **(Below) Woodsmoor, 12th November 1960.** The first in a series of views showing the 'Birkenhead' freight entering the Up goods loop with 8F No **48260** (6C) at the head. Buxton 8F No **48740** provides banking assistance, the clouds of smoke and steam emanating from the rear of the train which has just passed beneath Moorland Road. The brake van to the left in the Down goods loop brings up the rear of the return New Mills shunt, the train engine being 'Crab' No **42931** (9B). Both: ***J W Sutherland***

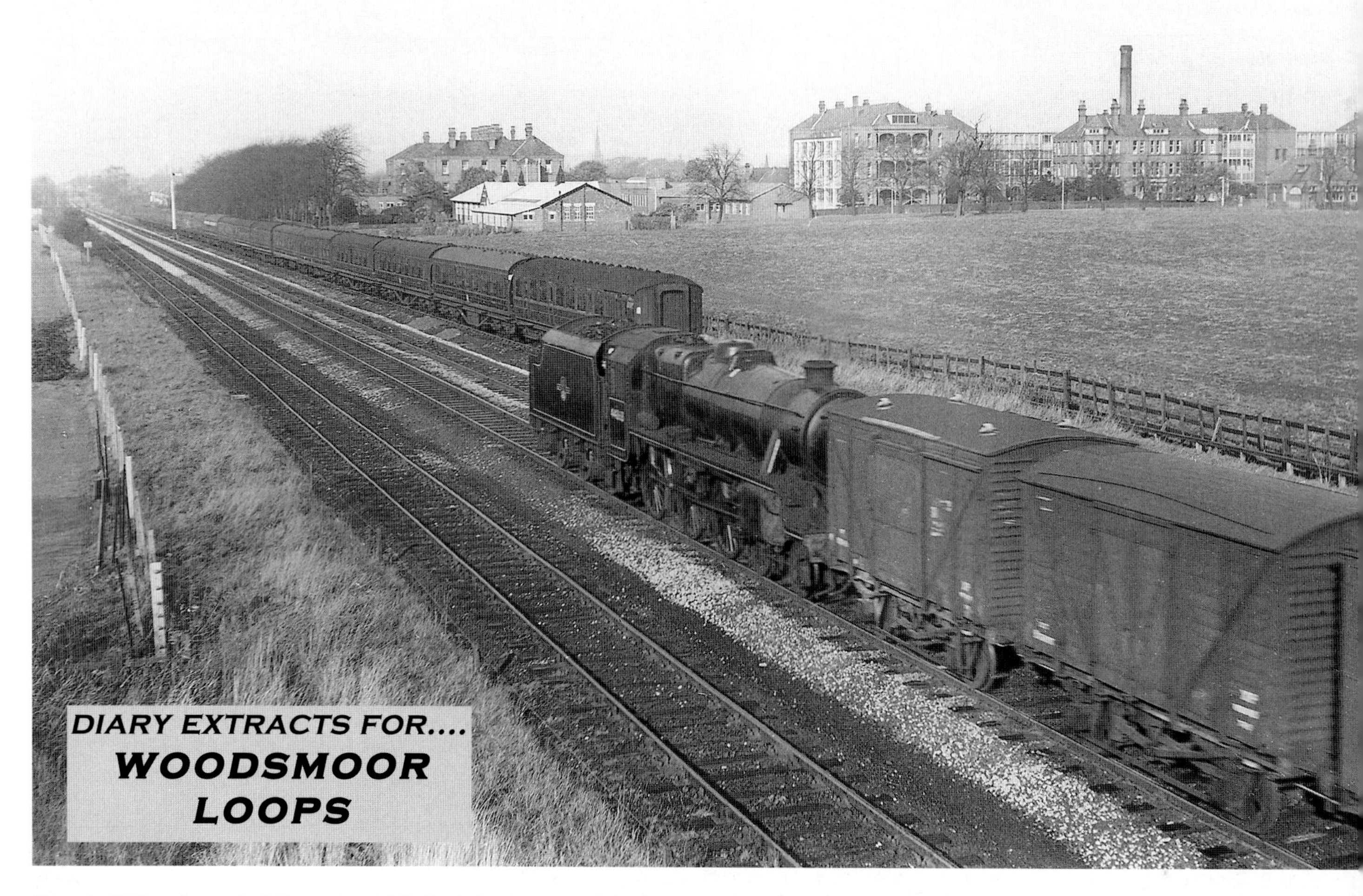

Bramhall Moor Lane, 3rd November 1962. Both the Buxton and the former Midland lines passed beneath Bramhall Moor Lane within a short distance of each other. In the case of the former, line capacity problems had resulted in the provision of goods loops here at Woodsmoor during the 1930's, resulting in removal of Woodsmoor Sidings (Hazel Gove) signal box. The view here from above the parapets of Bramhall Moor Lane bridge (Br. No 5), reconstructed in 1933 to cater for the additional lines, is in the direction of Stockport, showing a clean but unidentified Class 5 returning with the New Mills shunt, Bowaters vans in evidence. Stepping Hill hospital dominates the upper right of the picture in the days before it began to sprawl across the fields towards Bramhall Moor Lane. Formerly known as Stockport Union Infirmary, it was connected to the Buxton line by a siding on the site of the Up goods loop at a point roughly to the right of where the engine is. Access to and from the siding was under the control of the signal box mentioned earlier. The hospital siding was removed in 1914. Carriages were regularly stored in the Loops and details can be found elsewhere, particularly in the diary extracts. ***J W Sutherland***

3.10.59 Noted that there was a total of 24 coaches stored between Woodsmoor and Hazel Grove (16 on the Up goods loop and 8 on the Up side siding just before Hazel Grove. Another 10 were in the Down side siding beyond Hazel Grove.

27.2.60 Today there are no coaches stored in the Up goods loop between Woodsmoor and Hazel Grove but 8 coaches in the Up siding just beyond it.

7.5.60 Noted vans and empty mineral wagons stored in the Up Woodsmoor loop. There were, as usual, some coaches but this was the first time I have noticed wagons in this loop. A Down mixed goods train has been left in the Hazel Grove Siding - it had gone when I came back at lunch time.

18.6.60 Passed 90202 (I think) on Up train of vans in Woodsmoor Loop (As there was no train at New Mills, it was probably the New Mills shunt running very late).

12.7.60 (From 8.15 ex-Buxton). On the way down found 45067 on an Up goods in the Woodsmoor Goods Loop. Train consisted mainly of flats, each with three of the grey mineral type containers. 48744 occupied the Down loop with a very mixed goods including tank wagons. This had left Buxton, with an 8F banking at about 7.35 pm, probably a Rowsley - Garston train shown as "suspended" in last Winter Timetable. The Up train may have been the 7.20pm from Adswood or probably the Briggs running late, most likely, the 7.20pm. 48744 and train later went off towards Cheadle Village Junction.

1.10.60 Ex-9.35 Davenport. There were no less than 46 coaches stored in the Up side between Woodsmoor and Hazel Grove - 38 on the goods loop and 8 in the siding at the Hazel Grove end. There were a further 9 on the Down siding east of the station, while a 3-car diesel set to form the 9.53 to Manchester was in the siding by the old goods shed.

11.3.61 (Ex-8.35 Davenport) There were no steam coaches stored at Woodsmoor or Hazel Grove. Noted a banner signal just before the road bridge as a repeater of the Hazel Grove Up starting signal.

9.5.61 (Ex-8.20 from Buxton) There was a goods with an 8F in front in the Woodsmoor Down loop - presumably the train seen leaving Buxton earlier.

13.5.61 (Ex-Buxton Trip). On the way back saw 42391 on empty coaches in the Up loop at Woodsmoor.

16.8.64 (Sun) Making use of new off peak day return fares, which started today, Graham and I went to Buxton on 11.45 departure from Davenport. Noted a train of coaches in both Woodsmoor Loops.

t

Woodsmoor, 12th November 1960. (Above) Continuing the sequence of photographs - from page 45 - showing the Birkenhead to Buxton freight progressing through Woodsmoor Up goods loop. The view above shows 8F No **48740** (9D) in the rear of the train whilst BR Standard 9F 2-10-0 No **92048** (17C-Rowsley) passes on the Down line with a Buxton to Hooton freight. **(Below)** Awaiting passage of the 9.20am ex-Manchester Piccadilly to Buxton diesel passenger train, the 'Birkenhead', with another 8F, No **48260** (6C-Birkenhead), at the head, waits at the Hazel Grove end of the loop for the signal to proceed. The footbridge (Br. No 5A), replaced a footpath when the bridge was built in 1933 as a result of the quadrupling at Woodsmoor. The footbridge was built and erected by the Chesterfield company of Markham. ***J W Sutherland***

(Above) Hazel Grove, 31st December 1960. Storing of carriages in the loop lines and sidings is talk of folklore to those old enough to remember the occasions. This photograph does not disappoint, showing some forty vehicles in the Up goods loop, fivc of which were reported to be in chocolate and cream livery! There was another selection of eighteen carriages in the Down loop. This was spending New Years Eve with a difference. ***J W Sutherland***

(Right) Hazel Grove, 31st December 1960. Having been given the 'right-away', **48260** regains the main line with the 'Birkenhead' in readiness for the 1 in 60 climb to Disley. The carriages are stored in the siding accessed from Hazel Grove, whose signal box also controlled access to and from the Woodsmoor goods loops. This working, mentioned frequently in the diaries, was becoming a thing of the past. It was still an important service in 1962 but some twelve months later had been cut back to Arpley (Warrington), and a much reduced payload.

(Centre) Hazel Grove, 31st December 1960. Yet more activity at the Hazel Grove end of Woodsmoor loops. Far from home, Ivatt Class 4MT 2-6-0 No **43043** (55A-Holbeck) approaches Hazel Grove prior to picking up some empty coaching stock. It was just to the left of the picture where land had been acqired some thirty years earlier by the LMS to create a chord between the former Midland and LNW lines. It did not happen on this site and the present single line chord did not come about until 1985.

(Right) The Ivatt is now running back after crossing over from the Up line in order to collect coaches from the Down Woodsmoor goods loop.

All this page: ***J W Sutherland***

Hazel Grove, 8th June 1963 (Saturday)**.** The Up sidings are still being used for carriage storage as 8F No **48744** and crew, having safely descended the fourteen miles from Dove Holes, will be relieved to avoid the goods loops (and the consequential reduction in speed required) for a clear run to Davenport Junction where this, the 3.30pm (SO) Buxton to Garston freight will head for Cheadle Village Junction over the 'Khyber'. This Saturday afternoon train still displayed a reasonably healthy load but the writing was already on the wall and plans were in hand to transfer the remaining traffic on the line to the Midland route. Following proposals in 1963 to close the Edgeley Junction to Buxton route for both freight and passenger services, ongoing discussions looked initally at the rationalisation of freight services.
J W Sutherland

Hazel Grove, 11th August 1962. The summer has seen the growth of vegetation encroach across the Up sidings, but this does not affect the 'main' lines on which 'Jubilee' No **45564** *New South Wales* (55A-Leeds Holbeck) pulls away from Hazel Grove with a total of nine coaches on the 'Wakes' train for Scarborough. It was noted that pairs of LMS-built articulated vehicles were positioned at both ends of the train. These particular coaches, built in 1937 to diagram 1965, were familiar around the north-west but a restriction on them was placed for working into Blackpool North and Morecambe. The change from August (1962) to July in 1963 of the Stockport 'Wakes' fortnight resulted in the removal of the Bridlington - Filey - Scarborough train, thus ending a long association with the Yorkshire resorts. The wisp of steam in the distance is from the rear of a local train headed by 'Crab' 42921, a Stockport engine.
J W Sutherland

Hazel Grove, 12th August 1961 (Sat). From the safety of the Up siding, this low-level view shows departing 'Wakes' special on the first stage of its journey to Scarborough, Class 5 No **45426** (5A) providing the motive power. These excursions and special trains were approaching their 'Indian summer' as a consequence of the *Reshaping of British Railways* - the 'Beeching Report', which argued for the need to scale down occasional traffic such as these holiday specials. ***J W Sutherland***

Hazel Grove, 12th August 1961 'Jubilee' Class 4-6-0 No **45553** *Canada* (5B-Crewe South) waits to depart from Hazel Grove with the 8.25 ex-Whaley Bridge to Blackpool Central on the first Saturday of Stockport & District Holidays. In line with previous years, the special included Reddish South and Denton in its schedule, the latter having a long association with Stockport and its hatting industry. ***J W Sutherland***

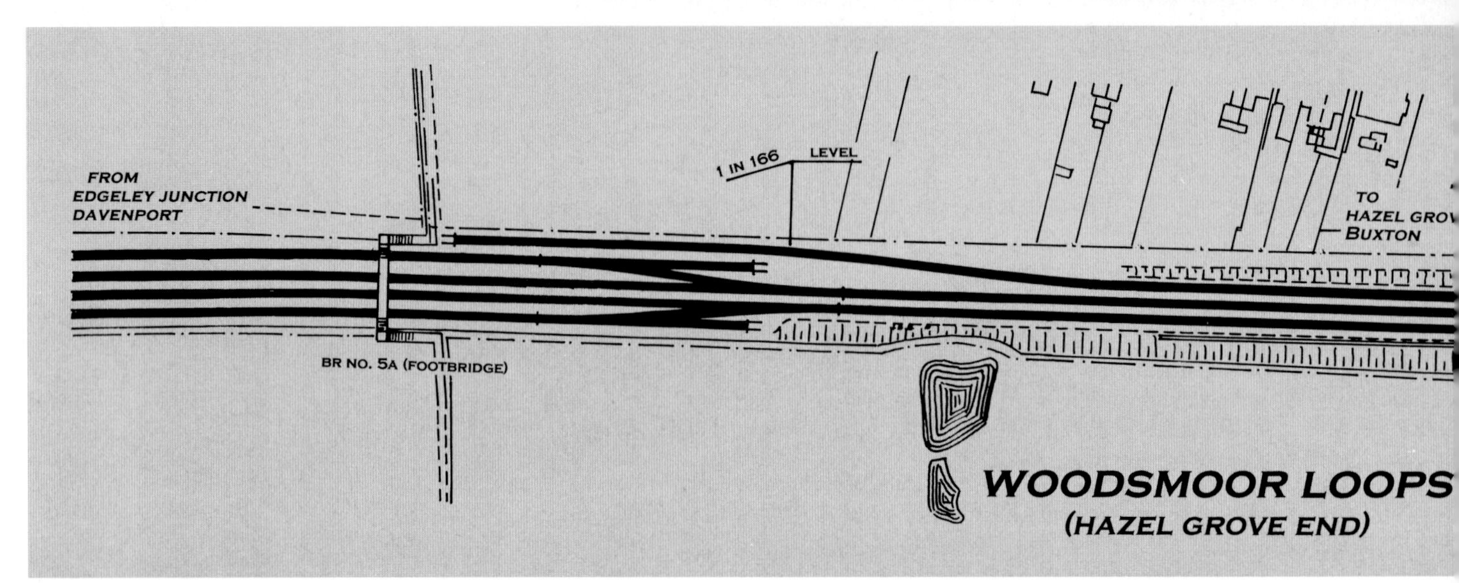

Hazel Grove, 26th June 1965. The first Saturday of the Stockport & District holidays produced a programme of 'Additional Period Trains' intended to serve most parts of the United Kingdom. The Beeching report was having drastic ongoing consequences although the programme of special trains was just about surviving at the expense of the daily 'trips by train' excursions. First 'through train' serving stations on the Buxton line was the 8.25am ex-Whaley Bridge, scheduled to call at Hazel Grove at 8.49. The same times had applied for years, but following closure of Blackpool Central in 11/64, the train was re-routed to North station. ......*continued across page*

...........Above we see Class 5 4-6-0 No **45225** (9B-Stockport) awaiting departure with nine carriages in tow. Alongside in the Up platform, a 3-car BRC&W set goes about its daily business with the 8.17 ex-Oxford Road to Buxton service.

(Left-centre) The two footbridges at the Stockport end of Hazel Grove platforms produce an almost tunnel like effect as Buxton 'Crab' No **42942** comes to a stand with a re-timed (for the holidays) 7.47am Buxton to Manchester London Road train on 1st August 1960. The bridge across the foreground (Br. No 7), a standard L&NWR wrought iron/cast iron structure dating from the 1880's, was removed in line with the reconstruction of the station in 1980. The arched bridge beyond (Br. No 6) carried the footpath between Hatherlow Street and the Hazel Grove Wesleyans cricket ground, etc., ***J W Sutherland***

Not quite a timeless scene but a station containing evidence of its hundred year-plus existance can be seen here in this view of Hazel Grove looking towards Buxton in May 1966. Station buildings of a fairly simple nature were provided by the Stockport, Disley and Whaley Bridge Railway when the line opened in 1857. The signal box and footbridge came courtesy of the L&NWR, with latter day embellishments by British Railways in the form of maroon enamel signs. Unusually, a 'totem' finds itself affixed to the front of the signal box. ***H B Priestley***

Hazel Grove, 22nd September 1956. The station will echo to the sound of wagon wheels clattering across rail joints from this train of empty mineral wagons on its way to Buxton, both crew and engine of Stanier 8F No **48188** (8B-Warrington) preparing for the first of the two steep gradients on the climb to the Derbyshire spa town. Some six months later, on 9th February 1957, 48188 made the news headlines for its role in the tragic accident at Chapel-en-le Frith which claimed the life of Driver John Axon. ***J W Sutherland***

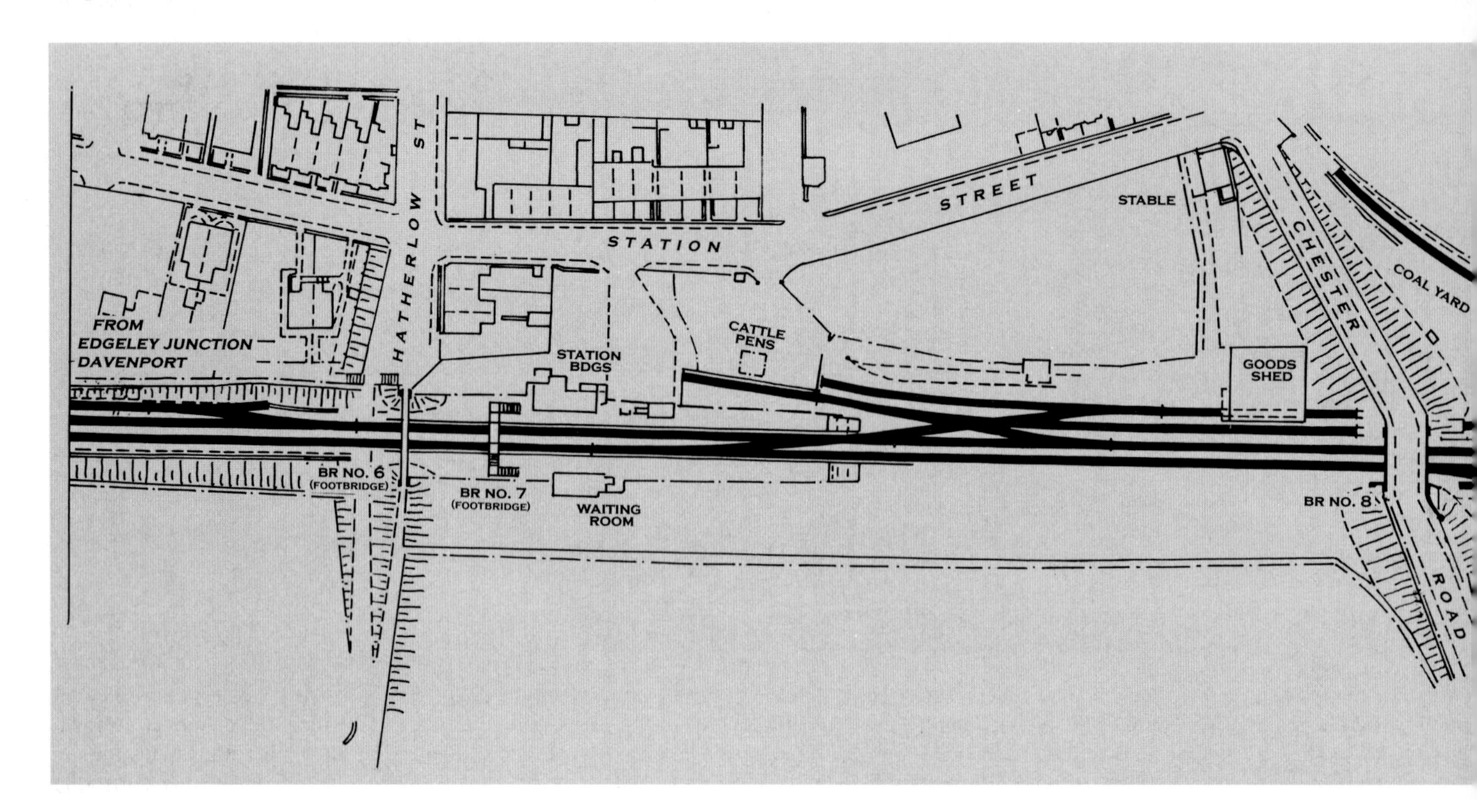

Hazel Grove station as it appeared on Saturday 22nd September 1956 in a state still basically as it was handed over by the LMS in 1948. The signal box retains the nameboard of a style introduced in 1936 together with the cast-iron letters on the front in a manner reminiscent of L&NWR practice. An LMS built locomotive, 8F No **48720** (8D-Widnes) carries its British Railways smokebox plate but otherwise, the station lies in wait of a new identity. The goods yard, or yards - the coal sidings were on the far side of Chester Road - were early closure victims (September 1950) although private siding facilities remained for some years. ***J W Sutherland***

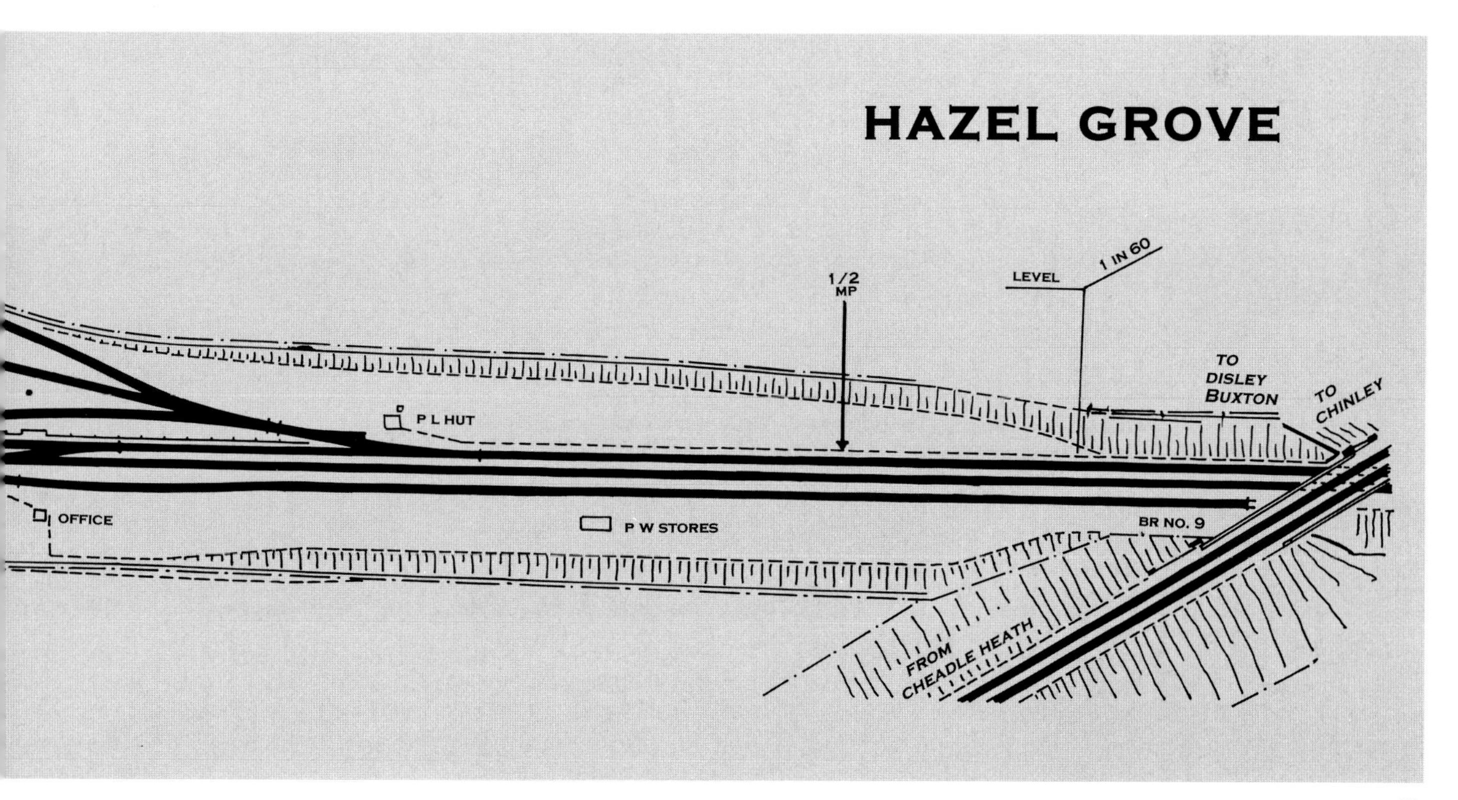

Hazel Grove, 11th August 1962. The crowds are still in evidence although casual wear, as we know it today, is still in the suitcases - it is still 'Sunday best' to travel to the seaside. The east coast of Yorkshire is still a magnet, particularly Butlin's at Filey, as the train with Leeds (Holbeck) 'Jubilee' No **45564** *New South Wales* enters the station with empty stock from the Down siding. This holiday special would also serve Bridlington and Scarborough, the former costing a weekly return fare of 55/- (£2.75p). Departure time of 9.15am was scheduled from Hazel Grove with the last picking up point being at Guide Bridge. ***J W Sutherland***

It was not always 'foreign' stock called upon to provide services for the Wakes exodus. In this view at Hazel Grove on 12th August 1961, the train entering the Down platform to provide the Lancaster/Morecambe service consisted of a Buxton 2x 3-car diesel set which, outside the Wakes period is understood to have run ECS to Edgeley. Commencing at Whaley Bridge at 9.55am and calling all stations to Stockport Edgeley, additional calls were made at Reddish South and Denton. Arrival at Lancaster was scheduled for 12.20 before a thirteen minute run to Morecambe Euston Road which included a call at Bare Lane. The special ran again in 1962 but twelve months on, the starting point became Edgeley. ***J W Sutherland***

(Left) Looking back in the direction of Stockport from Chester Road bridge illustrates the very rural (or urban) nature of Hazel Grove at the beginning of the 1960's. Very little in the way of development in what was to become the Newby Road industrial development has taken place probably because a substantial piece of the land had long been earmarked for the LMS 'Hazel Grove chord'. To the left, the sight screens and boundary highlights the cricket ground of long-time residents, Hazel Grove Wesleyans. This 1960 view shows a 3-car BRC&W set leaving Hazel Grove on its way to Buxton, the route code B3 being synonymous with the service. The distinctive yellow 'speed-whiskers' were fairly short lived, being replaced by yellow 'half-panelling'.

H Townley, courtesy J M Bentley

(Right-centre) A picture postcard scene from Chester Road bridge during the bitter and protracted winter of 1963. Having arrived at Hazel Grove on the 10.20am ex-Piccadilly train, the photographer first of all spent some time in the warmth of the signal box in the company of signalmen Bernard Shaw and Graham Neve before venturing out into the cold again to capture this view on film. Alongside the Down platform is an ex-Buxton diesel set waiting to depart. The simple nature of the track layout of both station and goods yard is defined well by the snow covering. Public goods facilites had been withdrawn many years earlier and the siding which entered the near side of the goods shed has also been removed. ***J W Sutherland***

(Left) What a difference three years makes. The allotments seen at the top of the page don't seem to be receiving the same amount of attention and the wooden 'post and rail' boundary fence of the railway has been replaced by the more utilitarian concrete post and wire type. The goods yard has ultimately lost its rails and a works train, powered by 8F No **48373** - short time resident of 9B (Stockport) - occupies the Down line whilst gangs of men recover the points and crossing components which formerly serviced the goods yard. Elsewhere, the development of the Newby Road area progressively fills the open land between the station and Bramhall Moor Lane. Comparing this view with that at the top of the page, it is interesting to note that during a period of uncertainty when the future of the route was being discussed, someone has deemed it sufficiently worthwhile to replace bullhead rail with flat-bottom, hardly the 'investment' one expects on a threatened railway. ***J W Sutherland***

Hazel Grove, 21st May 1959. The 5.50pm ex-Manchester London Road to Buxton service was still one of two Up trains still diagrammed for steam working, the other being the 5.40pm to Buxton, calling only at Disley and Whaley Bridge. Here we see Longsight 'Crab' 2-6-0 No **42889** pulling its train of five carriages away from Hazel Grove, twenty-one minutes after having left Manchester. Passenger steam operation ceased from 9/59. ***J W Sutherland***

Hazel Grove, 25th August 1962. So far we have seen numerous of the holiday specials on their outward jouneys. Weather permitting, sun-tanned (or weather beaten) holiday makers needed to be brought back. Recreating a scene somewhay reminiscent of the Asbourne line excursions, this returning Blackpool Central to Whaley Bridge special of ten carriages leaves Hazel Grove behind, double-headed by **42372** (9B-Stockport) and Class 5 No **44874** The close boarded fence to the right of the leading engine ran parallel with the Up line and offered protection to staff working in the coal yard which lay on the opposite of Chester Road from the station. The 'Lie-bye' siding to the left was also known as the Down Siding from which empty stock operated or as it was originally intended, a refuge siding - with a capacity of 43 wagon units - which was infrequently used. ***J W Sutherland***

(Above) The gradient post to the right of the engine marks the start of an unbroken 1 in 60 climb to Disley, the train comprising a mixture of coal wagons and vans, the latter catering mostly for Bowaters at Disley. This, the morning (SO) Stockport to Buxton freight, spent almost six hours making its (fragmented) way to Buxton Sidings. First port of call will be New Mills Newtown, spending a mere twenty-two minutes both dropping off and collecting wagons. Moving on to Whaley Bridge, two and a half hours is allotted, where shunting in the yard as required takes place together with a short trip down to Shallcross Yard over remnants of the erstwhile Cromford & High Peak line. On Saturdays, train crews resisted an early 'path' to Buxton, insisting on 'right-time' departure (at 2.16pm) to guarantee maximised pay. Refuge in the Up goods loop at Dove Holes allowed the 2.20pm ex-London Road to Buxton passenger a free run and Bibbingtons provided, again as required, the opportunity for wagon brakes to be pinned down. The April 16th 1960 view also shows, to the rear of the train, the tail end of a 3-car dmu waiting in the Down siding which will form the 10.09am Hazel Grove to Mayfield service.

(Centre) The intersection bridge (Br.No 8A on the Buxton line) at Hazel Grove, which carried the New Mills to Heaton Mersey Midland line of 1902 over the Buxton line, was a massive single skew span of 104feet 2inches. The routes crossed each other twice (the other 'crossing' is within Dove Holes tunnel just a few yards north of Dove Holes station) on their respective journeys south. Whilst trains on the Midland route benefited from uniformly graded and aligned infrastructure intended for fast trains, the LNW Buxton branch quite literally followed the contours of the land, producing scenes such as this as 'Austerity' 2-8-0 No **90173** (8F-Wigan Springs Branch) commences the 1 in 60 climb to Disley with the Birkenhead to Buxton freight on 25th March 1961.

(Right) The Saturday morning freight to Hooton (due Hazel Grove 10.43am) had left Buxton at 8.44 so was already two hours into its journey. Progress as usual was slow, most of the stoppage time being for the attention to wagon brakes (as necessary) at Bibbingtons, Whaley Bridge and Disley. Add to that a crew change at New Mills and it is not difficult to imagine time being eaten away. The LMS built Class 4F was no stranger to the line but No **44359** (6B-Mold Junction) is quite a way from home as she heads her train beneath the Midland line bridge on 25th November 1961.

All this page: ***J W Sutherland***

(Right) The Midland line through Hazel Grove was heavily engineered, achieving a constant 1 in 100 gradient between Cheadle Heath and New Mills where it rejoined the 'old route' to Manchester. This adverse gradient for trains in the Up direction was considerable but still allowed for a comfortable passage and timings for freight trains. Passing over the Buxton line at the head of the 7.20am ex-Walton (Liverpool) train of 'empties' is Rowsley (17C) 4F No **44327.** The LMS proposals for their version of the Hazel Grove chord would have seen a junction to the left of the structure. March 25th 1961. ***J W Sutherland***

The ICI Hopper trains were into their third decade of operation, plying between the limestone quarries at Tunstead and the processing plants in mid-Cheshire. Upwards of ten movements each day could occur, mostly serving Oakleigh Sidings at Hartford. Other destinations included Middlewich, Northwich and Wallerscote. On 25th November 1961 (Above), Northwich (8E) based 8F No **48693**, with a total of 15 empty hoppers trailing behind, heads back towards the Peak district with what is thought to be the 8.45am ex-Wallerscote working. On Saturdays (Only) a second train left the Cheshire location at 8.25pm. Many train crews were of the opinion that it was easier to drive the fully laden workings than the returning empties. ***J W Sutherland***

Having been given a clear road ahead, it is likely that the crew of LNWR built 0-8-0 G1 Class 6F No **49079** will be urging their engine on for an uninterrupted run through to Davenport Junction. Shortly to cross over Macclesfield Road bridge (No 9), the train is passing through an area of Hazel Grove still to be developed. The backs of houses in Chatsworth Road, a development of the late 1930's, are to the right of the embankment in this 1957 view, whilst on the left, open fields still give residents on Buxton Road a clear view of the railway. ***N K Harrop***

This 'tea-time' Buxton bound train is seen climbing away from Hazel Grove, rapidly gaining height to take the railway above the urban sprawl of greater Manchester. In this view, with Chatsworth Road this time on our left, Longsight 'Crab' 2-6-0 No **42889** is approaching a location locally known as Simpsons corner, so named after the long-time makers of meat products, including their renowned sausages, occupying the lineside buildings near Mill Lane. The Midland Railway built Norbury Viaduct strides across Hazel Grove to the right of the locomotive in this 1956 photograph. ***N K Harrop***

DIARY EXTRACTS FOR........HAZEL GROVE

10. 10. 59(Sat) Took two photos of Macclesfield Road underbridge, Hazel Grove. 48712 was on a Stockport to Buxton train. 42932 came down on the 'shunt' from New Mills. 42970 pulled the train from Birkenhead and 90699 pushed. 48435 was on the train to Hooton.

2.1.60 (Sat) Walked to Hazel Grove. 48348 was on the Birkenhead. A Crab was on the return 'shunt' from New Mills. 90369 was on the train to Hooton. 48712 was on a Down mixed goods, probably to Arpley while 42848 followed in on another Down mixed goods, probably Rowsley - Adswood with mainly railway equipment such as rails and sleepers. There are 32 corridor coaches parked - 3 lots in the Up loop and another 7 non-corridor coaches and two vans in the Hazel Grove dead end and just beyond. There were another dozen or so coaches visible in the dead end at the East end (Down side).

16.4.60 (Easter Sat.) Went to Hazel Grove. 48679 was on 'shunter' to Buxton. 42773 was on shunt from New Mills. 90227 was on train to Hooton. 48421 (9D) was on train to Arpley. In the afternoon en route to Millers Dale noted 42322 in the down goods yard.

29.10.60 (After Middlewood visit). Coming home noticed a new arm type signal post going up on the Up side just north (or west) of Hazel Grove.

12.11.60 (Sat) Walked up towards Hazel Grove to take photos. 42931 (9B) was on New Mills 'shunt'. 48260 (6C) was on the Birkenhead, which was banked by 48740 (9D). 92048 was on the Hooton.

31.2.60 (Sat) Went up to the Midland Railway bridge over the LNWR at Hazel Grove. 48106 (8B) was on the 'shunter' to Buxton consisting of 16 mineral wagons, vans and 'Return to Chelford' low side sand wagons.

31.2.60 42848 was on the return New Mills 'shunt'. The 10.20am diesel from Buxton consisted of 2 x 2 car units with the latest end roof train indicator. Later, 44327 (17C) was noted running up light. 48139 was on the Hooton train which included some large girders in the load. 45530 came down light (re-built Patriot) 48451 was on the Widnes train with several flats loaded with containers next to the engine and two old tenders (one still lettered LMS) no doubt water softening duties- next to the brake van. 48373 was on the Rowsley - Adswood. When I was walking home at about 12.45, 43043 (55A-Holbeck) came up light from Stockport direction, crossed over at Hazel Grove and went back on the Down line, then into the north end of Woodsmoor goods loop. From there, I was told, it would later remove 7 coaches. This morning there were 18 coaches on the Down goods loop, 40 (including one chocolate and cream Western Region) on the Up goods loop and about 10 in each of the two Hazel Grove Sidings - one on the Up side and one on the Down side. D72 and other diesels are noted on Midland line expresses while other engines, on goods use a 92XXX, several 4F 0-6-0's and 8F 2-8-0's. 44565 was photographed on the Up mixed goods.

11.2.61 The only coaches in the Hazel Grove area today was a set of 9 (probably excursion set) in the Up siding.

25.3.61 (Sat) Went to Hazel Grove. 42942 was on New Mills shunt. 48740 was on Buxton 'shunter'. 44770 was on Hooton train. 40173 was on train from Birkenhead. 48421 was on Widnes train. 42934 was on the Rowsley - Adswood.

8.4.61 (Ex-Middlewood Trip) Noted one cattle truck in the siding, alongside Hazel Grove Station and about 10 non-corridor in the Down siding. 10 corridors were in the Up Woodsmoor goods loop.

27.6.64 (Sat - Workers Holiday Started) Went up to Hazel Grove with Graham and photographed 45382 (9B) on the only special train from Whaley Bridge to Blackpool. (8 non-corridor including a push-pull vehicle at rear end reporting No. 3T70.

Approximately one and a half miles after passing through Hazel Grove, the line enters a picturesque wooded area commencing at **Norbury Crossing**. A narrow road linking Poynton with the A6 just north of High Lane passes over the line at this point, and generations of motorists using the route need little reminding of the 'traffic calming' nature of the approach roads. Until the installation in 1977 of a 'signal box' type structure, there had been a crossing keepers cottage, views of which can be seen on these pages. The crossing from the Down direction was protected by this pair of tubular posted co-acting 'home' signals, dating from 1941, that on left (in the Down cess) being sited in the conventional way whilst the taller posted signal on the opposite (Up) side assisted with sighting, a persitant local problem brought about by the encroachment of trees lining Norbury Hollow and no doubt the occasional fog. Both views on this page date from 24th January 1959. Although not exactly indicating a flurry of activity, the scenes illustrate the types of traffic passing the location within a two-hour period on a Saturday morning. **(Above)** A view looking in the direction of Hazel Grove with an Up (Buxton-bound) dmu approaching the crossing at approximately a quarter to the hour at hourly intervals. **(Below)** Creating a truly atmospheric scene is Heaton Mersey (9F) based 4F No **44379** climbing the 'bank' towards Middlewood and Disley with a Stockport to Buxton mixed freight, which, as previously mentioned, spent some three hours-plus at Whaley Bridge during its six hour journey to Buxton. At the time, Mr J Wood and his wife carried out crossing keepers duties as well as being occupants of the cottage. ***J W Sutherland***

An early 1970's view of the signal cabin at Norbury Crossing, the 'building' being a variation on the 'standard' L&NWR portable hut covered with an asbestos type cladding. There were four levers, none of which were spare, the co-acting signals being operated by lever 3. The replacement structure seen nowadays is a standard BR LMR type 15 signal box top and was constructed by a gang from Crewe in 1977. The present frame is a similar type to the LNW 446, containing five levers, the extra lever possibly for the gate lock. ***Graham Neve***

(Left) Not the banker of the train seen opposite (lower) but another scene reflecting the hard work carried out by assisting engines. On this occasion, Austerity No **90723** (56D-Mirfield) brings up the rear of an Up goods. 8F No **48448** (6C-Birkenhead) was the train engine.

NORBURY
CROSSING

(Centre) A fine elevated view of Norbury Crossing from the Up side embankment sees 'Crab' No **42932**, only recently allocated to Stockport, on the return journey with the New Mills 'shunt'. The coal wagon behind the engine is ready to be dropped off at Davenport coal siding, whilst the vans have no doubt come out of Disley Goods. ***J W Sutherland***

(Right) Some twelve years on and little has changed apart from the transition to British Rail blue livery of the diesel units (shortly to be classified as 104). Looking from the Up side road approach (High Lane) in the direction of Norbury Hollow, the crossing keepers cottage is looking a little worse for wear and would be replaced some six years later. Having survived 'Beeching' the branch service enjoyed the hourly interval service introduced in 1956. Up trains were due to pass over Norbury Crossing at two or three minutes past the hour Down trains on the half-hour. ***G K Fox***

Middlewood, or Disley 'bank' as it was known to different railway factions, was approximately half-way on the 1 in 60 between Hazel Grove and Disley. After being able to start on the level through Hazel Grove, the mid-point adjacent to Norbury Hollow (to the left) was when all the pulling and pushing of lengthy freight trains was at its most demanding. Freight working timetables latterly have omitted passing times at Middlewood and it has been necessary to refer to L&NWR documents for a look at scheduling for the passage of goods trains. Point to point timings from Hazel Grove to Middlewood varied between 10 and 15 minutes for 'fast' goods whereas ordinary goods trains were allowed up to 20 minutes for the two miles. It is perhaps unfair to compare too closely the timings of more than a hundred years or so ago but with passenger trains being allowed the same 4/5 minutes for the journey, it might not be critical to allow a similar view of freight timings. Therefore, allowing a generous 15/20 minutes for more recent steam hauled freights, the climb from Hazel Grove to Middlewood required a great deal of effort to achieve a speed not much greater double than that of walking pace.

All the views on this page depict the 1950's period, perhaps significantly showing the Horwich built 'Crab' 2-6-0's on both passenger and freight workings. The top picture shows No **42942**, a Buxton engine at the time of the photograph, hauling a train of 'empties' - mostly wooden bodied - through the tree lined Norbury Hollow. Passing Middlewood Low Level Junction's distant signal, this March 1952 view is also a reminder of requirements for track maintenance when carried out by local gangs. Contents of the stone chippings box to the right of the engine were available for packing the sleepers; also note the clear cess to the left.which doubled as a cycle path as well no doubt as an 'unofficial' short-cut from the station. ***C H A Townley***

(Centre) 42942 once again, this time on an Up passenger working, making a last effort before entering Middlewood Lower station (c.1954). The cess, mentioned above, was also used by lookout patrols made up of railwaymen brought in during holiday periods and weekends over many years, particularly between the wars, as visitors flocked to this isolated beauty spot, sometime in trainloads. ***A H Bryant***

(Right-lower) 'Crab' No **42856** (6C) on the 3.10am ex-Birkenhead freight approaching Middlewood on 28th November 1959. This view from the footbridge highlights the demands being made on two locomotives, with 8F No **48389** (9A) assisting at the rear. ***J W Sutherland***

(Right) Middlewood, c. 1954. A late spring/early summer shot of 8F No **48501** (9A) rounding the curve, past the 4 1/4 milepost, on the approach to Middlewood Lower station with an Up freight. The engine was transferred to Heaton Mersey in 1955 so was very likely to continue its presence in the area. Again notice the well maintained cess of ashes, nicely edged with fresh ballast. ***A H Bryant***

(Below) This pretty little station was, and still is, one of those rarities which was not accessible by road. Opened in 1879 concurrently with the station on the Macclesfield line, it appeared in the early timetables as Middlewood for Norbury. The view here is taken from the footbridge (Br No 11A) erected in in 1914 following safety considerations about an adjacent foot crossing. The lattice girder footbridge bridge (Br No 12) on this side the rail bridge (Br No 13, No 38 on the Macclesfield line) provided a pedestrian link with the Down platform (Marple bound). This 15th June 1958 scene, with a Manchester bound train in the Down platform, shows a very tidy and well maintained station, in contrast with the buildings on the platforms of the Macclesfield line. Diesel services on the Manchester-Buxton and Manchester-Macclesfield Central/Hayfield lines commenced at the same time in 1957 but the Buxton line journey time of approx 28/30 minutes into Manchester was always going to be more attractive than the fifty-minute 'round the houses' (via Hyde and Guide Bridge) route into Manchester. The Higher and Lower suffixes were added from 25th June 1951. ***J W Sutherland***

(Left) A somewhat 'weathered' WD 'Austerity' Class 9F No **90145** (41D-Canklow) passes through Middlewood Lower on 28th November 1959 on its way to Buxton with a freight from Stockport, apparently running late. The modest station facilities equalled most others on the line, the Up side buildings seen here containing Ladies Waiting Room, Waiting Room (which doubled as the Booking Hall) and Booking Office. Gentlemens toilets were on the near end. A resume of the mornings activities can be found in the diary extracts on page 70.

J W Sutherland

(Left-centre) Given that they were designed by two separate companies, the buildings, apart from window and other minor detail, are very similar. The wooden building in the background served the Up platform (for Macclesfield trains), being constructed on timber piles. The building serving the Down platform (for Stockport), again of timber construction, contained a centrally positioned Waiting Room, with Gentlemens toilets at this end, ladies being located in their own room to the right. The small wooden hut served was for ticket checks /collection. The horizontal weatherboarding was a feature of L&NWR station design and forerunner of a 'standardised' modular type adopted in 1882 and later seen at Disley. The platform - seen here in this c.1954 view - originally of timber construction, has been rebuilt utilising concrete components of LMS design.

A H Bryant

(Below) The low level station looking in the direction of Stockport with the Up platform building on the Macclesfield line to the left; c.1958.

Authors collection

(Left) Middlewood seemed to have an appeal for all seasons, particularly during winter after snowfall. It was remote, but the recent introduction of an hourly interval diesel service meant that a visit for the purpose of photography was not in anticipation of becoming frostbound. On Saturdays however, additional services in the lunchtime period meant that steam hauled trains came back into the fold and here we see Longsight based Fowler 2-6-4T No **42399** waiting in Middlewood Lower station's Up platform on 16th February 1957 with the 12.10 ex-Manchester London Road ready to depart for Disley on its way to Buxton. ***R E Gee***

MIDDLEWOOD
LOWER

(Right) Longsight based 'Caprotti' Class 5 No **44687** pulls away from Middlewood Lower's Up platform on Wednesday 8th June 1960 with the 5.50pm ex-Manchester Mayfield to Buxton train. The modernisation and re-construction of London Road station had been going on for some time and this train, along with a number of other Buxton workings was working out of nearby Mayfield. This minor disruption however was an improvement on the situation of some twelve months earlier when passengers were being bussed out to and collected from Longsight. **(Below)** From the truncated remains of the Middlewood 'Curve', a view towards Middlewood tunnel shows a departing 6-car diesel train, the 2.45 ex-Manchester London Road to Buxton service, heading off towards Disley on 15th June 1958.
J W Sutherland

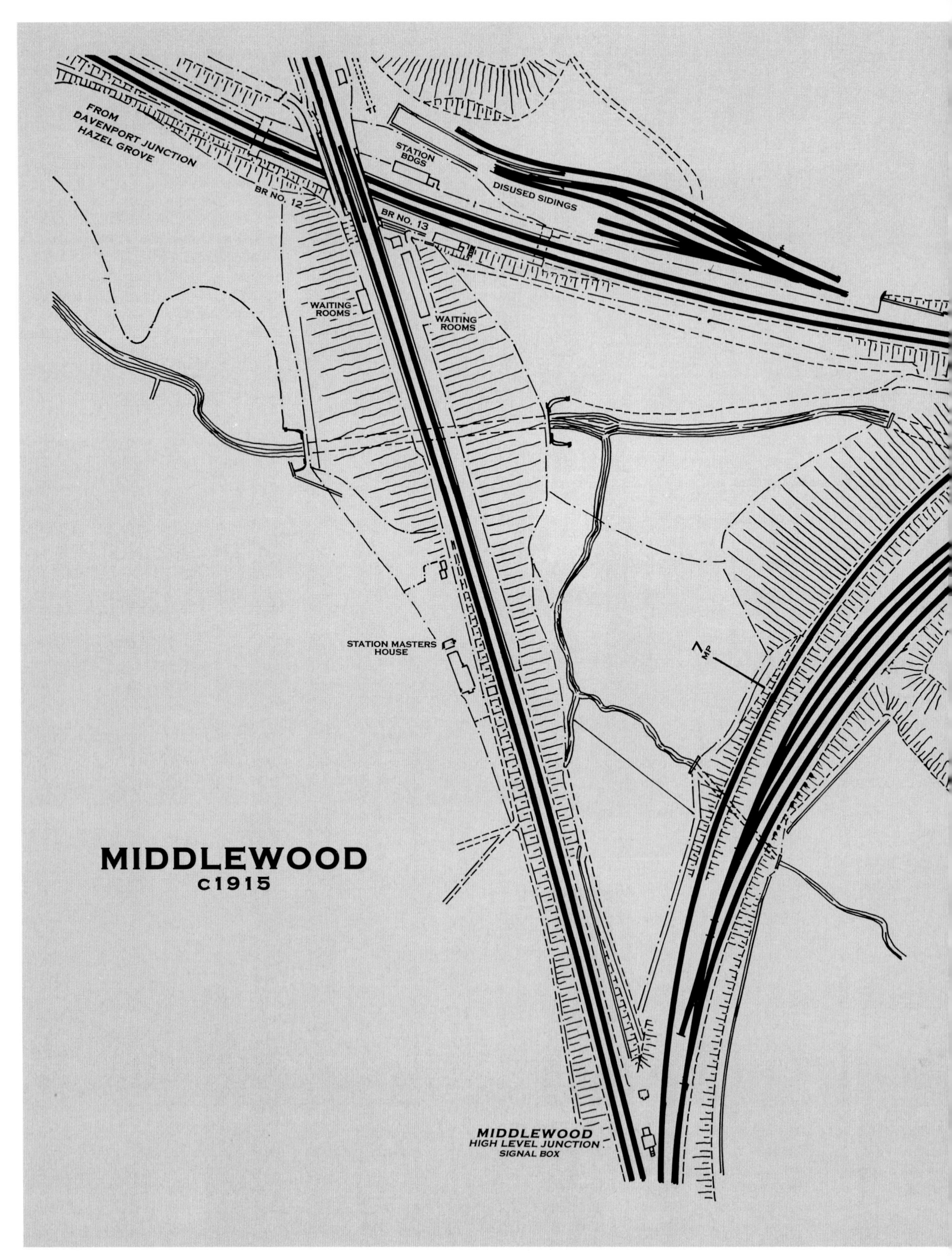

FROM
DAVENPORT JUNCTION
HAZEL GROVE
STATION
BDGS
DISUSED SIDINGS
BR NO. 12
BR NO. 13
WAITING
ROOMS
WAITING
ROOMS
STATION MASTERS
HOUSE
7
MP
MIDDLEWOOD
c1915
MIDDLEWOOD
HIGH LEVEL JUNCTION
SIGNAL BOX

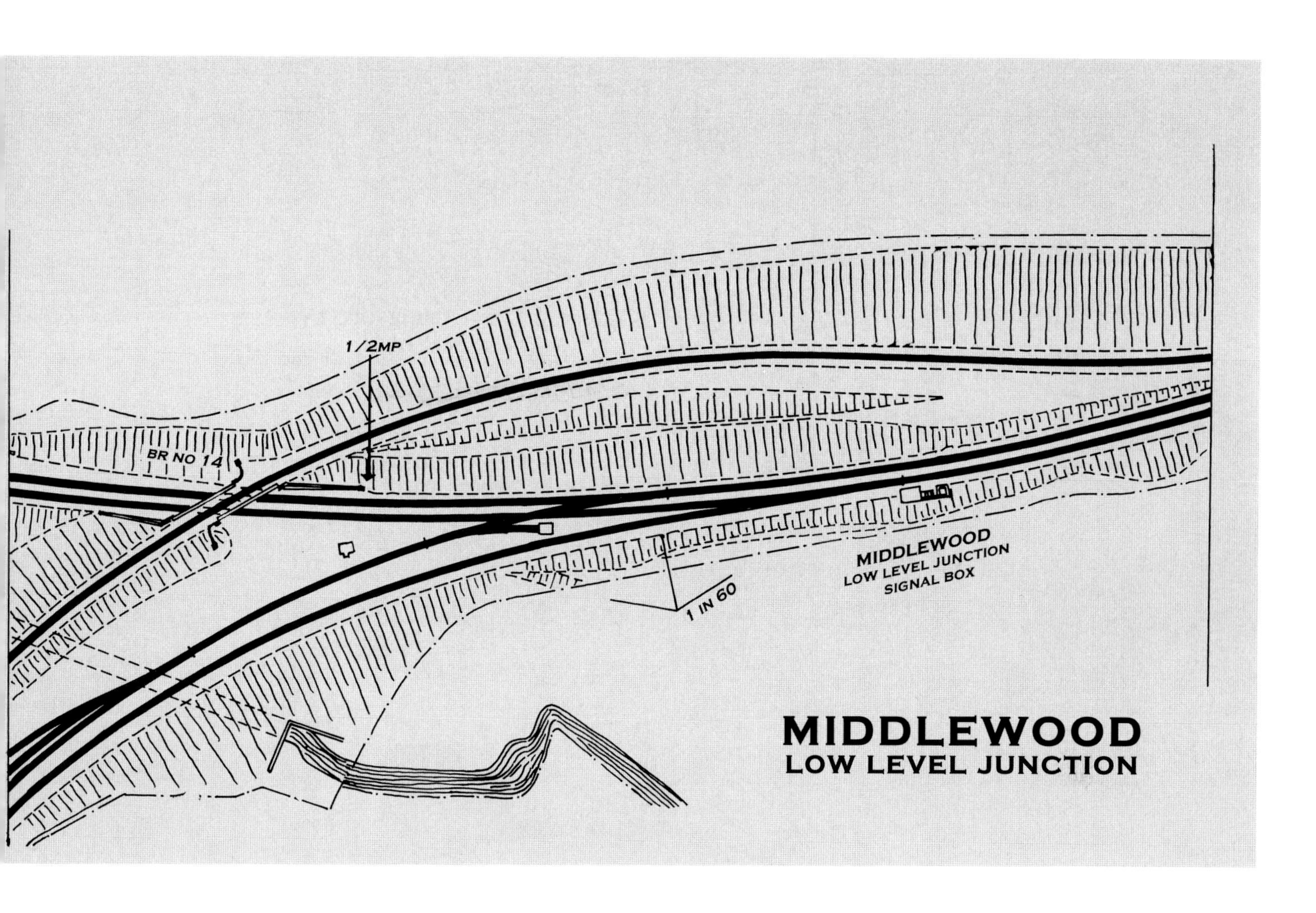

A stirring sight indeed as Buxton 'Crab' 2-6-0 No **42943** uses all its available powers to haul the 12.10 ex-Longsight train of empties up the 1 in 60 gradient through Middlewood Lower station (c.1954). The loco is working back to its Buxton base after having been diagrammed to work into Manchester the same morning with the 7.30 passenger working. The foliage to the right of the train has progressively covered the remains of a group of sidings that once served nearby Norbury Colliery. Little is known of its existance although references in the LNWR Working Timetables of 1885 indicate a 'dropping-off' of wagons by Up trains. There had been a long history of goods trains from Longsight albeit in minor variations over the years. A contemporary of the working seen above in 1889 would have been the 11.50am ex-Longsight to Buxton goods that was shunted into Middlewood sidings to pick up/detach traffic from the 'NS' line as well as to allow an Up passenger train to pass. ***A H Bryant***

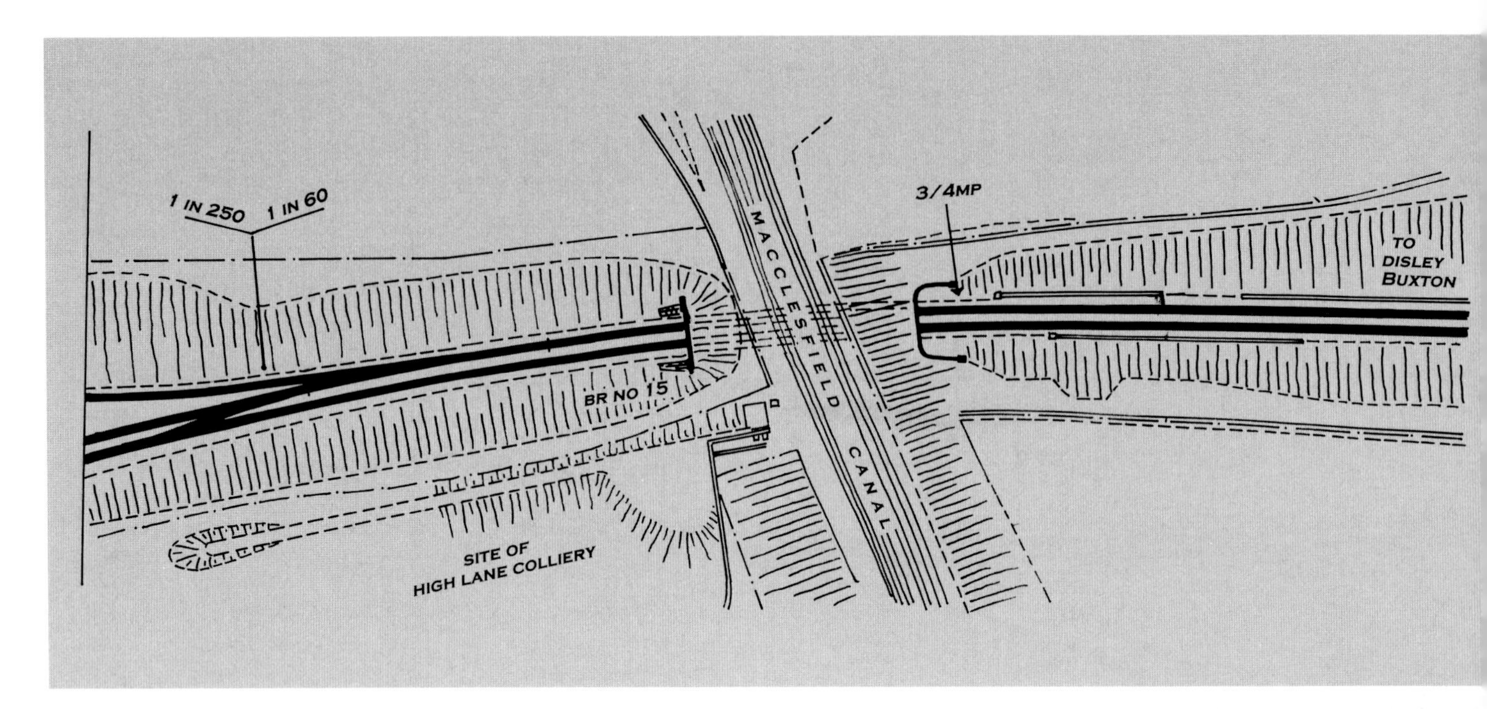

(Above) The Birkenhead to Buxton freight continues its climb up to Disley up the first of the two 'banks' it encounters on the line. To the rear of the train we once again see the abutments of intersection bridge No 14 some six years after the removal of its deck. Although now not a junction in the true sense of the word, Middlewood had its uses for the occasional storage of withdrawn carriage and wagon stock. On 23rd April 1960, Class 7F (LNW G2a) 0-8-0 No **49191**, a Wigan Springs Branch engine with 90622 assisting (out of sight) passes the signal box. ***J W Sutherland***

(Left) Looking totally at ease with its task, Class 7F No **49081** (8D-Widnes) takes a Down freight past Middlewood Low level Junction signal box one day in March 1952. The trees behind the signal box mark the site of the long gone High Lane Colliery, whilst the pair of chimneys opposite show the location of an erstwhile brickworks. ***J Peden***

(Left) A low level view towards Disley with the High Level connecting lines of the 'Middlewood Curves' fully operational in 1953. Home signals for both Up and Down Buxton lines are 'off' but it is more than likely the box is 'switched-out'. We have a clear view of Middlewood tunnel over which passes the Macclesfield Canal. The box, an LNW type 4 structure of 1885, contained a twenty-six lever tumbler frame and survived until 1971. ***Anon***

(Centre) A 'busy spell' on Saturday 29th October 1960 sees 4F No **44525** (6G-Llandudno Junction) has brought the Buxton to Hooton train to a halt opposite the signal box to enable a crew change with 8F No **48083** (17A-Derby), engine of the late running Stockport to Buxton 'shunter'. This procedure was normally scheduled for New Mills Newtown (see page 100), but for the reasons given above, was carried out at Middlewood, being a convenient changeover point within sight of the signal box. ***J W Sutherland***

(Below) An elevated view of Middlewood Low Level Junction (c.1950) from the Macclesfield Canal - above Middlewood tunnel - when the junctions still provided through running between the Macclesfield and Buxton lines. A Down passenger train is signalled to take the route towards Stockport. ***J W Sutherland collection***

28.11.59 Went up to Middlewood with Graham. At 9.30am 42328+5 was on the (higher) Down line with a Macclesfield to Manchester train. Later 49406 came through on the return 'shunt' from New Mills. The train from Birkenhead was headed by 42856 and 48389 banking in rear. 42374 was on the 11.8am Down train at the Higher station. Next came 90145 (41D Canklow) what was presumably the local goods from Stockport running late. 45093 came down on the Hooton train (probably the Class 5 noted on the Birkenhead yesterday). These two trains met at the signal box and they probably changed crews. 76048 was on the Up goods on the Macclesfield line at 11.25am. Then at 11.38am, 48519 (9D) came down on mixed goods (presumably the Arpley train).

13.2.60 Visit to Middlewood. Four coaches and a van were standing in the sidings awaiting dispatch to a works for breaking up. 48188 was on the Hooton train. 42886 was on the Arpley train. An 8F was on the shunt from New Mills. 48740 came down on another goods, I think Rowsley - Adswood, and later at Davenport saw 49277 (9D) on a special Buxton - Arpley. Spent much of time at Middlewood talking to a young signalman called Mr Mellor. 42970 was on the Birkenhead (no banker). Mr Mellor had helped put out a fire started in some coaches by youths a little while back. They said they had lit it because they were cold. I think 42889 was on the Stockport - Buxton shunt.

23.4.60 (Sat) Visit to Middlewood. Crab on New Mills 'shunt'. 48011 on 'shunter' to Buxton. 49277 on trip to Arpley. 48746 (8B) on train to Hooton. 49191 on train to Birkenhead (90622 banking).

8.6.60 In the evening went up to Middlewood. 48428 (9A) on the Down 'shunter'. 42925 + 4 on 5.37pm Mayfield - Buxton express. 44687 (Caprotti) on 5.50pm Mayfield - Buxton express. 48421 on the Stockport to Briggs train. 9F 2-10-0 was on the 4.10 Rowsley - Adswood.

29.10.60 Visit to Middlewood to take photos in view of Middlewood Higher impending closure (7th November 1960). A Crab was on the New Mills shunt.49083 (17A) was on the 'shunter' to Buxton. 44525 (6G-Llandudno Junction) was on the train to Hooton - they exchanged crews at Middlewood. A later Down train (to Widnes) from Rowsley was hauled by 48451. The Birkenhead was hauled by 90532 with a Crab banking. Was interested in some 1945 chairs on the old track in the Middlewood Sidings (formerly for trains to Macclesfield). Noted some fitted tarpaulin covered open wagons for New Mills marshalled to *The Bulk Packing Co.*, from Ellesmere Port West (Ship Canal Co)., Mr Clegg who was on duty in the box, suggested they would contain wood pulp from Scandinavia for paper and card manufacture. Mr Clegg was able to confirm that Turners Siding was where I thought, just down from New Mills. Apparently the place is now known as Wright Howarths. There was the usual string of coaches and vans in the siding.

8.4.61 (Sat) 48727 (9D) on Up shunter to Buxton. 48744 on the return New Mills 'shunt'. 42950 on the train to Hooton. 90369 (6C Birkenhead) on the Birkenhead, with 92050 banking. 48558 (9D) on train to Widnes. 44752 (Caprotti) On the Rowsley - Adswood.

16.9.61(Sat) Morning Visit. 92114 (18A - Toton) was on the Up 'shunter'. 44751 was on the return New Mills 'shunt'. 48106 was on the train to Hooton. 76087 was noted on a Down goods, Macclesfield - Marple line, at 10.42am. 48206 (8D) - or 48200 - was on the train to Widnes. At Middlewood the Down line had fairly recently been re-laid with 110lb rails on wooden sleepers with spring clip fastenings of the type sold by Exors of James Mills, Bredbury. In the 'old days', Middlewood was a popular terminus for special picnic trains and even more recently platelayers were specially employed there on Saturday afternoons to keep children away from the line. During the 1940's and early 1950's, there were regularly two football specials each year between Buxton and Macclesfield.

2.2.63 Mr Bernard Shaw, signalman at Hazel Grove, gave the following information, some obtained from his father. Middlewood Junction used to have the name marked out in egg-shells and is still sometimes known as 'Eggshell Junction'. Middlewood Junction used to be a relatively lively place. There was a regular daily shunt from Macclesfield to Buxton going up in the early morning and back in the late morning. This train did a lot of shunting at Bollington. Firebricks from Furness Vale were taken in the Macclesfield direction while traffic uphill included wagons of pulp.

(Right) The first link between the joint NSR/GCR Macclesfield and Marple line and the LNWR Buxton line was forged in 1879, ten years after the opening of the former and twenty-two years after the latter. Two stations, forming an interchange, were built at both high and low levels. The view here from the Down platform looking in the direction of Marple (Rose Hill) shows LNER/BR Class C13 4-4-2T No **67406** arriving at Middlewood Higher (c.1952), with an Up train bound for Macclesfield. The locomotive is just crossing over the intersection bridge which carries the line over the Buxton branch. The freshly ballasted Up line provides a reminder that the line was proposed for singling in the 1930's. Although the line lasted longer than most after Beeching, Middlewood higher lost its passenger trains on 7th November 1960. ***Authors collection***

(Top) The high level line looking in the direction of Marple from the Down side on Sunday 15th June 1958. The nameboard invites the passenger to *Change for Disley, Whaley Bridge and Buxton*. For another two years they could. ***J W Sutherland***

(Centre) Middlewood High level Junction signal box (c.1950), an LNWR design dating from 1885, on the Macclesfield, Bollington & Marple line looking in the direction of Marple with an unidentified Class C13 4-4-2T approaching on a Macclesfield bound train. ***Anon***

(Right) After the 1955 closure of the 'Middlewood Curve' as a through route, the line and sidings between Low Level Junction (Down line) and High Level Junction (Up line) were retained for storage of withdrawn /condemned coaches and other vehicles. The four bogied carriages seen here were all of LNWR vintage, all bearing builders plates from Wolverton circa 1915-1920. ***J W Sutherland***

(Right) This elevated view c.1951 from the Macclesfield Canal, above Middlewood tunnel, illustrates well the layout of the respective lines adjacent to Middlewood Low Level Junction signal box. The line coming in from the right, Middlewood Junction Railway No 2), left the Down Macclesfield at Middlewood High Level Junction. Popularly known as the 'Middlewood Curve', there were actually two independent lines, the other (Middlewood Junction (Railway No 1) bearing left at Low Level Juction, from the Down Buxton, to the Up Macclesfield at High Level Junction. This link, opened in 1885, allowed through running of trains between the LNWR and NS/GC Joint lines, including, in the early years, Euston/Buxton passenger services. Freight traffic would be the stable commodity throughout the remainder of its comparitively short life before closure in 1955 resulted in the flying junction line being removed, leaving a truncated stub of sidings that were accessed from the Down Buxton line. Used as storage for condemned vehicles, including carriages, the sidings rather surprisingly lasted for another ten years before being closed on the 29th September 1964. Recovery of the redundant track commenced on 13th August 1965. **(Below)** An undated LMS period view from a similar vantage point as that above sees Fowler 2-6-4T No **2368** (9D) climb towards Middlewood tunnel with what is presumably a Buxton bound train. It will be noted that the signalling arrangement is different, in that those - for Down trains - located above the second carriage are positioned on the opposite (Up) side for sighting purposes. Also, separate posts for the respective routes diverging at Low Level Junction followed LNWR practice, but when the junction was resignalled by the LMS, the new signals were mounted on a prefabricated steel bracket adjacent to the signal box. The crossover road was also moved nearer to the signal box. LNWR wooden posts were replaced by LMS pattern wooden types. ***Authors collection***

(Right) Middlewood, 30th May 1959. With 'Crab' 2-6-0 No **42856** (6C-Birkenhead) working hard with a Buxton-bound freight, an unidentified 8F passes Middlewood Low Level junction signal box with a working for Ince & Elton. In a surprisingly short time the vegetation in and around the cutting has proliferated almost beyond recognition when compared with the views on page 72. The abandoned formation coming in from the right of the Birkenhead train which had, until 1954, carried the Middlewood curve, has vanished beneath bushes and trees, although a connection to the left of the signal box, containing sidings, form the truncated remains of the Middlewood Curve (Low Level Jcn to High Level Jcn line). ***J W Sutherland***

(Left-centre) Middlewood Tunnel (Br. No 15) was in a shallow cutting interrupted only by the Macclesfield Canal which passed overhead. The cover between the waterway and brick arch of the tunnel was minimal, reflected in the short length (53yds) of the structure. This view is taken from the Down side looking in the direction of Disley. ***D Ibbotson***

(Below) Descending cautiously towards Middlewood tunnel from Disley on 26th October 1963, 'Austerity' No **90329** (56A-Wakefield), recently transferred from Sowerby Bridge, heads the 3.40pm (SO) ex-Buxton to Adswood freight towards Stockport. It seems quite extraordinary that a line speed as high as 50mph was in force (from $4\frac{1}{2}$ milepost-Middlewood); 60mph up to $4\frac{1}{2}$ milepost ***J W Sutherland***

(Above) The morning Adswood to Buxton 'shunter' leaves the Disley end of Middlewood tunnel in this Spring-time (Saturday 8th April) 1961 view, headed by 8F No **48727** (9D). Very noticeable is the extent to which the embankments are free of shrubbery or trees as a result of regular maintenance by local gangs who patrolled these lengths. Engine and crew would have been over three hours into their working day when the train arrived at New Mills (arr 10.28), but the Edgeley men would be relieved here by their Buxton counterparts from an eastbound Hooton train. **(Below)** Within a short distance of the tunnel, the line passes beneath bridge No 16, sometime known locally as Pearsons, and the 5 milepost which can be seen beneath the arch to the right.The distinctive front end of one of the BRC&W diesel sets, comprising six-cars, displays a white cab roof and B3 code to good effect. The bridge, seen also on 8th April 1961, was reconstructed with a new concrete deck in 1985. ***J W Suherland***

Having crossed the Cheshire plains, the daily freight from Birkenhead is part way through encountering the first gradient of any real substance since its early morning departure. **(Above)** Another in the fine series of pictures taken on that April (1961) day sees 'Austerity' 2-8-0 No **90369** (6C-Birkenhead) hauling its train beneath bridge 16. The rate of progress towards Buxton can again be judged by a scheduled time allowance of just over one hour betwen Edgeley Junction and Whaley Bridge, a distance of 10 miles. **(Below)** With pillars of smoke still bellowing from Middlewood tunnel, banking engine in the form of BR Standard Class 9F 2-10-0 No **92050** (17C-Rowsley) works its way, eventually to its home depot, makes a similar impact whilst passing milepost 5. ***J W Sutherland***

Buxton 'Crab' No **42814** appears to be taking the adverse gradient in its stride on the approach to Bullock's crossing with an Up Buxton passenger train on 6th October 1956. In the five years prior to views on previous pages, bullhead rail still remains along with a very tidy ballast shoulder. Note the signal wire in the cess which operated the Middlewood Low Level Junction Down distant signal (see below). ***N Fields***

A somewhat shorter 'Birkenhead' than normal is about to pass over Bullock's crossing on the approach to Disley on 27th February 1960. Stanier 'Crab' No **42973**, a long-time Birkenhead based engine, hauls the train single-handed whilst still managing to darken the skies. To the left, a concrete fog hut sits beneath the Middlewood Low Level Junction Down distant signal. ***J W Sutherland***

The Middlewood Low Level Junction Down distant signal was adjacent to the $\frac{1}{4}$ milepost ($5\frac{1}{4}$ miles from Edgeley Junction). The approaching diesel was due in Disley at 10.54am, having commenced its journey from Manchester's Mayfield station at 10.20, this being a Saturday (27th February 1960). Once again, route code B3 is displayed, although on Saturdays, there were a small number of Down workings from Buxton into Manchester with code B9, indicating that the train destination was Mayfield. The code A9 was also used to indicate express workings into Mayfield. ***J W Sutherland***

(Above) Our photographer has taken to the fields for this view of the morning Buxton to Arpley (Warrington) freight, 8F No **48421** (9D-Buxton) heading its train away from Disley on the descent towards Middlewood and Hazel Grove. On Mondays, the working ran to and was terminated at Longsight although the same timings applied as far as Davenport Junction. A stop at Disley was allowed (as required) for the pinning down of wagons brakes. The signal of course is the Middlewood Low Level Junction Down distant seen on the previous page. ***J W Sutherland***

(Centre) This well known photograph is included because of its 'Buxton line' connection. Having left Disley station a few moments before, the 4.25pm ex-Buxton to Manchester Piccadilly diesel service accelerates towards 'Park' bridge (No 20), as it was known to railwaymen, the point at which the line passed beneath the overbridge carrying the driveway to Lyme Park.The first three vehicles of this 6-car BRC&W set have possibly worked into the Manchester area from other north-west depots, this being a Sunday (5th April 1964) working. The three Buxton cars, recognised by the white cab ends, form the rear part of the train. The white cottage beyond the train gave an indication to crews working Up trains that the end of the climb from Hazel Grove was imminent. ***M Mensing***

(Below) The Up Refuge Siding alongside the approach to Disley was normally accessed following reversal by Up trains, although of course it wasn't unknown for Down trains to be stabled there. It was a very useful facility and on 3rd March 1962, a late running Up parcels train was 'set-inside' to allow for a scheduled passenger train, in this instance the 8.35am departure from Davenport, to pass on its way to Buxton. The parcel service, in the hands of 4F No **44042** (17C-Rowsley), was normally due to arrive at Disley at 7.27am, being allowed 2 1/2 minutes stopover. During the electrification of London Road station, the service worked to and from Manchester Victoria. ***J W Sutherland***

(Right) This time it is the turn of Buxton engine, 8F 2-8-0 No **48519,** on the Stockport 'shunter', to take refuge in the Up Siding at Disley. The date is 3rd March 1962 and it was quite obvious the weather was having an effect on timings. A description of the mornings workings can be found in the diary extracts for Disley on page 85.

(Centre) There is on occasions a story behind the photograph. Having travelled up to Disley from Davenport, our photographer made himself known to Mr Clegg, the signalman. Being Whit Friday (26th April 1961), an extra train, a 3-car dmu, had been included in the schedule to serve Disley, no doubt to cater for the folk wishing to visit Lyme Park........ ***continued below***

..........On this occasion, an Inspector Derbyshire was in charge of this extra, which made use of the Down Siding (in front of the signal box) while normal services continued. The view here shows the western approach to the station from the 'safety' of the Up Refuge Siding. Disley signal box was an LNWR type 4 structure of 1906 and contained a 15 lever Tumbler frame. The group of lineside buildings between water tank and signal box include lamp hut and concrete hut that probably served as toilet for the signal box

(Right) Neither did Whit Friday provide any barriers to freight operation as Stanier 'Crab' 2-6-0 No **42952** (5A-Crewe North) passes through Disley around 3.30pm with the 1.35pm ex-Buxton to Adswood train. Once again, time was allowed as required in order to stop and pin down wagon brakes. ***J W Sutherland***

The two views on this page show Disley from an earlier period, that to the left being prior to a fire, sometime around WW1, and which resulted in the rebuilding of the station above platform level. **(Left)** The somewhat motley collection of buildings, looking in the direction of New Mills from the Up platform, shows the main station facilities on the right hand (Down) side. These contained Porters (nearest), a general waiting room, Booking Office and Ladies. On the Up platform were Ladies Waiting Room (nearest) and a Booking Office with Waiting Room. Out of the picture behind the photographer was a substantial Gents urinal block.

(Left-lower) The replacement station buildings following the fire were, to say the least, a great improvement. Disley, a wealthy area of similar standing to Alderley Edge, would appear to have put pressure on the railway company for enhanced facilities. The L&NWR's offering was a compromise, erecting buildings of modular construction, solid and well built. Platform illumination was now the domain of gas lighting, a facility which would serve Disley patrons for the next five decades. The impovements included much needed canopy protection on both platforms. The Up side buildings (left) comprised Ladies Waiting Room (with toilets), General Waiting Room (with Gents toilets,etc) and Booking Office. The main buildings (Down side - for Manchester) had a separate Porters Room (hut seen here outside the canopy), General Waiting Room and Ladies Wating Room with access to toilets, combined Booking Office and Parcel Office. A bicycle hut was located adjacent to the entrance off the station approach. Furniture and fittings within the waiting areas were of a higher standard than elsewhere on the line and Disley remains to this day in one of the more picturesque settings of stations serving the south-east of Manchester.

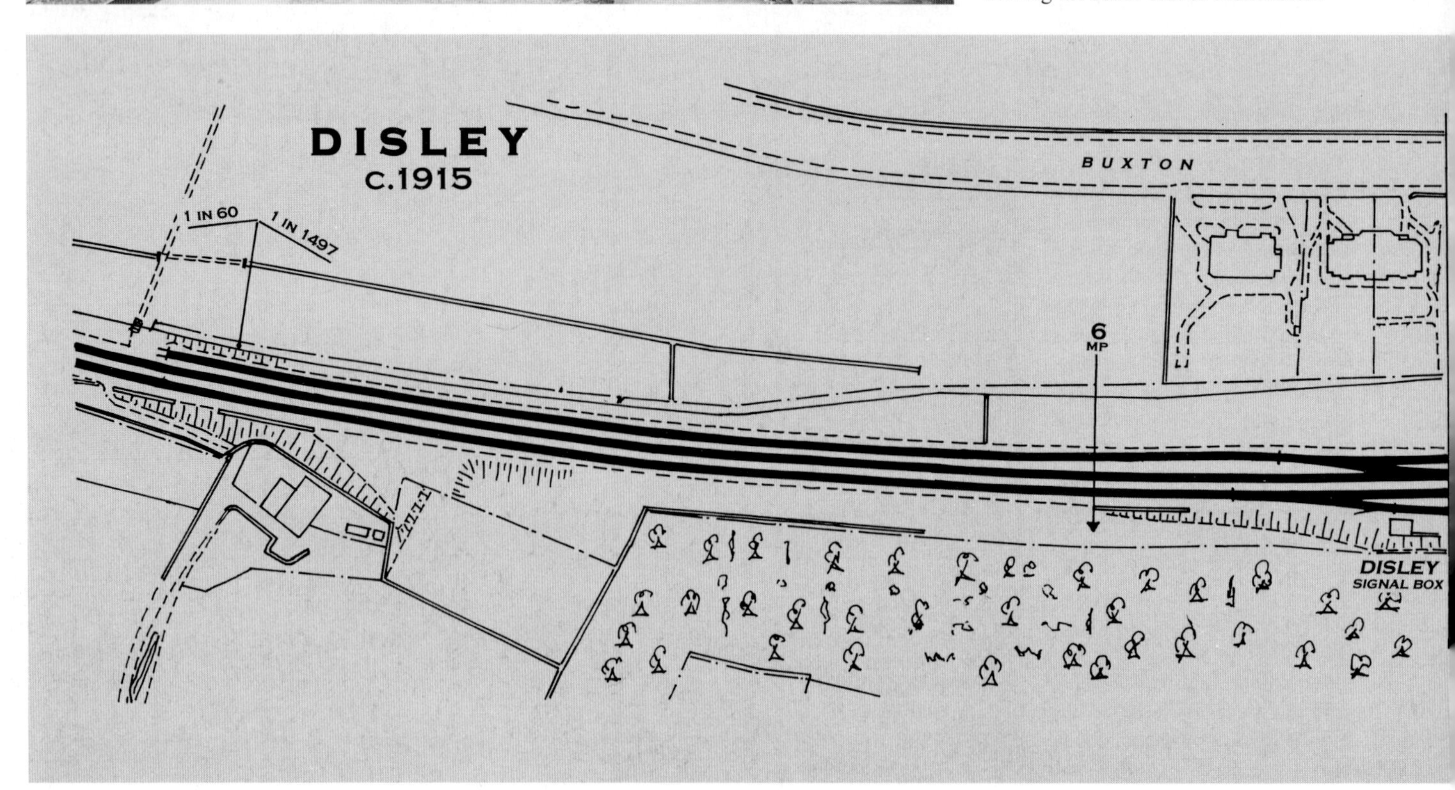

(Above) Longsight based Stanier 2-6-4T No **42430**, having completed the 3³/4 mile 1 in 60 climb from Hazel Grove, rolls alongside the Up platform with a Buxton train. It has just crossed with a Down freight, the engine of which is seen entering the station on page 83 (centre).

H Townley, courtesy *J M Bentley*

(Left) Steam has long since vanished from the Buxton line but this late afternoon view at five o'clock, one autumn day in 1972, shows a station still being well looked after. Destaffing of stations on the line had commenced during 1971 and further rationalisation was in the offing. The gas lighting seen here required the attendance of more staff than was deemed necessary and 'improvements' in the form of electric lighting were carried out to enable reduced levels of staffing. ***Stephen Shaw***

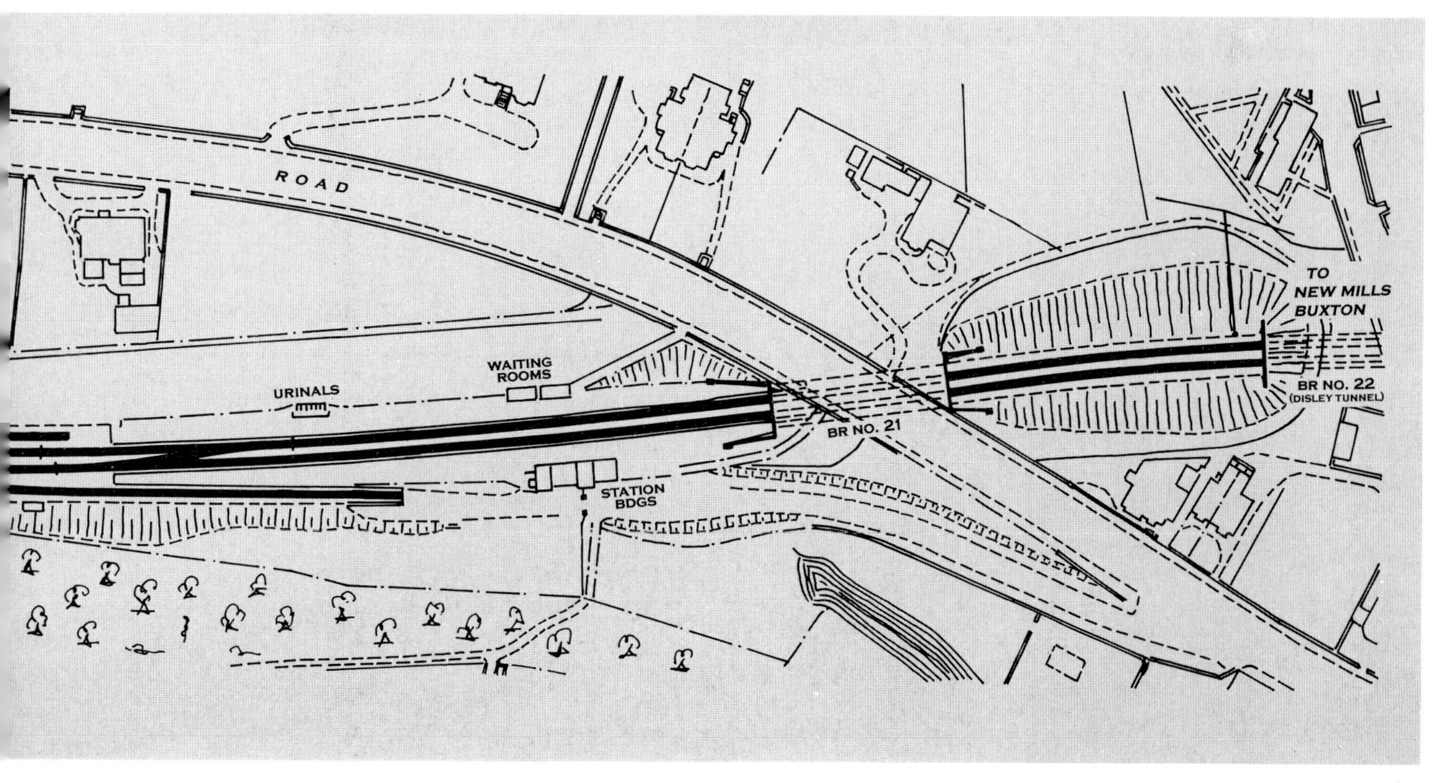

(Right) Smoking chimneys, coal fires, platform barrows and trolleys, poster boards, etc., all signs of a traditional railway that is unfortunately entered a state of decline. Having survived the Beeching 'axe', Disley station in this 13th January 1967 view from Buxton Road gives the appearance of everything being in 'apple pie' order. The modular layout of the structure is clearly seen, and ultimately, natural settlement would contribute to undulations in both roof and canopy (see centre view). Although slightly staggered, buildings on both platfroms were the same length. ***Authors collection***

(Centre) The rear elevation of the Down side station buildings. It is unclear, although not uncommon, to see the valancing continued around the building, here at Disley giving a more refined appearance to what in fact were at best functional but utilitarian structures. The small shed adjacent to the station entrance was originally provided for cycles but latterly used as a store. Dating from the 1880's, the design would see a multiplicity of uses such as waiting rooms, lamp rooms and even signal boxes.

(Below) The 'big freeze' of 1963 gave many an opportunity to record snow scenes and Disley, on February 16th, whilst looking in the direction of Stockport, was no exception. A careful look under the Up (right) side canopy will reveal an electric banner repeater signal located on the approach side of the Disley Up Starting signal which was some distance away. As the name implies, the signal repeats the indication of the signal ahead. Approaching the Up platform is BRC&W 3-car set, now sporting the yellow half panel markings beneath the cab windows. ***J W Sutherland***

(Right) One can almost here the garbled 'Tannoy' announcement at Manchester's London Road station prior to the departure of the 5.40pm train to Buxton....'*calling at Disley, Whaley Bridge and Buxton'*. The twenty-two minute non-stop schedule wasn't the quickest between the two stations (that distinction belonged to the 4.45pm ex-London Road which completed the journey in nineteen minutes including a call at Stockport), but it could merit a 'blue-riband' accolade amongst trains to Buxton. Longsight 'Crab' No **42887** has just arrived at Disley on 28th May 1958 with one of the two remaining steam locomotive hauled services to operate in a predominantly diesel railcar operation. For the casual traveller, a Cheap Day return fare Disley/Manchester was Two Shillings and Sixpence (12$^{1}/_{2}$p).

(Centre) A Down freight behind Buxton 8F No **48268** enters Disley station, passing beneath Buxton Road bridge (No 21) at a point where the A6 trunk road and Buxton line intersect for the first time after leaving Stockport. The view emphasises the shallow cover between arch and roadway. At the time, the route from Disley to Buxton came under the control of Derby North District although the Signal & Telegraph Engineer's boundary extended to Woodsmoor Crossing signal box. On the end of the Up platform is a water column supplied from the 'town' water supply. A number plate attached to the column provided details which engine crews were required to record the quantity of water used. Very few footplate staff seem to recall using the supply! A column at the Stockport end of the Down platform was catered for by a tank near the signal box.

(Right-lower) A clear view from the Down platform of the line looking in the direction of New Mills, bridge No 21 in the foreground. The Disley Up starting signal mentioned previously is located a short distance from the tunnel mouth, the advance warning of which was given by the banner repeating signal beneath the station canopy. Behind the signal is the Down Home 'board', positioned on the opposite (Up) side for sighting purposes. The stone-faced brick arch had a span of 30feet to accommodate the platform ramps.

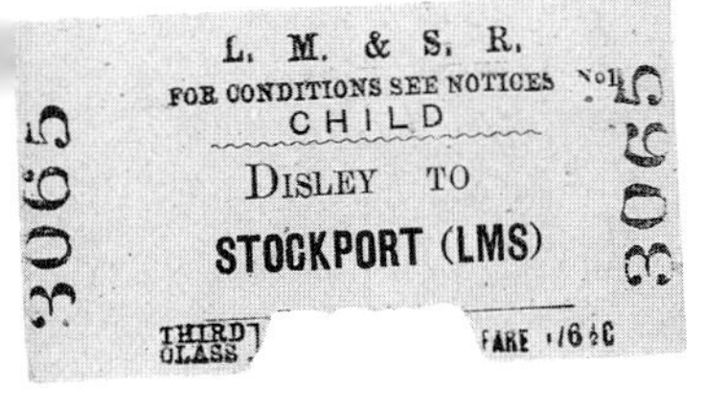

(Right) From above the parapet of bridge No 21 (Buxton Road), we see an unidentified 8F climbing the last few yards of a steady three mile ascent, of varying degrees, from Furness Vale with a Down freight. Clouds of smoke and steam envelop the portal of the 212 yard long Disley tunnel (Br No 22), almost to the point of blotting out the signals. Engine crews would certainly have needed the requisite route knowledge to pick out the signals adjacent to the tunnel entrance, in particular the Down home signal which could appear 'from nowhwere' if the tunnel was filled with smoke.

(Centre) A pre-WW2 close up of Disley tunnel's western entrance with long-time Buxton Fowler 2-6-4T No **2368** leaving behind the darkness on the run-in to Disley station at the head of a Down passenger train. The tunnel was built on a slight curve and falling gradient - towards Furness vale, commencing at 1 in 1497. This steepened slightly inside the bore to 1 in 453 and was quite noticeable for permanent way or tunnel inspection gangs when hand pushing trolleys or the like, as your author can verify from the periodic Saturday night/ Sunday morning sojourns.

(Below) The brief encounter with darkness through Disley tunnel will be in stark contrast to the bright snow covered slopes of Hagg Bank as a 6-car diesel set passes over bridge No 23 (Hollinwood Road) with the 9.20am ex-Manchester Piccadilly to Buxton working on Saturday 3rd March 1962. Just visible above the roof of the hut to the left of the train is the banner repeater for Disley Down home signal (seen above at the other end of the tunnel).

J W Sutherland

DIARY EXTRACTS FOR

..........DISLEY

27.2.60 Went up to Disley and walked back towards Middlewood to get some photos. An 8F was on the 'shunt' from New Mills. 42877 was on the train to Hooton. 48421 was on the train to Arpley. 42973 was on the train from Birkenhead. 42940 (5A) was on a late Down goods (probably Rowsley - Adswood).

5.3.60 Going up noted 48389 in the Up siding at Disley, with special goods (Widnes - Buxton). Noted that a Down diesel included one of the Buxton 2-car sets.

7.5.60 Went to Disley and walked to New Mills.

25.6.61 (Whit Friday) Went up to Disley and photographed 42952 (5A) on the early afternoon Down goods. Later 49144 was noted running up light. The later Down 'shunter' goods consisted of an unrecognisable Class 5 and a brake van. The extra 3-car diesel set was providing an additional service and at one stage was stored for about an hour in the Down siding at Disley station. Mr C. Clegg was in duty in the box and an inspector, Mr Derbyshire was in charge of the extra train.

3.3.62 (Sat) After a fairly heavy snowfall, I went up to Disley on the 8.35am from Davenport. 44042 was in the Up refuge siding at Disley with the parcels train, which followed my train, soon after the Birkenhead train came through (earlier than usual) headed by 48138 and banked by 48727. Next, 48519 (9D) came up on the 'shunter' and was put in the Disley Up refuge siding. 42849 (9B) was on the returning New Mills 'shunt' which spent some time at Disley Goods. After, 48519 eventually got away from Disley. 48558 came down with the Hooton train, followed by 48740 on the Widnes. Then 48138 came down light, followed later by 48106 (8B) on the Rowsley - Adswood. The Stalybridge diesel service working to Buxton today was in the form of a 2-car Birmingham set.

3.9.64 (Tue) 48089 in the Up siding with a Down train of mineral wagons except for the brake van which was in the Down siding. Heard later that the trouble was a failure of the brake van.

DIARY EXTRACTS FOR

.....DISLEY GOODS

17.10.59 (Sat) Got the 8.38 diesel from Davenport to Disley and walked to Disley Goods. Found the same well-spoken chap in charge as on my last visit. As usual the sidings were full of vans for Bowaters, together with one or two wagons for coal. Noted waybill destinations on the vans included Norwich, Liverpool, Barry (Glamorgan) Deighton and Wolverhampton. 49453 came down on the 'shunt' from New Mills and then after shunting vans, departed for Stockport. Thanks to kindness of the guard Mr Middleton I had a ride in the brake van................. ***continued on page 86***

Disley Goods, 16th February 1963. The view from Dryhurst Lane bridge (Br.No.24) of the morning New Mills shunt was familiar to residents of both Railway Terrace and Hollinwood Road (right) on a daily basis although plans were in hand to rationalise traffic which would result in closure of Disley Goods depot from 30th Novemer 1964. The train, comprising vans serving nearby Bowaters, on this snowy day in the extra cold winter of 1963 is being shunted by 'Crab' 2-6-0 No **42748**, (9G) an engine based at Gorton where it would see out its final days (w/d 10.64). The duration of this shunting procedure was approximately twenty three minutes between 9.52 and 10.17 in the morning as the 'shunt' returned from its trip to New Mills (Newtown). The last *Working Time Table (7th September 1964 to 13th June 1965)* shows the Disley Goods traffic being dealt with by the 1.30pm ex-Buxton to Adswood freight, scheduled to call at Disley between 2.58 and 3.16 in the afternoon, although that would have been curtailed due to withrawal of facilities in the November.

J W Sutherland

DIARY EXTRACTS FOR. ....DISLEY GOODS

continued from page 85.......We shunted at Davenport Sidings (put off one wagon of coal, and then went into Edgeley and backed into the enlarged Adswood Sidings where I left the train. At Disley Goods noted a gas lamp post was marked *"Midland Railway Company."*

7.5.60 Went up to Disley, walked to New Mills. The crane at Disley Goods was being demolished, perhaps to facilitate movement of Bowaters large road van when loading vans on the shed road. 48519 (9D) + 39 + brake to Hooton; 48679 (9D) to Arpley; 42886 (9B) + short train, with Rowsley to Adswood a special; 48465 (9D - I think) on Birkenhead - Buxton 92786 banking. 49281 (9D) on Stockport - Buxton' shunter'.

1.10.60 (Sat) From 9.35 ex-Davenport). An 8F was on the shunt at Disley Goods while 48684 was on the train to Hooton. We walked down from Long Hill, Whaley Bridge, and looked in at Shallcross Yard.

5.9.59 Photographed 49191(9B) on the 'shunt' from Stockport.

3.10.59 49191 was on the' shunt' at New Mills.

2.2.60 8.38am ex Davenport. On the way up noted a 'Super D' at New Mills, 49453 I think.

5.3.60 42937 was on the shunt at New Mills. 42778 (6C) was on the Hooton train, banked up to Buxton by 48278 (9D).

30.4.60 En-route to Bibbingtons noted 42937 at New Mills on the 'shunt' service.

7.5.60 (Sat) Went to Disley and walked to New Mills. 49401 (9B) with tender cab and new o/head warning signs was on the New Mills 'shunt', which spent some time shunting Disley Goods (the man in charge said they were busy with Bowaters traffic and had loaded 160 wagons this week. There is also a regular inward coal traffic. Located what I think was Turners Siding near New Mills. Noted two wagons (vans) of China clay at New Mills.

4.6.60 Ex-8.38 from Davenport. 49401 (9B) was on the 'shunt' from Edgeley. Noted the yard crane was 10 tons and had a plate *"LNWR 2971"* but no sign of builders or date, except for 'Manchester' embossed in one place.

7.6.60 42786 at New Mills on the Down 'shunter' from Buxton. 92008 was on the 4.10pm Rowsley - Adswood. 45409 (26F) was on the 5.37 pm Manchester - Buxton express and a "Crab" on the 5.50 pm. 49281 was on the Stockport - Briggs goods and 45505 (unrebuilt Patriot) on what is said to be the Buxton - Arpley.

(Below) Disley Goods, Saturday 7th May 1960. ***J W Sutherland***

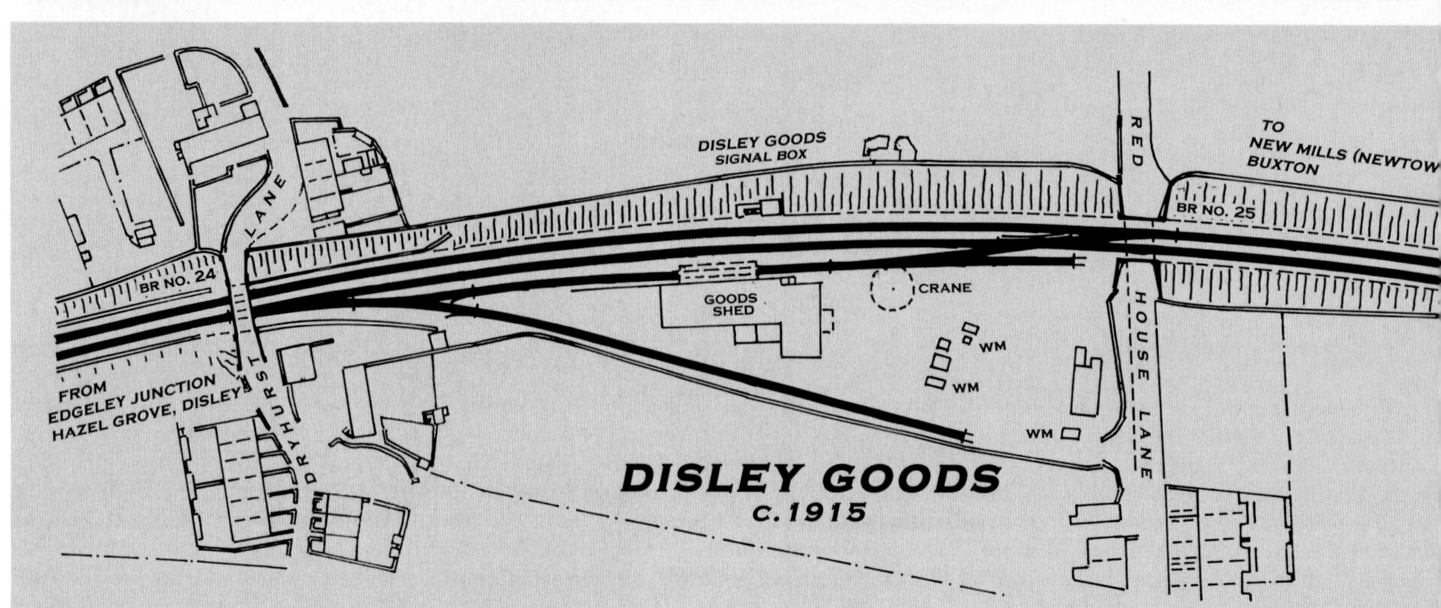

In contrast to the plush tree-lined hillsides surrounding the passenger station, Disley Goods was somewhat hidden away amidst the the more local community housing that was to be found on the Manchester to Buxton road as it wound its way from Cheshire into Derbyshire. The goods yard was hemmed in on three sides away from the railway by Dryhurst Lane, Red House Lane and Meadow Lane, the latter which spreads itself across the background in the photo on page 86.

Until 1934, access by rail to the sidings was controlled by a signal box located on the Up side opposite the goods shed (see diagram - page 86). There was a crossover at the New Mills end which enabled Up trains to reverse both into the yard or the Down line. The facility for Up trains appears to have been confined to 'refuge' requirements, allowing freight trains to be shunted out of the way to enable passenger trains to pass unheeded. Goods workings affecting the yard itself always always seem to have been of trains working in the Down direction. In the mid 1880's, two afternoon workings, firstly a local Whaley Bridge to Davenport Junction goods, called for a ten minute spell, the limiting factor being the restriction on the number of wagons allowed (15) in the train this side of Whaley. The second, from Buxton to Longsight, spent twenty minutes at Disley catering for traffic that had arrived too late for the earlier train. A typical latter day's working of the depot can be found on page 85.

Until 1964, Bowaters, whose factory was in nearby Red House Lane, utilised both rail and road transport for their packaging products. Consignments by rail were widespread and the company vehicles could be seen on their daily routine ferrying between factory and both Disley Goods and New Mills Newtown station goods yard. By the very nature of Bowaters traffic, their numerous road vehicles and the railways' vans took up most of the space available at Disley. The scene over on page 86, Saturday 7th May 1960, although showing the somewhat restricted nature of the yard, illustrated Bowaters commitment to rail at the time. That said, the logistics of double handling, improvements and investment in the national road network, and a desire by government to rationalise the railway system would only mean one thing, withdrawal of freight facilities.

(Above) The returning New Mills 'shunt' arrives at Disley on the morning of Saturday 30th August 1958 in readiness to perform the morning's routine activities. On this occasion, 4F No **44271** (9B-Stockport) provides engine power.

(Right) Shunter for today's train, New Mills Newtown Leading Porter Edwin 'Teddy' Greenhough, crosses the line having detached vans and wagons from the brake van in readiness for the shunting manoeuvre. ***J W Sutherland***

(Above) The Brake Van, remaining on the main line, stands idle whilst the engine and train are involved in shunting operations beyond the goods shed. This Saturday 30th April 1958 scene also records the passing of the 9.20am ex-London Road to Buxton service in the hands of a 6-car BRC&W set. Still comparatively new, the units are in original green livery and yet to be adorned by the 'speed-whiskers' beneath the cab windows.

(Centre) The entrance to the depot from Red House Lane gives a clear indication of how coal wagons were positioned on the siding in order to serve the merchants handling needs. Former resident of Dryhurst Lane, Ian Parker, recalls coal being brought initially to Mr Isaac (Ike) Ford, and then to Mr Travis, whose lorry is seen 'bagged up' prior to deliveries. A Bowaters vehicle is being unloaded at the far end of the yard, with every possibility that van drivers Geoff Haughton or Bob Lomas could be involved in the exercise.

(Right) The 'Super D's' were regular performers on the New Mills 'shunt', this Saturday 17th October 1959 view showing **49453** (9B-Stockport), tender first, hauling a long train alongside Disley Goods where it will come to rest. Bowaters are obviously enjoying a busy spell if the number of vans is anything to go by.

All (3); ***J W Sutherland***

The peace and tranquility of a wintry Saturday morning (3rd March 1962) will be disturbed by Class 8F No **48558** (9D-Buxton) climbing past Disley Goods on a short stretch of 1 in 236 gradient with the Buxton to Hooton freight. The New Mills 'shunt' has been and gone by some twenty minutes, leaving clear signs of vehicles parked overnight. To the left of the picture above the rooftops is Bowaters factory on Red House Lane, highlighting the close proximity of the works to the railway. What is not quite clear however is if the steam/smoke emission above the factory is from Bowaters or in fact across the valley from a passing locomotive in the vicinity of New Mills Central.

A slight detour around the Disley Goods site on the same day provides a quiet moment and shows a snow covered landscape but which indicates nicely the marshalling of vans and coal wagons to suit the appropriate users. Because of the restraints caused by siding capacity, it was sometimes necessary to split the number of wagons/vans to aid shunting. The Buxton line at this point was within a few yards of both the Midland line, between Manchester and Derby, and the Peak Forest Canal winding its way between Marple and Whaley Bridge.

Both this page; ***J W Sutherland***

With capacity for both road and rail very much at a premium, Bowaters is taking full advantage of the space between the goods shed and coal stacking ground to utilise both sidings. Entering the picture from the right is a BRC&W 3-car dmu set on a Down passenger working which is also seen passing Disley station's Down distant immediately before passing over Red House Lane bridge. (3rd March 1962) Above and below; ***J W Sutherland***

Bowaters Disley factory is to the left as Class 8F No **48106** (8B-Warrington) makes the ascent towards Disley with a Rowsley to Adswood coal train. the headroom sign in the bottom left of the picture is affixed to Red House Lane bridge (No 25) through which the Bowaters vans made their short trip by road to Disley Goods. To the left of the engine, in the distance, are some of the mill chimneys, locating manufacturers in the Newtown area above New Mills. The encroaching trees to the right, beyond the train, mark the route of the A6 road adjacent to Seven Springs Garage between Disley and Newtown.

(Above) The Stockport to Buxton 'shunter' makes its way down the gentle grade towards New Mills Newtown on Saturday 7th May 1960 with 'Super D' No **49281** (9D-Buxton) in charge. To the left of the picture, the outline of Albert Mill indicates a site once connected by rail to the Down line and given the name of Turners Siding after the then owner of the mill for some forty years, Mr J W A Turner. The principal activity was bleaching. Messrs Wright Howarth took over the mill in 1912 but the siding had long since been taken out of use. The Grove Mill Paper Company (waste paper recycling) took over the premises between 1940 and 1954 but it was as Rose Vale Manufacturing that then New Mills (Newtown) Junior Porter Derek Ashworth recalls visiting the works to either collect or deliver consignments of foil containers, cake paper cases and cake frills. While at Newtown, in Derek's words, his mother never ran short of 'doyleys'. The site is now occupied by private housing alongside Peveril Mews and Peveril Gardens. In the days when Turners Siding functioned, there were two afternoon trains in the Down direction.

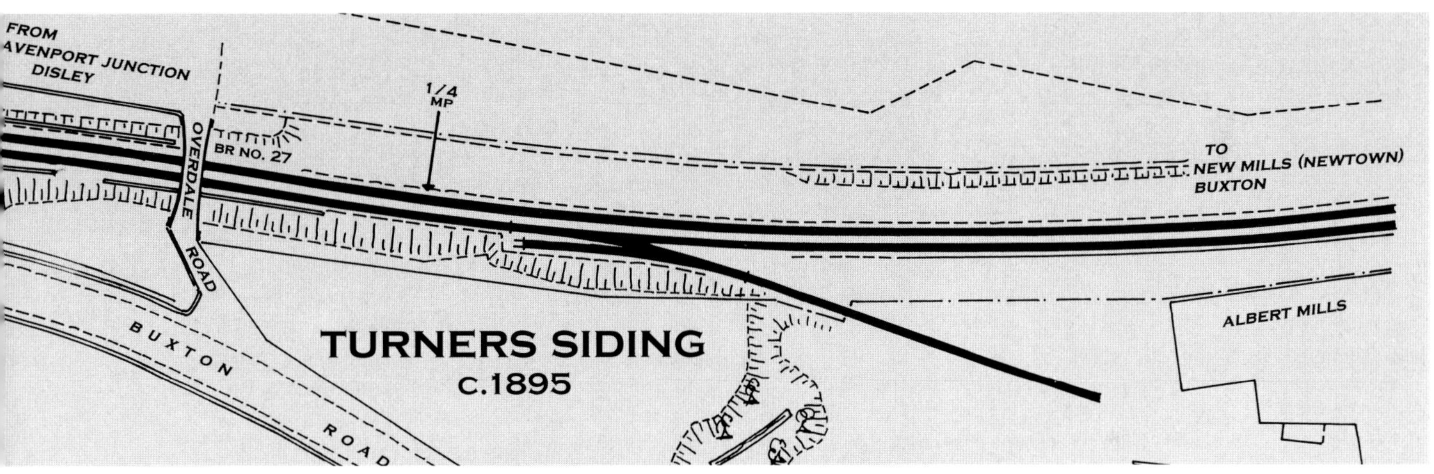

NEWTOWN

(Right) The 'Wessy', as it was popularly known, frequently saw use at the weekends by the ICI Hopper trains, sometimes due to engineering work on the Midland main line, in particular repairs to Dove Holes tunnel, but also to keep the flows of Limestone needed to keep the mid-Cheshire processing plants operational. An atmospheric exit from New Mills (Newtown) is produced as Northwich (9G) 8F No **48613** grapples with the 1 in 136/218 gradient towards Disley, possibly with a payload of 15/16 wagons. This frosty scene was recorded on 6th February 1954 to the rear of gardens in Maple Avenue and Meadowside. The chimney to the right of the telegraph pole stood above the Matlow Brothers and Swizzels works of Brunswick Mill.

N K Harrop

(Right) Albion Road bridge (No 28) was an excellent vantage point for both watching trains and for Up train crews to focus on the platforms just ahead at New Mills (Newtown). A day on from our previous photograph (*bottom-page 91*) and the snow has provided another of its overcoats on this part of the High Peak. This Sunday, 7th February 1954 view shows Stanier 2-cylinder Class 4 2-6-4T No **42467** (9A-Longsight) on an Up passenger train with one of the four scheduled return workings on the Manchester/Buxton service.

N K Harrop

DIARY EXTRACTS FOR.......

NEW MILLS (NEWTOWN)

12.7.60 (Tues) from 5.37 ex-Davenport. Passed a 4F, possibly 44237 - at New Mills, apparently on the 3.30pm Buxton - Stockport goods.

8.9.60 48408 was on the 'shunt' at New Mills. I travelled on the 7.50 departure from Davenport and noticed a lot of school children for Buxton get on en-route.

15.10.60 (to Whaley Bridge). 42773 at New Mills on shunt. 44413 (17C) was on the Up parcels running late (2 vans). There was a Crab on the Birkenhead. It was a long train, banked by 48679. 48726 was on the train to Hooton. 48506 was on a Down train, probably due out from Rowsley.

11.2.61 (8.35am ex-Davenport). Noted 48310 on the 'shunt' at New Mills.

11.3.61 (8.35am ex-Davenport). 42886 was at New Mills on the 'shunt'.

9.5.61 Ex-Disley. Noted 48451 in the sidings at New Mills on a Down goods - evidently the 3.30pm Buxton - Stockport goods.

13.5.61 (Sat) Ex-7.51am from Davenport. 48744 (9B) was on the 'shunt' at New Mills.

24.2.62 (Sat) Went up to New Mills Newtown on the 9.20am from Piccadilly. Did not see what engine was on the New Mills 'shunt' - passed between Disley Goods and New Mills. 48437 (9E Trafford Park) was on the 'shunter' passed on the Up loop at Woodsmoor on the way up. I had a chat with the Station Master at New Mills Mr J. Harrop, according to the sign on the door, then went out and found 90532 (6B-Mold Junction) on the Hooton waiting at the signal by the box. It consisted of the usual tanks, coal wagons and some other wagons, also a rake of Palvans, all apparently being allocated to margarine traffic and on their way back to Port Sunlight. The shunter arrived and backed into the loop. Then, presumably the shunter was still at Disley Goods, the Hooton went forward and backed out on to the Up line so that the Down diesel could get past. Then it departed as also (later), did the shunter after a little shunting. 42946 followed behind the Hooton with the Widnes, presumably, then 48746 with the Rowsley - Adswood. A little later 76087 (9F-Heaton Mersey still, as far as I know) came down light. Next I returned to the goods yard and noted the waybills on some of the wagons. They included coal for the Disley Goods (Ford Bros). Some fitted open sheeted wagons were from Bowaters U.K. Pulp & Paper Mills at Ellesmere Port via Edgeley and worked under consignee *"Disley Drums"*. A van from Lostock Gralam via Broadheath was to *"Bowater Packaging"* and contained 300 x 10 Gal. Wire Hampers. There was one or two vans from Burngallow to J J Makin at New Mills and described as *"Bags Clay"*, Mr Harrop told me this was for a local paper mills. He also drew my attention to some stone sleepers lying in the grass rear of the Up station building and which he thought had been taken out of one of the siding lines. Also showed me a new sign at the nearby NORTH WESTERN HOTEL in the form of quite a good painting of "Cornwall" in black LNW Livery.

3.3.62 Walked to New Mills along the A6 road. En-route noted 44867 running backwards, with a brake van on the Up line. When I got to New Mills found it was the morning 'shunt' which had come up late.. There is a lady in the signal box there at present. Saw no signs of the Birkenhead train. Went home on the 12.20pm from Buxton.

21.8.64 (Fri) 45632 *Tonga* was at New Mills on the shunt.42892 was on the Down goods at New Mills. A very pleasant mainly sunny day.

20.8.64 (Tue) 42782 was on the morning Arpley to Buxton train (2 vans and tank wagons).

3.9.64 (Fri) Had a chat with Signalman Lee (the woman has left the job). 45015 came through on the Arpley - Buxton (tanks only) 44867 left for Disley Goods, with 3 vans only. There were two wagons of coal consigned to Lord Brothers in the yard. Was told that the goods shed would become an "off - rail" depot in November and the sidings disconnected. It will be used for smalls traffic which will be taken by road to and from Stockport-as is largely happening now I gathered. Also it is said that Disley Goods and Whaley Bridge will be closed for all goods. Bowaters traffic will probably go to New Mills East. 45380 came through light from Buxton returning from moving the parcels train. Walked to New Mills East. Gathered they are quite optimistic about the future of this depot which mainly handles wagon load traffic. There were several British, Belgium and German train ferry vans there, handling plastic material brought from Memmingham in Germany for a firm called Fletcher, apparently bound to a plastics factory at Compstall, near Marple. 48501 (9F-Heaton Mersey) was waiting in the yard on a semi-fast from Gowhole.

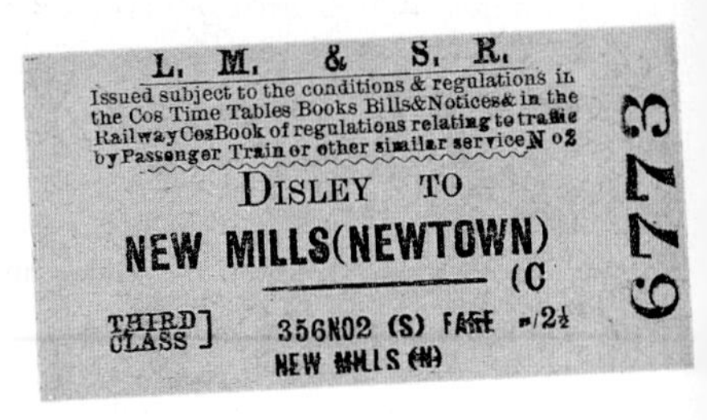

L. M. & S. R.
Issued subject to the conditions & regulations in the Cos Time Tables Books Bills&Notices& in the RailwayCosBook of regulations relating to traffic by Passenger Train or other similar service N 02
DISLEY TO
NEW MILLS(NEWTOWN)
(C
THIRD CLASS
35GN02 (S) FARE -/2½
NEW MILLS (N)
6773

New Mills (Newtown) as viewed through the single span opening of Albion Road bridge (No 28) on Friday 1st September 1961. The forty-chain radius through the station, coupled with a falling gradient of 1 in 136, induced a substantial cant in the rails and a gap between carriages and platform that could occasionally unnerve unsuspecting passengers who were alighting. That leaning experience can be imagined by looking at the slight angle of the diesel railcar set in the Up platform prior to departure for Buxton. The tall signal was the New Mills home 'board', operated by lever 19 in the signal box.

New Mills (Newtown) on Saturday 18th July 1959 as an Edgeley to Buxton freight passes alongside the Up platform, hauled by 8F No **48106** (8B-Warrington). The station clock reads five minutes past ten (in the morning) so it would appear that we have a late running train which was scheduled to arrive around 9.30am. The main station buildings at Newtown, here on the Up platform, have been modified at an early stage by the L&NWR by 'filling in' the one time open waiting area as well as the addition of a Porters Room to the right of the loco. Station Master at the time was Mr J Harrop who put Newtown station on the map in 1961 when it was awarded the Station Gardens Competiton Shield, organised by the District Manager, Manchester. Both this page; ***J W Sutherland***

(Right) This 1958 photograph is reproduced with thanks to lifelong rail wayman Derek Ashworth, native of New Mills but nowadays a resident of Chapel-en-le-Frith. Derek is the bespectacled youngster fourth from right on the occasion of the retirement of Station Master Bill Stubbs, suited, immediately to the right of his award, a mantel clock. Derek, who at the time was Junior Porter, describes SM Stubbs as a good boss who was always dressed very smartly. The individuals, from left to right, are Dennis Smith *(Station Master, Disley)*; Bob Dutton *(Station Master, Whaley Bridge)*; Maurice Wild *(Relief Signalman - making the presentation)*; Bob Keighley *(Relief Station Master 1956-64 - from Stockport)*; Bill Stubbs *(Station Master, New Mills Newtown)*; Derek Ashworth; Edwin 'Teddy' Greenhough *(Leading Porter, New Mills Newtown)*; Millie Jennings *(Signalwoman, New Mills Newtown);* and Bill Oulton *(Signalman, Whaley Bridge).* On a more personal footing, both Derek and Bob Keighley had cause to remember their visits to Newtown when Millie Jennings (and pet poodle) were on duty. Apparently, the pet was a mite excitable and was very protective of its owner when in the signal box. Derek recalls approaching the pet on numerous occasions, the excitement being so great that the welcoming became decidedly wet. Similarly Bob, upon offering his hand in friendship, received a nasty nip ! Signalman Bob Oulton worked at Whaley Bridge for many years, sharing duties with his brother. The railway fraternity was still very committed to both the organisation and the localities it served, in fact the railway industry was built on a strong base of family involvement. The traditional role of the Station Master, and the railway, being at the heart of the communtity was still valid, having evolved generations of service. Passenger and Freight services on the Buxton line were administered commercially on a District basis from the respective managers at Hunts Bank in Manchester. Locally, the respective station masters were accountable for running their 'patches' although at New Mills, the volume of traffic through the goods depot warrented a Goods Agent. Derek's duties as Junior Porter involved a variety of tasks which included going out and about assisting the driver with the C&D (Collection & Delivery) van, lamping, general cleaning around the station, overseeing train departures. Another job took Derek to a notice board at the bottom of Union Road, where posters from both Central and Newtown stations were displayed..

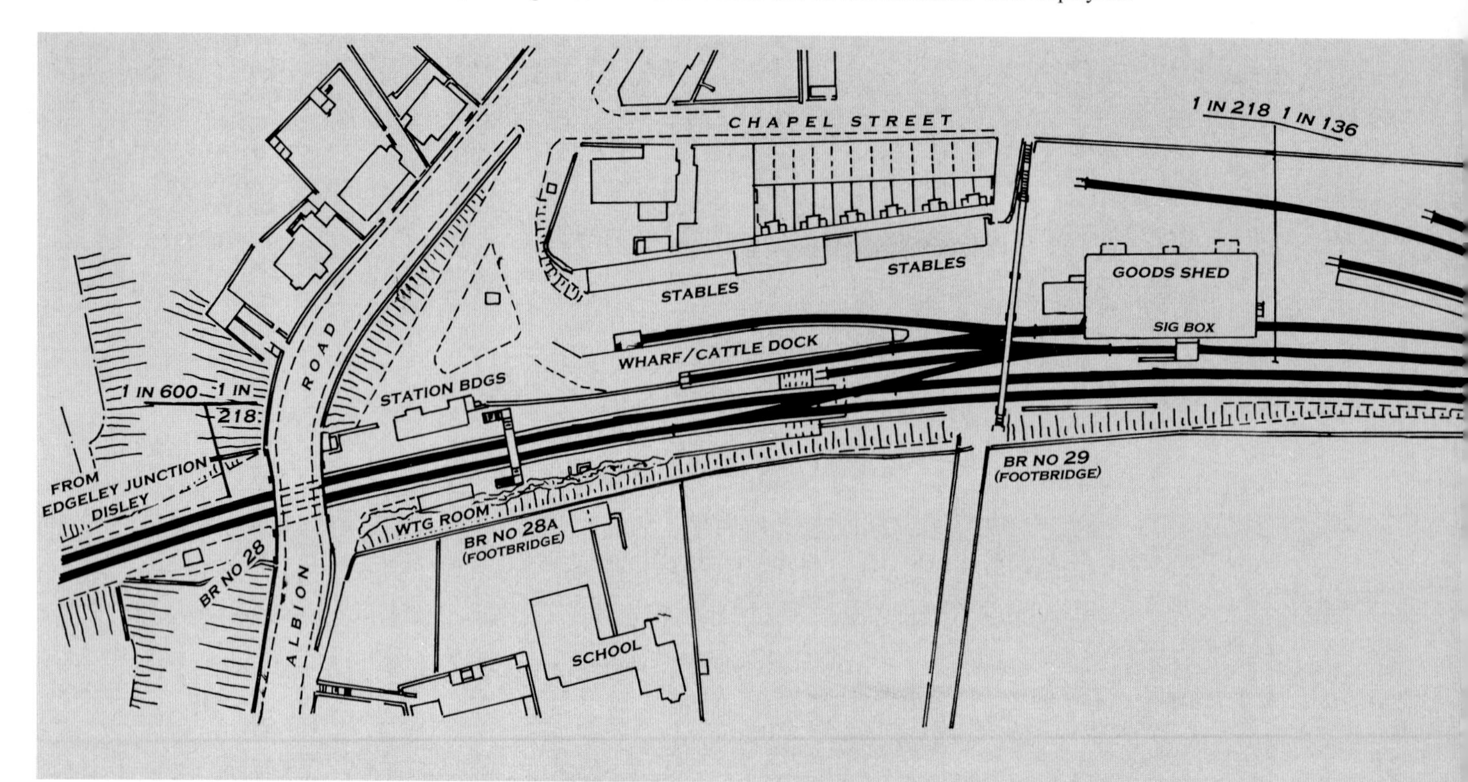

Unfortunately, the photograph seen here is one of those that comes into one's possession without any details, therefore much of the description is based on calculated guesswork. That this is New Mills Newtown is beyond doubt and the date is thought to be c.1956/57. The signalling is such, both home (beyond Albion Road bridge) and starting signals being in the 'off' position, that this could be a Sunday and Newtown box is switched out. It certainly seems quiet enough, with little evidence of custom to suggest trouble for Longsight based Stanier 2-6-4T No **42594** and its five coach train bound for Buxton. The coaching stock, all LMS design and build, commencing from the vehicle immediately behind the engine, is as follows; **1**) Period 3 Non-Corridor Brake Third; **2**) Diagram 1761 Period 1 Non-Corridor Lavatory First; **3**) Period 3 - as coach (1); **4**) Period 3 - as per coach (1); **5**) Period 1 Non-Corridor Third, ex-works; Presence of the cattle wagons is something of a mystery as livestock generally was latterly dealt with at Chapel-en-le-Frith. However, with the presence of two slaughterhouses in the New Mills area, there remains the possibility that a small number of beasts could have been brought in for that reason and that the wagons were waiting for collection. ***Authors collection***

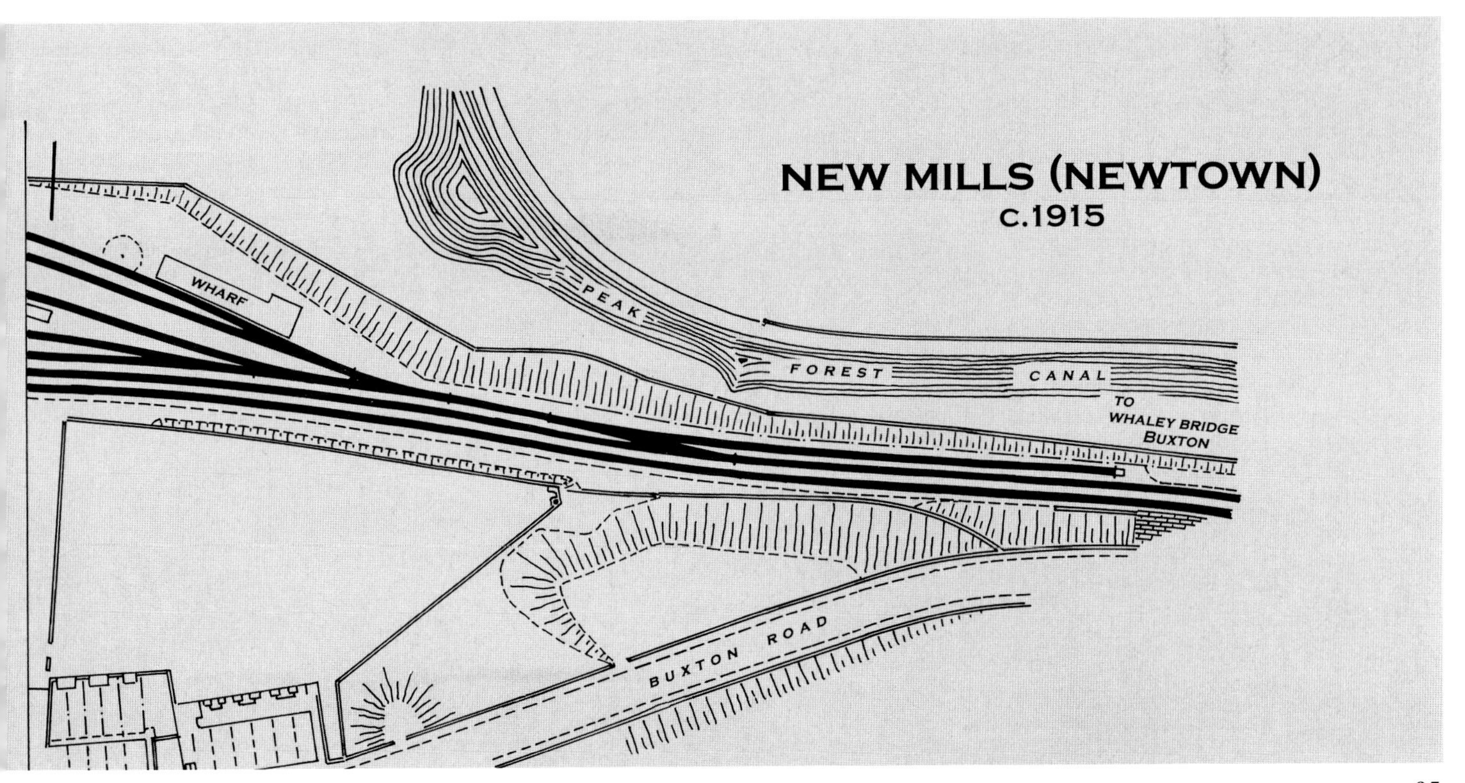

(No. 1) 2nd-SINGLE | SINGLE-2nd (No. 1)
New Mills (Newtown) to
New Mills (Newtown) Disley | New Mills (Newtown) Disley
DISLEY
(M) 0/4 FARE 0/4 (M)
For conditions see over | For conditions see over
0817 | 0817

(Above) Springtime at New Mills and a young Graham Sutherland stands on the Up platform on one of the many trips on the line. Apart from the regional maroon signs erected by British Railways, the station shows little change from its previous owners, the LMS. Unlike other locations, the timetable display case of the North Western Road Car Company (behind the fence on the side of the hut) is not as prominent ***J W Sutherland***

(Centre) The Whaley end of the Up side station buildings, stone built but with the LNWR infill (1971). ***G K Fox***

(Right) In contrast with many railways built during the mid-Victorian period, stations on the original line to Whaley Bridge and subsequent Buxton Extension did not have a company 'style' about them. The L&NWR carried out numerous minor modifications which stamped an identity on the buildings but it was of the very 'ad-hoc' nature seen here at Newtown on the Down side platform (1971). ***G K Fox***

2nd - SINGLE | SINGLE - 2nd
Furness Vale to
Furness Vale Whaley Bridge, etc. | Furness Vale New Mills (N'town), etc.
NEW MILLS (Newtown) or WHALEY BRIDGE
(M) 0/4 FARE 0/4 (M)
For conditions see over | For conditions see over
5988 | 5988

(Above) The crossover at the Whaley Bridge end of Newtown station gave direct access to the Down line from the goods yard seen in the backgound. The station platforms had been raised and lengthened in 1912, resulting in a re-arrangement of the track layout in this area and relocation of the starting signal and cattle dock. Gas lighting and large stone platform flags highlight another era as British Railways early attempts to implement its modernisation plan appear in the form of diesel multiple units, the first stage in the replacement of steam traction. Approaching with a Down train is the 4.15pm ex-Buxton to Manchester working on 14th June 1958. The somewhat lightweight structure, a footbridge (No 29) of three spans, carries a footway between the two sections of Redmoor Lane. It also provided the vantage point from which a view **(below)** on 3rd June 1962 (Sunday) shows a Manchester Piccadilly to Ashbourne excursion passing through Newtown station. This special excursion, comprising eight (original) Derby Lightweight cars, was organised primarily for the Tissington Well Dressings. Last pick up point on its way to Dovedale was Hazel Grove (dep 10.23am), having called at Levenshulme, Heaton Chapel, Stockport Edgeley and Davenport en-route. The itinerary included Parsley Hay (arr 11.16), Hartington (arr 11.22), Tissington (arr 11.18), Thorpe Cloud (arr 11.54), with arrival in Ashbourne scheduled for 11.59; As an example, the return fare second class - Hazel grove/Hartington was Five shillings (25p), giving the visitor just over eight hours to explore the dales. Wallace Sutherland, who with his family, travelled on the excursion, noted also that there were two other diesel excursions and a steam hauled special, which crossed at Alsop in both directions with a Nottingham (16A) 'Crab' 2-6-0 in charge. The deserted appearance is reminiscent of the scene on page 95. ***J W Sutherland/A Moyes***

Over the years, there have been photographs that appear and then re-appear. Three in particular are included on this page that are from the period when custodianship of the Buxton line was in the hands of the LMS. Despite the minor difference in liveries, both scenes would stand the test of time for a period of some thirty years. **(Right)** Local photographer R D (Dougie) Pollard recorded this view standing on bridge 29 and which shows Fowler 2-6-4T No **2398,** displaying a 9A (Longsight) shed code and headlamp code indicating an 'ordinary passenger' or stopping train, waiting to depart for the remaining stations and Buxton on Saturday 5th June 1937. The work of Mr Pollard appeared in the *Railway Magazine* during the 1930's as well as the occasional railway book and concentrated on the New Mills area, particularly on routes radiating from the town within a few miles of the locality. He was a railwayman who in the early 1950's was Head of Freight Trains, Manchester London Road (Eastern Section), a prominent managerial position. His interests also included being organist at a New Mills church. Whilst the work of E R Morten (lower) is well known, and rightly so, R D Pollard's contribution has gone largely unnoticed, mainly through its scarceness. **(Centre)** Same locomotive as above, different angle. Of particular interest however are the stables in the background, the designs which, although of LNWR origin are from different periods. Compared with the view on page 95, the cattle docks appear to have seen recent use. ***J W Sutherland collection***

(Right-lower) E R Morten, the well respected Buxton dental practitioner and railway photographer *par excellance*, travelled widely on Britain's railway network, often with friend and fellow cameraman Harry Townley. This view of a 'Super D', LMS No **9357** at Newtown in 1934 deserves to be given the term 'classic'. Almost everything about the scene, showing a Down freight, suggests a ruggedness relating to this part of Derbyshire's High Peak. The station was hewn out of a rock strewn hillside above an area teeming with a variety of industries. Hardly the normal impression one gets of Derbyshire with its plethora of Dales but an essential ingredient across a varying landscape. Signal box, locomotive, station signs and the like are still steeped in the L&NWR tradition some eleven years after the company name had disappeared. ***E R Morten***

Redmoor Lane footbridge is once again the focal point for the photographer as 'Super D' No **49453** (9B-Stockport) leaves Newtown on 18th July 1959 with the return New Mills 'shunt'. The reason for the short train was due to Bowaters being on holiday, therefore no vans. New Mills Newtown signal box was erected on an overhead gantry spanning the Up siding, the framework being built into the side of the adjacent goods warehouse. It was an LNWR type 5 structure with 20 levers dating from 1910, replacing a signal box situated immediately alongside on the end of the warehouse. ***J W Sutherland***

A sunny, wintry Saturday morning of the 2nd March 1963 emphasises the appearance beneath Redmoor Lane footbridge of the 8.3am ex-Manchester Piccadilly to Buxton train, due to depart from Newtown at 8.31. From this elevated position in the signal box, it is interesting to compare the track layout with the diagram on page 94 which shows a direct connection between the goods warehouse and left hand side of the cattle/loading dock. ***J W Sutherland***

(Above) Late morning activity on 18th July 1959 beneath New Mills (Newtown) signal box witnesses the meeting of freight workings as the Stockport to Buxton 'shunter' (left) and the Buxton to Hooton train (right) prepare for a crew change that will enable Buxton and Stockport men to work back to their respective depots. Stanier 8F No **48534** (8B-Warrington) stands at the Down home signal whilst **48106**, another Warrington engine, pauses alongside at the booked changeover point beneath the signal box, during which time the crews will 'swap' footplates. **(Below)** Almost three years have passed, but the Up 'shunter' and 'Down' Hooton trains prepare to give a repeat performance, albeit with different motive power. On 24th February 1962, the approaching 'shunter' has 8F No **48437** (9E-Trafford Park) doing the work, whilst Austerity No **90532** (6B-Mold Junction) lets off steam at the Down home signal. To the right, a couple of 'Palvans' carry labels which read "Empty to Port Sunlight - Margarine". Both this page; ***J W Sutherland***

Only ten months separate the two views on this page although the short train, with **49453** on the New Mills 'shunt', already seen on page 99, stands in the Up siding awaiting departure time with the return working to Stockport on Saturday 18th July 1959. Also used as a 'Lie-Bye' or refuge siding, it could accommodate trains of 45 wagon units from both Up and Down directions. The sweeping forty-chain curve, which commenced on the Disley side of Newtown station, continued beyond the photographer for some distance. **(Below)** The 'shunter' - Stockport to Buxton - seen previously on a number of occasions, finds refuge at New Mills in the Up siding, ready to head off to Whaley Bridge, and possibly Shallcross Yard, on its fragmented journey. 'Super D' No **49281** (9D-Buxton), having previously seen service at Stockport before a spell in St Helens, was approaching the end of its life, having only some five months left 'in harness' before withdrawal in October 1960. Both; ***J W Sutherland***

The extent of the goods yard at New Mills (Newtown) can be judged by the sequence of photographs on this and the opposite page. **(Above)** The tender cab of **49401** (9B-Stockport) identifies almost straight away that this is the engine off the New Mills 'shunt', Saturday 4th June 1960. The large warehouse highlights the extensive undercover storage facilities on three floors (inclusive of the basement). In the distance to the right of the warehouse, a large gable end marks the site of stables for the horses that at one time served New Mills and district. The stables comprised two separate buildings adjacent to the goods yard entrance - see pages 97 (lower) and 98 (top), each providing for eighteen and fourteen horses respectively. **(Below)** Bowaters blue liveried road transport vehicles could easily be identified as they plied betwen the factory at Disley and the Newtown area above New Mills. A slight change led to the appearance of the lettering *Bowaters Packaging* on the van sides which was not as prominent as previously (see page 86). This Saturday 18th August 1962 view shows the limited room between sidings in which the vehicle could manoeuvre, no doubt made more difficult when there were rail vehicles in each siding.

Both; ***J W Sutherland***

Two panoramic views adjacent to the goods yard at Newtown from nearby Buxton Road. Both taken on Saturday 24th February 1962, an almost fully occupied railway unfolds. **(Above)** In the foreground, the Buxton to Hooton freight (again), headed by Austerity No **90532** (6B-Mold Junction) - the wisp of steam/smoke to the left indicates the position of the loco - moves forward slowly through Newtown station prior to a movement that will see it reverse on to the Up line, enabling the 10.20am ex-Buxton to Manchester Dmu to pass (see below). **(Below)** The Hooton train, having moved on to the Up line, pauses for a time to allow the 3-car BRC&W set to pass unhindered towards Newtown station and subsequently all stations to Stockport. Meanwhile, 8F No **48437** (9B-Stockport) has arrived on the scene with the Stockport to Buxton 'shunter' and stands across from the Dmu in the Up siding. The Brunswick Mill complex of Matlow Brothers and Swizzels is to the extreme right of the picture. Both; ***J W Sutherland***

(Left) The 'road' side elevation of New Mills (Newtown) warehouse in 1962, a C&D lorry taking advantage of the canopy. The warehouse contained four 30cwt deck cranes, one 10cwt electric jigger and one 10cwt gravity jigger. The building in its final form certainly existed in 1891 (*Ref: Railways of New Mills - D Brumhead*), with the upper floor being used for cotton and grain storage at the time. The ground floor catered for pulp paper and skips of yarn. Until reorganisation of British Railways in 1966, maintenance of buildings and structures between Buxton and Disley came under the District Engineer, Derby.

(Right-centre) For once, the 'Super D' (**49401**-9B) is not the centre of attention, prominence being given to LNW 10-Ton yard crane No 2971, which became redundant from 5th October 1964 following conversion of Newtown yard into a non-rail connected freight depot. **(Below)** As previously mentioned, Newtown goods depot had a small compliment of lorries engaged in collection and delivery services. The popular cream and carmine livery survived longer on the road vehicles than their rail counterparts by a number of years and here, sometime in 1962, a Fordson Thames flat-bed lorry rests beneath one of the warehouse canopies. However, following major reorganisation within the railway industry, these vehicles would soon be transferred into a new Road Motors department under the control of the Chief Mechanical & Electrical Engineer, Derby. The second two letters of its registration, WRO 438, indicate that the vehicle licensing authority was Hertford County Council. Many London Midland Region road vehicles carried these same letters, as well as AR, also Hertford. It is likely that the service on offer through New Mills originated with the LMS 'Country Delivery' branding. Vans for Bowaters traffic are to the right. Below and right; ***J W Sutherland***

Before we leave New Mills (Newtown), a reminder (Friday 1st September 1961) of how busy the goods yard could be before rationalisation over the next few years made freight operation of this nature obsolete. Carrying out shunting duties in the Up siding is **48161** (9F-Heaton Mersey) on the 3.30pm Buxton to Stockport goods. Scheduled time of arrival at New Mills was 5.23pm, allowing some fifty-five minutes to re-arrange as necessary its train for the onward journey. The conversion of Newtown to a 'non-rail' connected freight depot on 5th October 1964 was the start of a fairly rapid decline in the yard's fortunes. Almost two years to the day after the 'conversion' (10th October 1966), Newtown closed completely as a rail facility as part of the *Reduction in Freight Terminals* programme. The Freight Sundries traffic formerly dealt with here was concentrated on two collection and delivery areas. Business originating at New Mills, Furness Vale, Disley, Hayfield, Marple and Marple Bridge would be dealt with by Heaton Norris (Stockport), whereas traffic from Chinley, Chapel-en-le-Frith and Whaley Bridge would now go via Buxton Central. Following closure of Newtown, a plan to abolish the signal box was prepared and subject to slight retiming of trains, the box closed on 24th May 1967.

A healthy payload is still in evidence as the 3.30pm Buxton to Adswood freight approaches New Mills (Newtown) behind 'Stanier Crab' No **42961** (5D-Stoke). Somewhat ironically, discussions were already taking place about the reduction of both passenger and freight services between Edgeley Junction and Buxton in the light of closure proposals for the route. It was intended to re-direct remaining services via Chinley over the Midland route, which coincidentally, runs from left to right just above the train. New Mills South Junction signal box can be seen above the second van. Both; ***J W Sutherland***

(Left) Approaching the 8 milepost, the line reverses its alignment commensurate with a short steep (ish) descent at 1 in 136 past the New Mills (Newtown) headshunt and the Up outer home signal. Although not apparent in this or the pictures below, both dated 18th August 1962, the railway is pitched on a ledge between Buxton Road - top of the embankment to the left - and the Peak Forest Canal - over the fence to the right. In the distance, 'Crab' No **42892** (9B) occupies the Up siding, with the Stockport to Buxton 'shunter'. ***J W Sutherland***

(Below-centre) Taking advantage of the downward grade, 8F No **48389** (9D-Buxton) heads towards Furness Vale and Whaley Bridge with the daily Birkenhead freight on the next stage of its journey to Buxton. ***J W Sutherland***

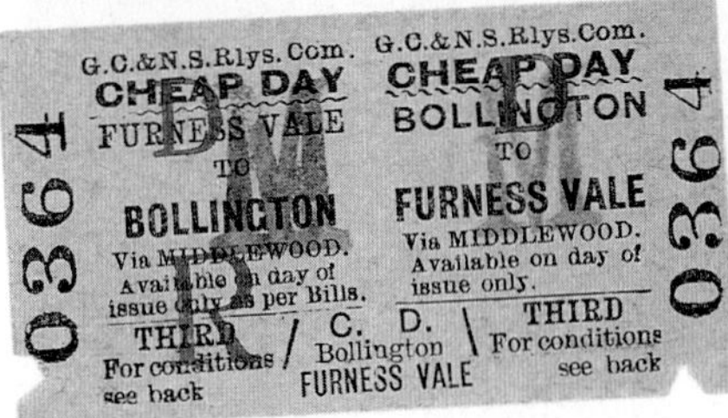

(Right) Escaping steam disturbs dry dusty ballast on a summer's day, 13th August 1955, as Fowler 2-6-4T No **42397** - a Longsight engine at the time - races through New Mills towards Furness Vale with the 11.50am Manchester London Road to Buxton train. This Saturdays Only working ran non-stop between London Road and Disley (arr 12.13) and then called at only Whaley Bridge for the remainder of the fifty-one minute journey. ***E R Morten***

From being almost on top of each other, canal, railway and road temporarily seek wider and less constrictive routes towards Furness Vale where the river Goyt is also vying for space in the valley bottom. The river, having followed a fairly sinuous route from its junction with the Tame in Stockport, is now approaching the upper reaches, where, beyond Whaley Bridge, its waters have been harnessed by two reservoirs, namely Errwood and Fernilee. In this view from Bank End bridge (No 30) on 24th February 1962, BR Standard Class 4 No **76087** (9F-Heaton Mersey) is seen running light from the Furness Vale direction. The Midland line again cuts across the hillside at Gowhole on the opposite side of the valley, with only a minute white pall of smoke indicating the whereabouts of these substantial freight marshalling sidings. ***J W Sutherland***

A short distance further south along Buxton Road provides an opportunity to view the New Mills landscape above the confluence of the Goyt and Sett rivers. The spire of New Mills Parish Church stands prominently in the centre of the picture. Housing development towards the upper right marks the route of Marsh Lane on its way between New Mills and Furness Vale. The Midland line (Manchester Line - Old Route), in particular New Mills East (or Midland) Goods Depot, can just be distinguished above the locomotive - **42946** (6C-Birkenhead) - in this picture taken on Saturday 24th February 1962 showing the Buxton to Widnes freight on the ascent to New Mills (Newtown). ***J W Sutherland***

This pastoral setting, recorded on 28th September 1956 looking east from Buxton Road, shows a Down freight hauled by Fowler 'Crab' 2-6-0 No **42848** (9A-Longsight) passing New Mills (Newtown) distant signal (extreme right) shortly after passing through Furness Vale. Extremely well camouflaged are the Gowhole Sidings, the main body of which are within the hillside and running parallel with the Buxton line above the train. ***Norman Jones***

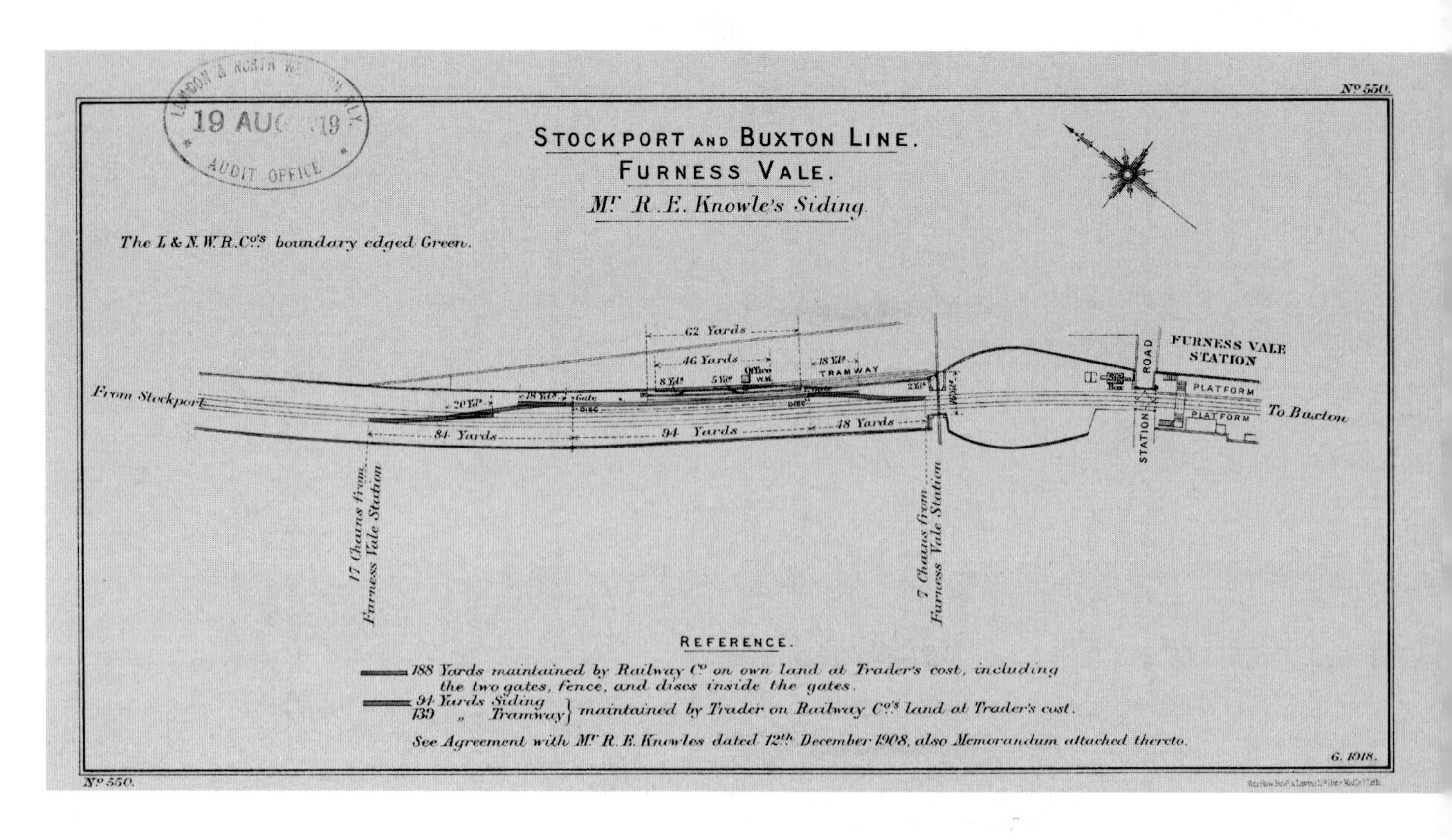

This short, level, stretch of line aproaching Furness Vale from the New Mills direction will be the last encountered by Down trains before Hazel Grove (as well as Bibbington's for trains in the Up direction). **(Above)** A BRC&W 2-car set (M50422/M50426), with exhausts puthering away, leaves Furness Vale on the next stage of its all-stations journey to Manchester on Saturday 4th June 1960. To the right is the gated compound which, according to the LNWR *Diagrams of Private Sidings,* contained a short length of siding used by Mr R E Knowles, one time brick manufacturer at Furness Vale. The siding included a loading dock with 'tramway' which enabled wagon to wagon transfer (see diagram opposite). The type of brick manufactured remains unconfirmed although the LMS sidings diagram of 1926 describes the siding as being used for 'bricquettes'. It is unclear when the siding was removed. **(Below)** On the same date, an elevated view (from the crossing footbridge) of the line heading away from Furness Vale in the direction of New Mills shows a Rowsley to Adswood freight, hauled by 'Crab' No 42829, clearing the section. The site of the private siding is clearly defined as is the Up side parapet of a bridge (No 32) under which the 'tramway' ran. The then freshly painted signal box, which survives to this day by courtesy of the adjacent level crossing, contained an LNWR Type 4 frame with twenty-two levers, dating from 1884. Both; ***J W Sutherland***

DIARY EXTRACTS FOR.......FURNESS VALE

4.6.60 Walked from New Mills to Furness Vale where 42886 (9B) with a "Loco" wagon and brake was standing while coal was unloaded into station coal drop. Apparently the engine had run down from Buxton to New Mills to pick up the wagon and take it to Furness Vale (it left New Mills just before I arrived) then after unloading both at the signal box and the station, eventually made its way back to Buxton. Rather an expensive way of supplying 10 tons of coal to Furness Vale, although they did 'bank' the Birkenhead from Whaley Bridge. Chatted with the crew on the engine (Mr W Weston of Buxton was the driver) while they shunted to and fro over the crossover, keeping clear of trains before they finally got away. The driver said 'Crabs' good enough engines but rough at speed. 48498 (6C) was on the train to Hooton. 48691 (9C) was on the Birkenhead train. 48165 was on the train to Arpley. 48322 (9D) on the 'shunter' to Buxton. 42849 was on Rowsley - Adswood train. 42306/70/71 are the only Fowler tanks (2-6-4) or 'Crab' Tanks as we called them at Buxton now. He said, re; morning steam business trains, that engine of 7.26am (formerly 7.30) train goes back on the mid-day goods from Longsight (usually a 'Crab' while that on the 7.47 (formerly 7.50) has gone on the early morning mail train (usually a 'named' engine).

3.4.61 (Easter Monday) Went to Furness Vale and back to visit Gowhole. The diesel coming back (3-car) was absolutely packed even in the guards section where I stood. This is in spite of a half hour service instead of the usual one hour being on at the time.

2.8.64 (Fri) Noticed a decorative sort of plaque by the Down Platform at Furness Vale Station.

(Left) A 'standard' wooden sectioned permanent - way hut, freshly painted, occupies a site on the some-time connection with the private siding. Details of the train, 42886+coal wagon+brake, are to be found in the diary extracts for 4th June 1960 (above-left). The crossover located beneath the engine was worked by signal box point levers 17 (Up) and 18 (Down), lever 19 operating the ground disc for crossing between Up and Down lines.

(Below) The level crossing at Furness Vale is clearly shown in this view of the 5.50pm ex-Manchester London Road to Buxton train on 22nd May 1959. When the gates were open (to trains), the footbridge provided both access to the station platforms as well as an alternative for pedestrians crossing the lines. The wicket gates - the Down side set is seen on the left - were locked by levers 1 (Up) and 2 (Down). The gates themslves, opened/closed by by a hand operated 'gate' wheel in the signal box overlooking the crossing, had 'stops' which were operated by lever 3 and locked by lever 4. The restricted height signal (Up line) to the left was operated by lever 7. Both; ***J W Sutherland***

(Above) By this time (30th March 1959), British Railways had some kind of mark on the station with a range of maroon enamel signs. Buildings, structures, furniture and fittings however still carry the LNWR influence. The LMS 'statement' was confined to the restricted height signal (Down starter) just beyond the footbridge. Trains tend to come and go so the appearance of a 3-car BRC&W set would only momentarily blur the scene. A careful look at the wall beneath the Waiting Room sign will focus on a very much modified 3/4 milepost, comprised normal cast metal numerals on a small strip of wood.

J W Sutherland

(Right) The backs of the Up platform buildings overlooked ground falling away quite steeply towards first, the canal and then the valley bottom along which the river Goyt cut its course. The 'swan neck' electric lighting has replaced its gas counterpart in this 1971 view as a prelude to partial de-staffing ***G K Fox***

(Above) Early spring sees the station garden being tidied up by the station staff although it was the stations at Disley and Davenport that usually ran off with the prizes in the gardens competition. All the buildings at Furness Vale were clustered around the four corners of the level crossing. The station masters house was directly opposite the signal box whilst on this side of the crossing the Booking Office and Waiting Room occupied the Down (left hand) buildings. The large roof ventilator - for toilets - above the roof to the left is very similar to those found at Whaley Bridge. On the Up platform, the larger of the two buildings provided General Waiting Room facilities. The small building was the Lamp Room. Note also the variation in the name application on the backrests of the station seating. It may be interesting to note that maintenance of these platform seats was the domain of the Carriage & Wagon Department, as was office furniture.

(Centre) Looking in the direction of Whaley Bridge in this 1971 view, the Up starter (to the left) was operated by lever 20, the Down home signal by lever 6. Towards Buxton, the need to maintain a consistent alignment of the railway necessitated a modest diverson of the Buxton road between Furness Vale and Bridgemont. As a result, the 'new' road level was required to fall sharply to the left in order to pass beneath the railway (Bridge No 35) before rejoining the original road.

(Right) Between 1971 and 1973, Bridge No 35 (Bridgemont) was progressively reconstructed, requiring the gauntletting or interlacing of Up and Down lines. The earlier cast iron ribbed arch, strengthened and partially rebuilt in 1908, was replaced by steel main and cross girders with a concrete deck infill. This view from the Whaley Bridge end of the structure helps clarify the reason for the diversion of the Buxton road in 1857.

Six years separate the two views on this page. That comparison however is not as important as the difference in height the railway has risen since Middlewood where the water level of The Macclesfield Canal remains consistent with that of Whaley Bridge canal basin, transshipment point with the erstwhile Cromford & High Peak Railway until 1892. **(Above)** Entering Whaley Bridge on 19th May 1959 is 'Crab' No **42848** (9B-Stockport) with the 5.50pm London Road to Buxton train, due in Whaley at 6.34pm. Above the engine and first carriage is the water tank which originally formed part of the early engine shed of the SD&WB Railway when the line opened in 1857. The tank is seen below in the upper right of the picture. Both the Stockport to Buxton 'shunter' - Up train, and the Whaley 'shunt' - from the Buxton direction, would work both this yard as well as Shallcross Yard. Both station and goods yards came under the control of the Whaley Bridge Station Master. **(Below)** At the canal side, with transshipment shed to the left, the route of Buxton Road (now A5004) can be traced by following the tall street lighting on its way towards Market Street in the town itself. The car is parked on the continuation of the aptly named Canal Street. Reference to the water tank has already been made but confirmation of its presence is seen in the upper right of the picture.

Both; ***J W Sutherland***

DIARY EXTRACTS FOR..........WHALEY BRIDGE

5.9.59 Noted 42398 on empty stock train from Buxton to Stockport, a 'Crab' on the Hooton train. 48278 on the Stockport - Buxton 'shunter' and 48451 which went down about 11.8am and the train to Arpley. The ex-Birkenhead train was double headed by 48081 and 90369.

3.10.59 Noted a train at Whaley Bridge with stickers 'More ICI Fertiliser'.

10.3.60 John Moss told me he saw 92111 (2-10-0) on the Up goods passing Whaley Bridge soon after 9pm one night this week.

30.4.60 On the way home from Dove Holes, passed the Birkenhead running late in the station siding at Whaley Bridge. 48740 (9D) at head and 44562 in rear.

11.2.61 Having left Dove Holes at 12.26, the Birkenhead train was in the sidings at Whaley Bridge headed by 44247 (2E Northampton), no brakes. The ballast train still headed by 48451 was on the Shallcross line near the junction.

11.3.61 Ex-8.35 Davenport. The parcels train was running late and we passed it at Whaley Bridge after it had been shunted onto the Down line. It was headed by 44334 (17C) Rowsley and photographed it later at Chapel. (From Chapel) I walked back down the track to Whaley Bridge, or rather as far as the main road overbridge where I diverted so I could walk through Shallcross Yard. On the way down from Chapel passed the following trains: 90242 (8D) on Widnes train (mineral wagons only); 48170 on Birkenhead train (banked by 48008 (17C); 44748 (Caprotti) on Rowsley - Adswood.

11.3.61 48119 on the Buxton 'shunter'. NB. Easter this week I noted a 9F banking the Birkenhead one day.

1.9.61 (Fri) I caught the 12.31 departure for Whaley Bridge to get some photos. It was a hot perfectly sunny day. Unfortunately the Up empties from Longsight, also the one from Dundas Sidings were both not running; 48322 (9D), on the 1.35 from Buxton to Adswood ran early and picked up a rake of vans for Disley off the Shallcross loop where they had been left for another train. 48161 (9F-Heaton Mersey) was on the 3.30 from Buxton to Stockport also early and loaded, apparently, with lime from the High Peak. It shunted down to Shallcross. Kindly gave me a ride in the van back to Whaley Bridge and then down to New Mills where they went into the loop, in order to shunt later and finally leave after the rush with the diesels had finished. I caught the 5pm diesel back to Davenport. John Mellor was on duty at Whaley Bridge and I had quite a chat with him. Don't remember noticing it before but the siding which formerly went off the Shallcross line has obviously been taken up for some time.

16.8.64 11.45 ex-Davenport. At Whaley Bridge the siding to the water tank and the stock loading platform has been lifted, apart from the connecting points in the main line.

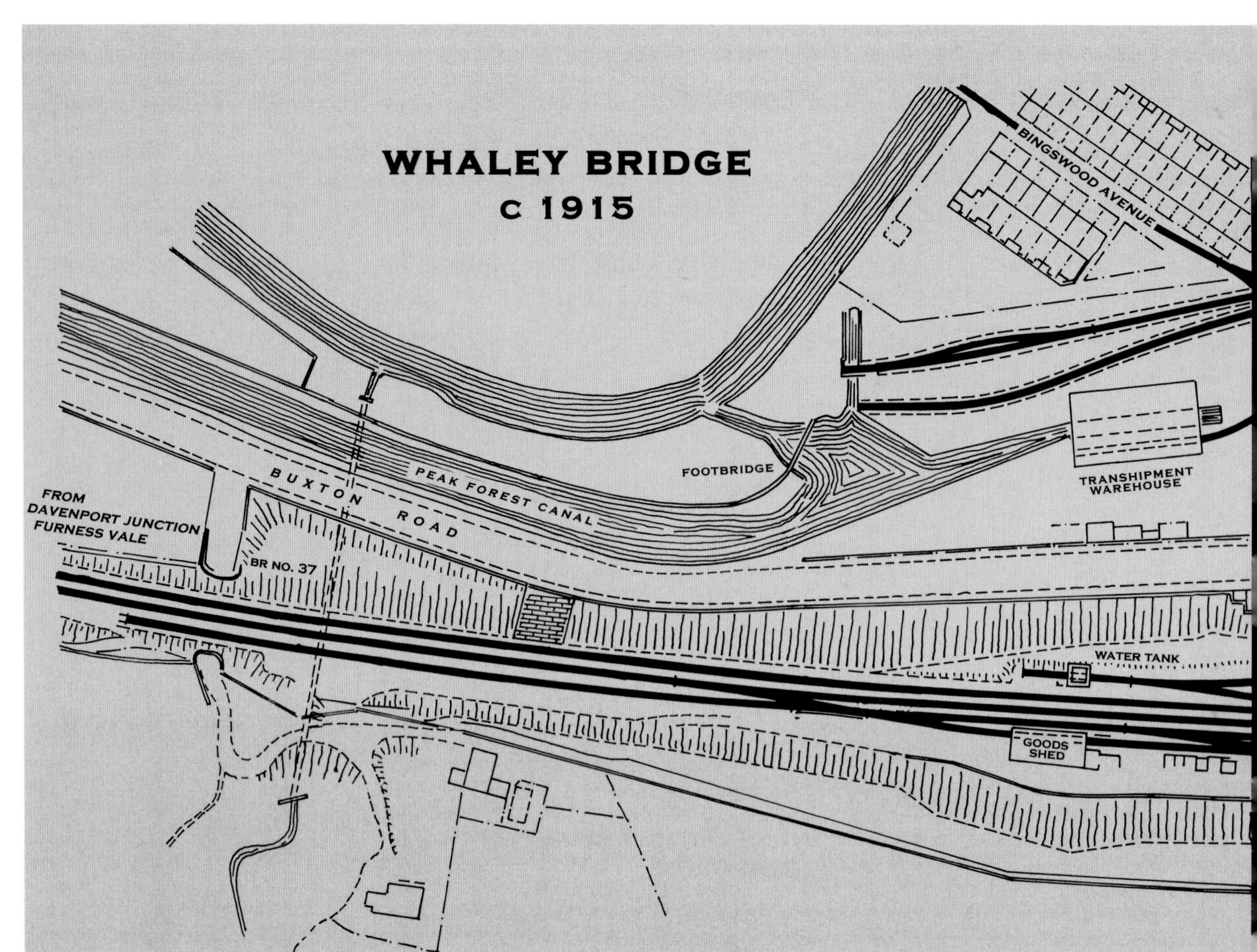

Perhaps slightly out of context when compared with the period generally under discussion, but with Buxton line services historically remaining almost unchanged between the wars, we take the opportunity to focus on one particular working. The 12.25pm (SO) Manchester London Road to Whaley Bridge was a well established train that only ended with the introduction of regular interval services by diesel multiple units in 1956. There had been some slight variation in the departure times over the years and general slimming down of services during WW2 saw the Saturdays Only 'lunch-time' train cut back to Hazel Grove. By 1930, the Fowler 2-6-4T's had virtually commandeered Buxton line services but additional resources required to support Saturdays Only trains resulted in some anomalies. 'Precursor' tanks, at one time regulars on the line, covered this working and this 13th May 1933 view shows No **6824** arriving at Whaley Bridge following its fifty-five minute all stations run from Manchester. After WW2, the service commenced its journey from Mayfield, also destination for the the return working from Whaley. ***E R Morten***

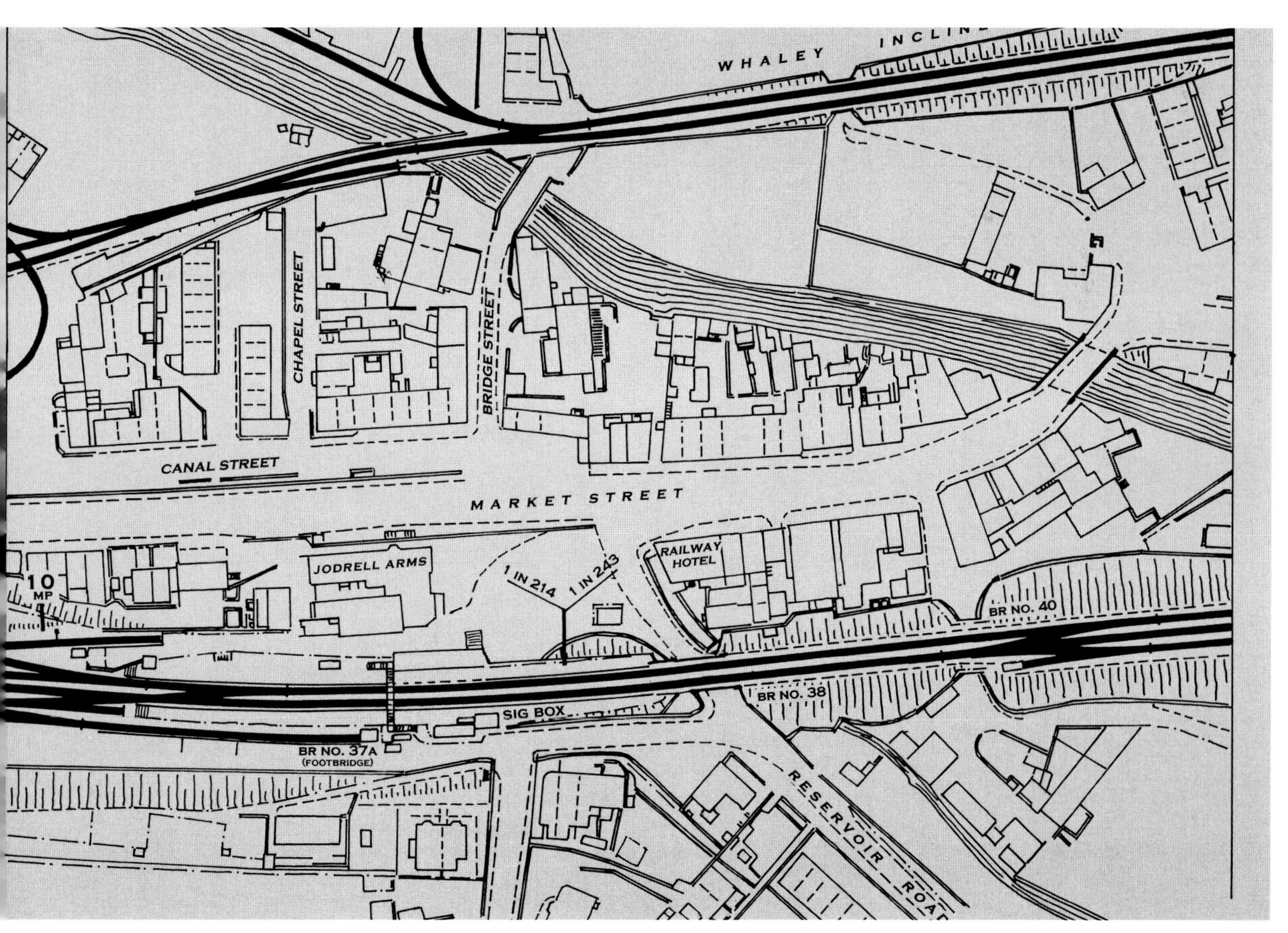

PLEASE RETAIN FOR REFERENCE

PROGRAMME

OF

SPECIAL PERIOD TRAINS

FOR

STOCKPORT

AND DISTRICT HOLIDAYS

11th to 25th AUGUST 1962

Travel in Rail Comfort

LONDON MIDLAND

E 585

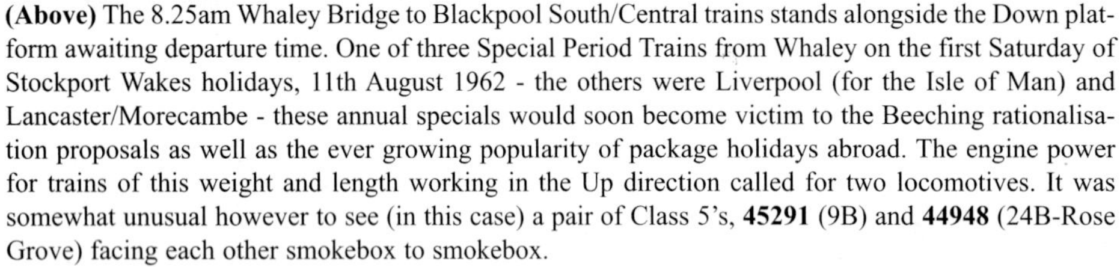

(Above) The 8.25am Whaley Bridge to Blackpool South/Central trains stands alongside the Down platform awaiting departure time. One of three Special Period Trains from Whaley on the first Saturday of Stockport Wakes holidays, 11th August 1962 - the others were Liverpool (for the Isle of Man) and Lancaster/Morecambe - these annual specials would soon become victim to the Beeching rationalisation proposals as well as the ever growing popularity of package holidays abroad. The engine power for trains of this weight and length working in the Up direction called for two locomotives. It was somewhat unusual however to see (in this case) a pair of Class 5's, **45291** (9B) and **44948** (24B-Rose Grove) facing each other smokebox to smokebox.

(Below) The shunter, ready with pole, waits on a chilly Up platform at Whaley Bridge after Austerity No **90328** has propelled two vans of sugar beet pulp into the Down siding (in the distance). By now, the freight business had declined dramatically and this, the 8.30am from Adswood, was one of a dwindling band of goods trains on the Buxton line. The Saturday (4th January 1964) schedule still allowed in the region of $2^{1/2}$ hours shunting at Whaley Bridge, including as necessary, a trip to Shallcross Yard. Both; ***J W Sutherland***

The crowds gather on the morning of Saturday 18th October 1958 for the arrival of the 9.09am ex-Buxton to Manchester express service. Whaley Bridge signal box, manned for many years by the Oulton brothers, was an LNWR Type 4 structure dating from 1877 with a twenty-eight lever frame. It closed on 18th November 1984. The footbridge and station building were subsequently listed as structures of historical interest. ***J W Sutherland***

The main station buildings at Whaley Bridge in 1971, virtually unchanged since it opened in 1857 as then terminus of the line from Stockport. Until 1896, a level crossing at the station allowed Whaley Lane to continue across the railway and where the cars are parked in this photograph. As a result, Whaley Lane was diverted to form a junction with Reservoir Road. Stone setts, forming drain channels, were certainly visible well into the 1980's showing the alignment of the former roadway across what became the station car park. Access to the platform was up a steep flight of steps to the Booking Hall at the near end of the building. The Booking Office occupied the middle section of the building and Waiting Rooms faced the platform at the far end, the roof ventilators (for toilets) indicating their position. ***G K Fox***

(Above) The Railway Hotel, Market Street, Whaley Bridge on 4th January 1964 portraying a scene identifiable to generations. The railway station and adjacent Jodrell Arms remain synonymous with this part of Whaley Bridge, neither having changed greatly since the railway arrived in 1857. It is easier to visualise in this view how Whaley Lane formed a junction with Market Street prior to the station level crossing being eradicated in 1896.

(Below-right) Robinsons, a long established Stockport brewer, have many public houses in the region and have managed to produce the attractive sign seen here depicting Richard Trevithick's high pressure tram engine, built for the *Pen-y-Darren* Iron works in South Wales. What price these days for something commemorating the nearby Peak Forest Tramway or even closer still, the Cromford & High Peak Railway. ***J W Sutherland***

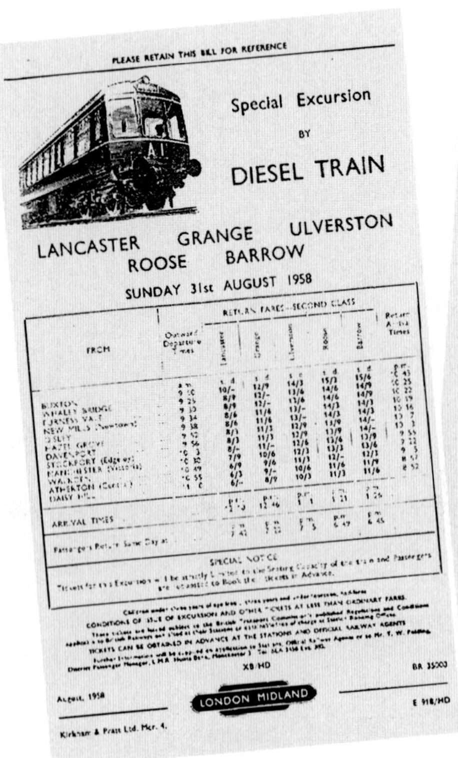

PLEASE RETAIN THIS BILL FOR REFERENCE

Special Excursion

BY

DIESEL TRAIN

LANCASTER GRANGE ULVERSTON
ROOSE BARROW

SUNDAY 31st AUGUST 1958

FROM	Outward Departure Times	Return Fares—Second Class: Lancaster	Grange	Ulverston	Roose	Barrow	Return Arrival Times
	a.m.	s. d.	s. d.	s. d.	s. d.	s. d.	p.m.
BUXTON	9 50	10/-	12/9	14/3	15/3	15/6	10 43
WHALEY BRIDGE	9 25	8/9	12/-	13/6	14/6	14/9	10 25
FURNESS VALE	9 30	8/9	12/-	13/6	14/6	14/9	10 22
NEW MILLS (Newtown)	9 34	8/6	11/6	13/-	14/3	14/3	10 19
DISLEY	9 38	8/6	11/6	13/-	14/3	14/3	10 16
HAZEL GROVE	9 52	8/3	11/3	12/9	13/9	14/-	10 7
DAVENPORT	9 56	8/3	11/3	12/9	13/9	14/-	10 3
STOCKPORT (Edgeley)	10 3	8/-	11/-	12/6	13/6	13/9	9 55
MANCHESTER (Victoria)	10 30	7/9	10/6	12/3	13/3	13/6	9 32
WALKDEN	10 49	6/9	9/6	11/3	12/-	12/3	9 5
ATHERTON (Central)	10 55	6/3	9/-	10/6	11/6	11/9	8 57
DAISY HILL	11 0	6/-	8/9	10/3	11/3	11/6	8 52
ARRIVAL TIMES		p.m. [illegible]	p.m. 12 46	p.m. 1 1	p.m. 1 21	p.m. 1 26	
Passengers Return Same Day at		p.m. 7 42	p.m. 7 22	p.m. 7 5	p.m. 6 47	p.m. 6 45	

SPECIAL NOTICE

Tickets for this Excursion will be strictly limited to the Seating Capacity of the train and Passengers are advised to Book their Tickets in Advance.

CONDITIONS OF ISSUE OF EXCURSION AND OTHER TICKETS AT LESS THAN ORDINARY FARES.

TICKETS CAN BE OBTAINED IN ADVANCE AT THE STATIONS AND OFFICIAL RAILWAY AGENTS

XB/HD BR 35003

August, 1958

LONDON MIDLAND

E 918/HD

Kirkham & Pratt Ltd. Mcr. 4.

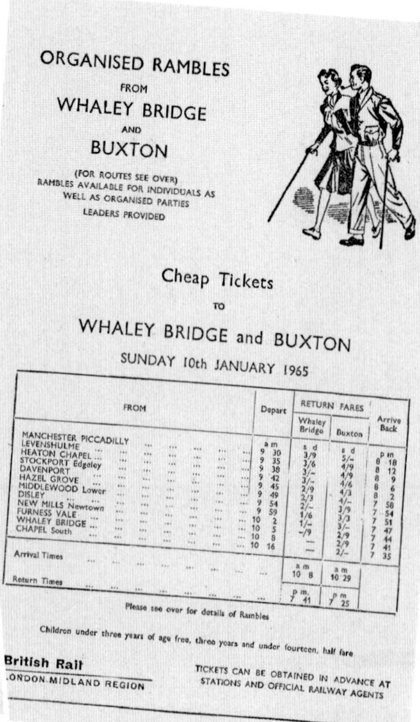

ORGANISED RAMBLES

FROM

WHALEY BRIDGE

AND

BUXTON

(FOR ROUTES SEE OVER)
RAMBLES AVAILABLE FOR INDIVIDUALS AS WELL AS ORGANISED PARTIES
LEADERS PROVIDED

Cheap Tickets

TO

WHALEY BRIDGE and BUXTON

SUNDAY 10th JANUARY 1965

FROM	Depart	Return Fares: Whaley Bridge	Buxton	Arrive Back
	a m	s d	s d	p m
MANCHESTER PICCADILLY	9 30	3/9	5/-	8 18
LEVENSHULME	9 35	3/6	4/9	8 12
HEATON CHAPEL	9 38	3/-	4/9	8 9
STOCKPORT Edgeley	9 42	3/-	4/6	8 6
DAVENPORT	9 45	2/9	4/3	8 2
HAZEL GROVE	9 49	2/3	4/-	7 58
MIDDLEWOOD Lower	9 54	2/-	3/9	7 54
DISLEY	9 59	1/6	3/3	7 51
NEW MILLS Newtown	10 2	1/-	3/-	7 47
FURNESS VALE	10 5	-/9	2/9	7 44
WHALEY BRIDGE	10 8	—	2/9	7 41
CHAPEL South	10 16	—	2/-	7 35
Arrival Times		a m 10 8	a m 10 29	
Return Times		p m 7 41	p m 7 25	

Please see over for details of Rambles

Children under three years of age free, three years and under fourteen, half fare

British Rail
LONDON MIDLAND REGION

TICKETS CAN BE OBTAINED IN ADVANCE AT STATIONS AND OFFICIAL RAILWAY AGENTS

E 4/R

(Right) Buxton (9D) 8F No **48421** stands in the Down siding with the Buxton to Hooton freight on Saturday 5th July 1958, having been set inside to allow the 10.15am ex-Buxton to Manchester diesel service to pass. The Down siding at Whaley also served as connecting line with Shallcross goods but for the first hundred yards or so, all three lines ran parallel on the same gradient with the slight rise away from the station (1 in 150) before increasing suddenly to the 1 in 60/70/60/58 at the (10)$^{1}/_{4}$ milepost. As the main line climbed away at this point, the siding to Shallcross maintained a lower level, first at 1 in 243 and then 1 in 636/630 for the short distance to the yard, giving the distinct 'falling away' impression. After a short distance, a small hut and intersection bridge (No 43- C&HP No 64) appear on the left hand side, indicating the point at which this diverted section of the C&HP came in from the head of Whaley Bridge Incline/Canal basin. **(Below)** On Saturday 5th September 1959, 8F No **48278** (9D-Buxton) commences the climb towards Chapel-en-le-Frith with the Stockport to Buxton 'shunter'. To the right is the abandoned formation of the Cromford & High Peak Railway that until 1952 connected Whaley Bridge Incline with Shallcross Yard. This particular section was a diversion of the original route, a situation brought about by the opening of the Buxton extension in 1863. The somewhat overgrown parcel of land, in more recent times occupied by Z & W Wade (a company also providing plant and other equipment to the railways), also contained sidings that were removed in 1910. A wing wall of the intersection bridge to be seen on page 120 appears in the bottom left hand corner of this picture. Both; ***J W Sutherland***

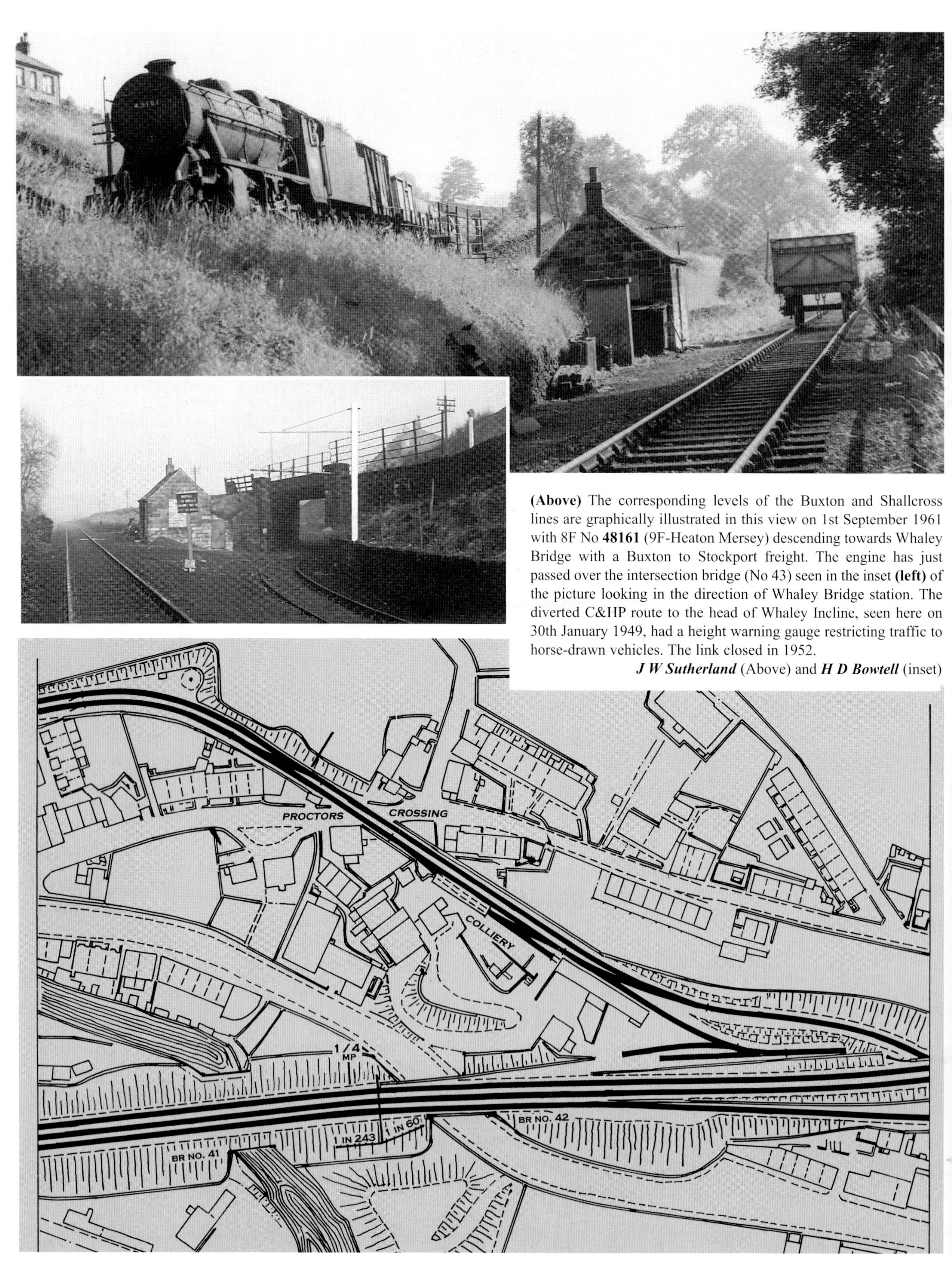

(Above) The corresponding levels of the Buxton and Shallcross lines are graphically illustrated in this view on 1st September 1961 with 8F No **48161** (9F-Heaton Mersey) descending towards Whaley Bridge with a Buxton to Stockport freight. The engine has just passed over the intersection bridge (No 43) seen in the inset **(left)** of the picture looking in the direction of Whaley Bridge station. The diverted C&HP route to the head of Whaley Incline, seen here on 30th January 1949, had a height warning gauge restricting traffic to horse-drawn vehicles. The link closed in 1952.

J W Sutherland (Above) and ***H D Bowtell*** (inset)

The truncated remains (northern end) of the Cromford & High Peak Railway winding its way through the Horwich End district of Whaley Bridge - looking in the direction of Whaley Bridge - is seen in this 10th March 1956 view from the parapet of Chapel Road (B5470) bridge (No 63). The loading gauge is intended to afford protection to the bridge opening over which the photographer is positioned. A careful look along the base of the retaining wall will also reveal a wire cable from the Checkers cabin (at Shallcross) to a warning gong that was actuated when shunting operations were taking place in the yard.
H D Bowtell

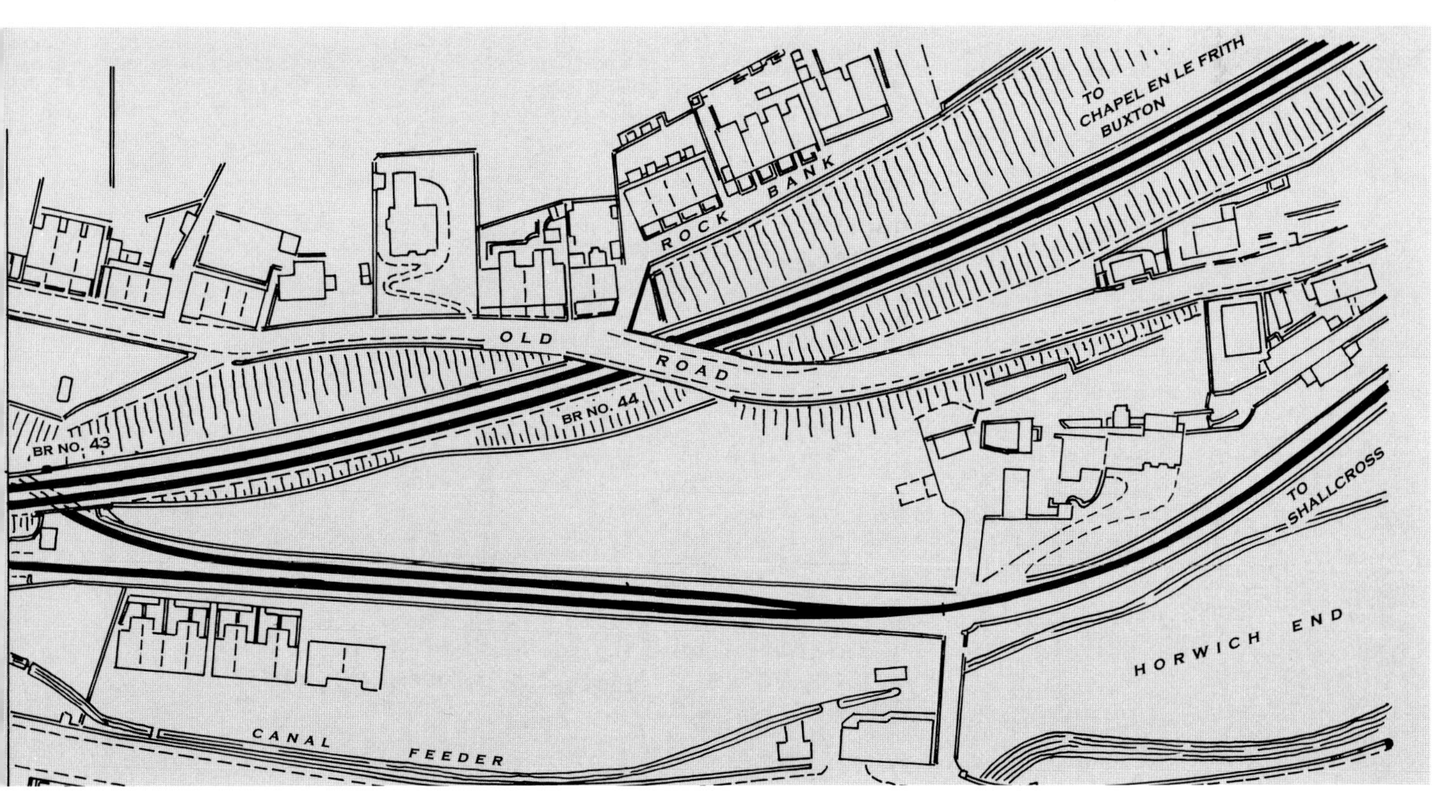

(Above) Lonsight (9A) based Class 5 4-6-0 No **45404** propels its train over the last few yards towards Shallcross Yard where it will drop off two wagons. Chapel Road bridge casts a shadow over the first few vehicles. **(Right)** The loco seen on page 120 descending from Chapel-en-le-Frith with the 3.30pm ex-Buxton to Stockport freight is now having to carry out the part of its schedule which included shunting Shallcross Yard. Partially hidden beyond the wagon is the tall chimneyed Checkers cabin, from which Frank Birch carried out his duties checking wagon numbers and their loadings. This small building was by all accounts kept in immaculate condition. Following closure of the yard in 1965, Mr Birch saw out his days on the railway at Norbury Crossing. Both; ***J W Sutherland***

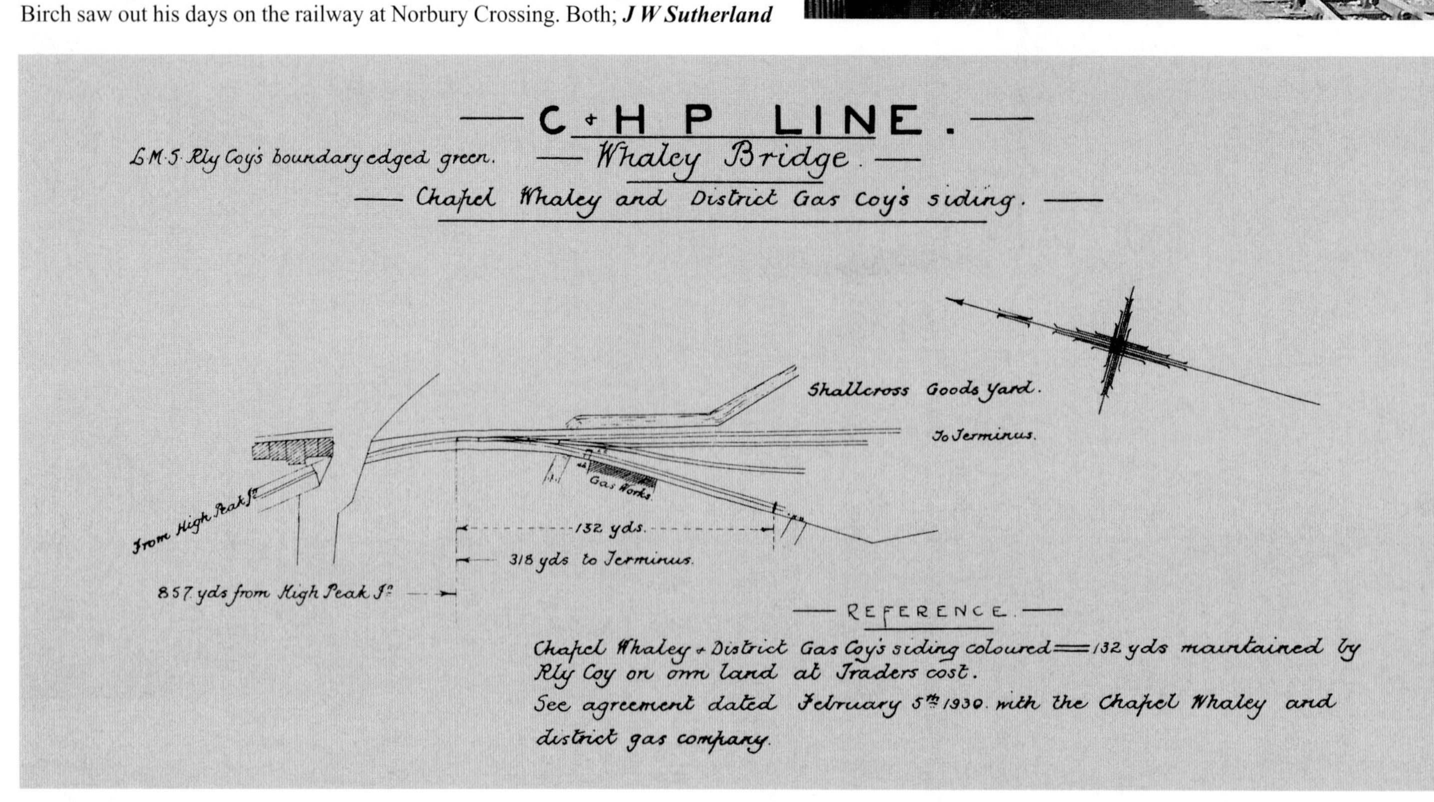

An elevated view of Shallcross yard from Chapel Road bridge in the direction of Fernilee. The single line from Whaley Bridge 'fanned' out into four sidings, three serving the goods shed and that to the right providing standage for wagons to and from the Gas Works, the buildings of which are to the right of the picture. The long abandoned Shallcross Incline continued beyond the goods yard. This view taken on 10th March 1956 shows the intact alignment of the incline beneath undergrowth before piecemeal building across the trackbed. The surviving gas works buildings were subsequently taken over by Dorothea Restorations Ltd. ***H D Bowtell***

A third view in almost as many pages of Heaton Mersey's 8F No **48161** with the 3.30pm ex-Buxton to Stockport train, this time preparing to leave Shallcross yard for the short trip to Whaley Bridge to regain the main line. A somewhat surprisingly short time, around thirty minutes, was scheduled for the shunting at Shallcross and that included reversal from the main line to and from the depot. ***J W Sutherland***

Both upper and lower views show a busy Shallcross yard, with that above, on 25th February 1961 (Sat), on the occasion of the Stockport to Buxton 'shunter' filling its allotted time at Whaley Bridge. It was the day when a small group, including Wallace Sutherland, arranged a brake van trip as part of the proceedings, details of which will appear in part two. The yard is almost fully occupied, mainly with vans, some of which had been left adjacent to the main line at Whaley by a Down train and which were then propelled into Shallcross. **(Left-centre)** Reproduction of the notice informing the public that freight facilities were to be withdrawn. Whaley Bridge Station Master at the time, Mr Jim Satchell, attended a meeting in August 1965 to discuss the disposal of redundant assets, 135 years after the railway had first reached Whaley Bridge. ***J W Sutherland***

BUXTON LINE

Diesel Multiple Units - the early days

(Above) A pamphlet that no doubt appeared on a nationwide basis prior to the introduction of DMU services. This particular copy covered the Manchester London Road / Mayfield and Stockport to Buxton, Macclesfield and Wilmslow respectively. A similar version covered the services between Manchester London Road and Hayfield / Macclesfield respectively via the Hyde or Reddish routes. Note the use of 'speed whiskers' on this early publicity

The impact of British Railways 1955 Modernisation Plan very soon became apparent to local passenger services in and around Manchester, as 'first generation' Diesel Multiple Units started to appear in 1956, integrating with the existing steam hauled trains. Ultimately, the Manchester London Road to Buxton route would become the domain of the Birmingham Railway Carriage and Wagon Company's vehicles (later Class 104). Notable for the white cab roof, the sets would provide an almost unbroken continuous three decades of service. Before the regular interval timetable was introduced on the line in autumn of 1956, many of the services had been taken over by the diesel units, accounting also for driver training, which had commenced in July 1956.

(Below) Original Derby Lightweight set, units **79185/79190,** is seen passing Davenport coal siding on 13th October 1956 (Saturday) with the 1.54pm ex-Buxton to London Road service. This was the end of the first week of regular interval (hourly) services on the line following introduction of a new timetable (Leaflet on page 127). Interestingly, *British Railways LM Timetable of Passenger Services 17th September 1956 to 16th June 1957 (or until further notice)* continued to advertise the service as Manchester (London Road), Buxton, Ashbourne and Uttoxeter, indicating that the journey between Buxton, Ashbourne and Uttoxeter - rail service withdrawn November 1954 - was still possible using North Western Road Car Company, Stevensons Transport and Trent Motor Tracton Company buses. The Uttoxeter rail service via Macclesfield would continue until 1960. The units seen here formed a 'twin' set from Lots 30324 and 30325 to Diagrams 633 (DMBS - Driving Motor Brake Second) and 510 (DMCL - Driving Motor Composite with Lavatory). The white cab roof so well associated with the later Buxton allocated Birmingham R C & W (Class 104) sets has been applied here also. A former Buxton driver commented that the white finish reflected the sun and helped keep the driving compartment cool. One suspects that application of the white paint to the trailing ends would have helped cool the Lavatory and Guards compartments in the respective units, positioned as they were.

J W Sutherland

The first of the designs to appear in numbers however were the original Derby Lightweight units of the 79XXX series, virtually taking over the line during the months of October and November 1956, mostly as paired units but occasionally as four-car sets. As production of these and other companies DMU's increased, the Buxton line would take on the appearance of a test route, or track, enabling them to be put through their paces whilst contributing to revenue earning duties.

The list below is included to illustrate the 1955/56 construction programme of diesel multiple unit stock ordered. It represents but a small proportion of the 4600 vehicle envisiaged in the Modernisation plans as the number eventually petered out after topping 4000. However, it is interesting to note that examples of these types would appear at some early stage of the programme on the Buxton line.

No	Type of Vehicle	Builder
36	Motor cars	Cravens
36	Control Trailers	Cravens
20	Motor Cars	Gloucester R C & W
20	Control Trailers	Gloucester R C & W
227	Motor Cars	Birmingham R C & W
43	Control Trailers	Birmingham R C & W
123	Trailers	Birmingham R C & W
205	Motor Cars	Metro-Cammell C & W
44	Control Trailers	Metro-Cammell C & W
90	Trailers	Metro-Cammell C & W

courtesy the Railway Observer (RCTS)

The following sightings have been extracted from the note books of Wallace Sutherland. The 79XXX units were from Lots 30321/22/24 and 25 and were maintained initially at Reddish Electric Traction Depot, which of course had been constructed for the Manchester, Sheffield and Wath Electrification scheme.

Date.	Unit numbers	Train.
10.10.56	**79185/79190**	on 5.45pm Buxton - London Road
10.10.56	**79673/79172**	on 9.20pm London Road - Buxton
12.10.56	**79189/79184**	on 7.55am Hazel Grove - London Road
13.10.56	**79188/79631**	on 8.34am Buxton - London Road (joined to **79171/79672** at L.Rd for next run)
13.10.56	**79190/79185**	on 1.54 pm Buxton - London Road.
17.10.56	**79184/79680**	on Hazel Grove - London Road train (7.55am)
18.10.56	**79174/79683**	ditto
22.10.56	**79680/79186**	ditto
22.10.56	**79188/79179**	on 5.45pm Buxton - London Road.
22.10.56	**79681/79177**	on 9.20pm London Road - Buxton.
23.10.56	**79184/79178**	on 7.55pm Hazel Grove - London Road
25.10.56	**79180/79675+79171/79672**	on 8.41am(SX) Whaley Bridge - L. Road
2.11.56.	**79178/79677**	on 5.45pm Buxton - London Road
2.11.56	**79683/79174**	on 10.50 pm London Road - Buxton.
7.11.56	**79172/79186**	on Hazel Grove - London Road

These alloy bodied vehicles and the concept of the diesel multiple unit had been well received on the many services where they were being introduced. Passenger numbers, year on year for 1956 and 1957, would increased beyond expectations, particularly on the Buxton /Macclesfield line services which saw patronage increase by 169%

Davenport, 13th October 1957 (Sunday). Although sightings had been noted as early as 17th April, new Birmingham Railway Carriage & Wagon units continued to appear on the line as allocated. Here we see (later 104) units **M50501/M59157/M50449** pulling away from Davenport with the 11.45am ex-Manchester London Road to Buxton train. Looking resplendent in its dark green livery with unique white cab roof, the sets would proceed to give many years of reliable service although the vehicles here were subsequently allocated to Stoke (Cockshute). The make-up of the three-car set is a well acknowledged formation, the trailing vehicle **M50501** being designated DMCL (Driving Motor Composite - 1st/2nd) with Lavatory; The second or centre vehicle, **M59157** is a Trailer Composite (1st/2nd) with Lavatory. The leading vehicle, **M50449** is a DMBS (Driving Motor Brake Second), ensuring that the novelty of sitting in the compartment behind the driver was not confined solely to First Class passengers. ***J W Sutherland***

BRITISH RAILWAYS

NEW DIESEL SERVICES

MANCHESTER
LONDON ROAD
and
BUXTON

For service between Manchester Central and Buxton see separate folder

8th OCTOBER 1956 to 16th JUNE 1957
or until further notice
Subject to alteration

B.R. 35031/54 STAFFORD & CO. LTD. FOLDER E 25/A

BUXTON TO MANCHESTER LONDON ROAD

The services will be worked by Diesel trains except where otherwise shown

WEEKDAYS

	am	am	† am	am	† am	† am		† SX am	SX am	SO am	am	am	am	am		am	am	pm	pm
BUXTON dep.	..	..	7 05	..	7 30	7 50	..	8 20	..	8 24	8 34	9 12	..	9 54	..	10 54	11 54	12 54	1 54
Dove Holes ,,	..	..	7 11	..	7 36	..	..	..	..	8 31	8 41	..	..	10 01	..	11 01	12 01	1 01	2 01
Chapel-en-le-Frith South ,,	..	..	7 16	..	..	7 59	..	..	..	8 35	8 45	9 21	..	10 05	..	11 05	12 05	1 05	2 05
Whaley Bridge ,,	6 30	7 08	7 25	..	7 47	8 06	..	..	8 41	8 41	8 51	..	..	10 11	..	11 11	12 11	1 11	2 11
Furness Vale ,,	6 33	7 10	7 28	..	7 50	..	..	..	8 45	8 45	8 54	..	..	10 14	..	11 14	12 14	1 14	2 14
New Mills, Newtown ,,	6 36	7 14	7 32	..	7 54	..	..	..	8 48	8 48	8 58	..	..	10 18	..	11 18	12 18	1 18	2 18
Disley ,,	6 40	7 17	7 36	..	7 59	8 13	..	..	8 52	8 52	9 01	..	..	10 21	..	11 21	12 21	1 21	2 21
Middlewood Lower ,,	6 43	7 21	7 41	..	8 03	8 17	..	..	8 55	8 55	9 05	..	..	10 25	..	11 25	12 25	1 25	2 25
Hazel Grove ,,	6 47	7 24	7 46	7 55	8 08	8 21	..	..	8 59	8 59	9 08	..	9 59	10 28	..	11 28	12 28	1 28	2 28
Davenport ,,	6 50	7 28	7 51	7 59	8 14	8 26	..	..	9 02	9 02	9 12	..	10 02	10 32	..	11 32	12 32	1 32	2 32
STOCKPORT Edgeley arr.	6 54	7 32	7 56	8 02	..	8 33	..	8 49	..	..	9 15	9 40	10 06	10 36	..	11 36	12 36	1 36	2 36
STOCKPORT Edgeley dep.	6 55	7 33	7 59	8 03	..	8 34	..	8 50	..	..	9 16	9 41	10 07	10 37	..	11 37	12 37	1 37	2 37
Heaton Norris ,,	6 57	..	..	8 05	..	..	..	..	..	..	..	..	10 09	10 39	..	11 39	12 39	1 39	2 39
Heaton Chapel & Heaton Moor ,,	7 00	..	..	8 08	..	..	..	..	..	..	..	..	10 12	10 42	..	11 42	12 42	1 42	2 42
Levenshulme North ,,	7 03	..	..	8 11	..	..	..	..	..	..	..	..	10 15	10 45	..	11 45	12 45	1 45	2 45
Longsight for Belle Vue ,,	7 06	..	..	8 14	..	..	..	..	..	..	..	..	10 18	10 48	..	11 48	12 48	1 48	2 48
MANCHESTER London Road arr.	7 10	7 42	8 10	8 18	8 29	8 44	..	9 01	9 14	9 14	9 24	9 49	10 22	10 52	..	11 52	12 52	1 52	2 52

	WEEKDAYS pm	pm	SX pm	SO pm	pm	SX pm		SO pm	pm	pm	pm	SO pm		SUNDAYS am	am	pm	pm	pm	pm
BUXTON dep.	2 54	3 54	4 35	4 54	5 45	6 30	..	6 54	7 56	8 54	9 45	11 00	..	8 54	11 54	3 54	4 54	7 54	9 25
Dove Holes ,,	3 01	4 01	4 41	5 01	5 52	6 37	..	7 01	8 03	9 01	9 52	11 07	..	9 01	12 01	4 01	5 01	8 01	9 32
Chapel-en-le-Frith South ,,	3 05	4 05	4 45	5 05	5 56	6 41	..	7 05	8 07	9 05	9 56	11 11	..	9 05	12 05	4 05	5 05	8 05	9 36
Whaley Bridge ,,	3 11	4 11	4 51	5 11	6 02	6 47	..	7 11	8 13	9 11	10 03	11 17	..	9 11	12 11	4 11	5 11	8 11	9 42
Furness Vale ,,	3 14	4 14	4 54	5 14	6 05	6 50	..	7 14	8 16	9 14	10 07	11 20	..	9K 14	12K 14	4K 14	5K 14	8K 14	9K 45
New Mills, Newtown ,,	3 18	4 18	4 58	5 18	6 09	6 54	..	7 18	8 20	9 18	10 11	11 24	..	9 18	12 18	4 18	5 18	8 18	9 49
Disley ,,	3 21	4 21	5 01	5 21	6 12	6 58	..	7 21	8 23	9 21	10 15	11 27	..	9 21	12 21	4 21	5 21	8 21	9 52
Middlewood Lower ,,	3 25	4 25	5 05	5 25	6 16	7 01	..	7 25	8 27	9 25	10 19	11 31	..	9 25	12 25	4 25	5 25	8 25	9 56
Hazel Grove ,,	3 28	4 28	5 08	5 28	6 19	7 05	..	7 28	8 30	9 28	10 23	11 34	..	9 28	12 28	4 28	5 28	8 28	9 59
Davenport ,,	3 32	4 32	5 12	5 32	6 23	7 09	..	7 32	8 34	9 32	10 27	11 38	..	9 32	12 32	4 32	5 32	8 32	10 03
STOCKPORT Edgeley arr.	3 36	4 36	5 16	5 36	6 27	7 13	..	7 36	8 38	9 36	10 31	11 41	..	9 36	12 36	4 36	5 36	8 36	10 07
STOCKPORT Edgeley dep.	3 37	4 37	5 17	5 37	6 29	7 15	..	7 37	8 39	9 37	10 34	11 42	..	9 37	12 37	4 37	5 39	8 37	10 08
Heaton Norris ,,	3 39	4 39	5 19	5 39	..	..	..	7 39	8 41	9 39	..	..	..	..	..	..	..	..	..
Heaton Chapel & Heaton Moor ,,	3 42	4 42	5 22	5 42	..	..	..	7 42	8 44	9 42	10 39	..	..	..	..	..	..	..	..
Levenshulme North ,,	3 45	4 45	5 25	5 45	..	..	..	7 45	8 47	9 45	10 42	..	..	9 42	12 42	4 42	5 44	8 42	10 13
Longsight for Belle Vue ,,	3 48	4 48	5 28	5 48	..	..	..	7 48	8 50	9 48	10 45	..	..	..	..	..	..	..	..
MANCHESTER London Road arr.	3 52	4D 52	5M32	5 52	6 38	7 25	..	7 52	8 54	9 52	10 49	11 50	..	9 47	12 47	4 47	5 49	8 47	10 18

D—Saturdays excepted arrives Manchester Mayfield
SO—Saturdays only
K—Commences 31st March, 1957
SX—Saturdays excepted
†—Steam train
M—Manchester Mayfield

Extracts from the handbill introducing the new diesel services betwen Manchester London Road and Buxton. The hourly interval service was an innovation on the line but was still shared with the *Steam train,* succinctly included in the footnotes.

Buxton, 6th February 1957. It had been almost three years since the first of the original Derby Lightweights had completed their trial runs and been introduced to the travelling public and it was the 79XXX series that had provided Buxton with its first taste of the new trains. Following the trials and tribulations of the 'first generation' of diesel multiple units, the 1955 Modernisation Plan put into place requirements for maintenance facilities such as the one at Buxton, seen here in an embryonic stage. Construction of the servicing depot was to take the best part of two years before it was fully operational. The depot comprised a two road shed with inspection pits, workshops, stores, fuelling installations and staff amenity buildings. The 240 ft long shed would be equipped for normal maintenance, being designed to service an allocation of nine three-car sets. Ample siding accommodation alongside the shed will enable stabling and external washing. Trains allocated at Buxton according to *Railway Magazine (January 1959)*, would operate between Buxton and Manchester London Road, to and from Millers Dale, and between Manchester and Crewe, and Stoke via Macclesfield. Despite the depot being incomplete, the presence of a two-car Gloucester RC&W set, M50358/M56113 was noted 'on shed' on 14th September 1958. ***E R Morten***

While the Derby Lightweights were busying themselves with day to day operations, the scene was set for the appearance of numerous other new units manufactured by outside contractors. First to arrive were the Birmingham RC&W Co sets on 17th April 1957, noted on the 7.55am Hazel Grove - London Road working. These were followed in quick succesion by Metro-Cammell sets, M56093/50137 being noted on 29th April 1957, also on the 7.55am Hazel Grove to London Road service.

Noted at Manchester London Road on 4th May 1957 was a new three-car Birmingham RC&W set, comprising units M50425/M59133/M50421. Of passing interest, steam in the form of Fowler 2-6-4T No 42370 was to be seen at the head of a five-coach train forming the 12.30pm(SO) Mayfield to Buxton .

During the month of May, the 7.59am departure from Davenport (7.55am ex-Hazel Gove to London Road) was noted on four occasions with varying combinations of three-car Birmingham RC&W units.

Date	Composition
8.5.57	M50420/M59132/M50424
9.5.57	M50421/M59132,M50424
23.5.57	M50427/M59135/M50423
30.5.57	M50425/M59133/M50421

This selection of units was part of Lots 30290/91/92

Although steam was still the dominant force throughout British Railways, diesel multiple unit trains continued infiltrating on an increasing scale. Loco 'spotters' generally remained unconcerned.

Hazel Grove 12th August 1961. Although slightly later than the first sightings of Metro-Cammell units in 1957, and 'electric flash' signs permitting, it is possible to imagine the sight - if not the sounds - of these very distinctive units (later 101), their bodyside alloy framed windows being one of a number of noteable features. Examples of these units outlasted all other Modernisation Plan designs on the main line network. The train here is actually a Stockport - Stalybridge set en-route to Buxton for servicing. ***J W Sutherland***

Stockport, 5th July 1958 (Sat). Threading its way amidst the dust and grime of partially demolished Edgeley Tunnels, a pair of three-car 'Birmingham' sets, led by M50424, heads towards Edgeley Junction prior to commencing the climb to Buxton with the 2.20pm departure from London Road. ***J W Sutherland***

At the beginning of June however, a somewhat surprise arrival on the scene witnessed vehicles manufactured by the Gloucester Railway Carriage & Wagon Co., Sent on loan to Longsight, the units, intended for use on the Scottish Region, fulfilled duties on the Buxton line in both 2-car and 4-car formations, although not always as the same combinations. On 1st June 1957, the 2.54am Buxton to Manchester train was formed of SC56095/SC50341+SC50340/SC56096 (Lot 30278). Also noted at London Road on the same day, the 5.20pm to Buxton comprised Metro-Cammell sets M56093/M50137+M50135/M56091. On 4th June, the 7.59am departure from Davenport consisted of a 'Gloucester' set SC50339/56094. Later in the day, the 8.54pm Buxton to Manchester was made up of units SC50431/SC56096. Noted at Davenport on 29th June, was a five-car train formed of Metro-Cammell 2-car set M50134/M56090 and 'Birmingham' set M50429/M59137/M50481.

(Above) Heaton Norris, 1st June 1957. This Saturdays Only working, the 4.20pm from Manchester London Road to Buxton, departs from Heaton Norris for its scheduled two minute trip to Stockport Edgeley, most of the 'journey' being aloft the town's famous viaduct. This train was booked to call at 'all stations' between Manchester and Buxton, including the now closed Longsight and Heaton Norris. In the circumstances, an end to end journey time of 68 minutes was very creditable performance. Built for service on Scottish Region lines, a small number of Gloucester Railway Carriage & Wagon Co. units were placed on loan to Longsight. Four of the new units are seen here forming 2x2-car sets with **SC56095** (DTC - Driving Trailer Composite (1st/2nd) trailing. The other vehicles are, left to right, **SC50341** (DMBS - Driving Motor Brake Second), **SC50340** (DMBS) and **SC56096** (DTC). This four car combination had earlier worked the 2.54pm Buxton to Manchester train. The cantilevered colour light signals ahead of the train were part of the Stockport resignalling scheme commissioned on 7th March 1955 which saw the displacement of manual signal boxes at Heaton Norris (No's 1, 2 & 3) and Heaton Chapel. Another vehicle, **SC50339** (DMBS) was seen running in tandem with with **SC56094** (DTC) on the 2nd July.

J W Sutherland

BRIEF DIARY EXTRACTS FOR....
DIESEL MULTIPLE UNITS

1.6.57 2.54pm Buxton - Manchester train consisted of SC56095, SC50341, SC50340, SC56096 - Gloucester RC&W (Lot 30278).

1.6.57 5.20pm London Road - Buxton on some days consisted of M56093, M50135, M56091 - Metro Cammell.

11.12.57 Diesel M50512 (BRC&W) noted in London Road. The 12.30 diesel from Mayfield consisted of M50504, M59160 and M50452.

11.1.58 The 10.20 am London Road - Buxton train consisted of M50432, M59140, M50484, M50433, M59149, M50441 (all BRC&W of course).

The pioneering Derby Lightweight diesel multiple units made an early appearance in Buxton on 5th January 1955, less than six months after the first trains had been introduced on the Eastern Region. Platform 1 at the former LNWR station played host to at least one of the second batch (Lot 30123) built at Derby in December 1954. The leading car, M79017, operated as Driving Motor Brake Second (DMBS), a twin-unit (2-engines) with Brake compartment and seating for sixty-one (2nd Class) passengers. These were normally paired with 796XX powered trailer units designated DTCL (Driving Trailer Composite - with Lavatory), which again, with two-engines catering for nine First and fifty-three Second Class fare paying passengers. Curiously, this group visiting Buxton comprises three vehicles, but unfortunately neither centre or rear cars have been identified. The visit was arranged for local dignataries and members of the public as a prelude to the introduction of diesel services although surprisingly it would be the best part of two years before regular services commenced. For the record, M79017 was destined for the West Cumberland lines of the LMR, the horizontal door window bars affixed to counter potential accidents on the Maryport & Carlisle section with its limited clearances. ***H Townley*** per J M Bentley

(Below) Full commissioning of the new diesel maintenance facility is imminent in this 28th March 1959 (Saturday). Two 'Birmingham' sets occupy the storage sidings whilst a Metro-Cammell is about to enter the depot. Note the carriage sidings to the right. ***J W Sutherland***

THE BUXTON LINE DIARIES OF *J W SUTHERLAND*

Davenport, 13th October 1956. Although not the earliest of views taken by Wallace, it is thought appropriate to include one which is referred to in the first of his three 'diaries' which recorded events on the the Buxton line. Davenport of course was his 'home' station and a great many of the references were based on sightings at the location. Above we see **48554**, a Widnes based 8F, at the head of a Down goods train making a cautious approach to Davenport Junction where it will take the route to Cheadle Village Junction over the 'Khyber' line. *J W Sutherland*

1956 - 1962

12.9.56 42366 (9D) + 3 bogies on 9.16am London Road - Buxton.

15.9.56 42344 (9D) + 4 bogies on 8.20am (SO) Buxton - London Road.
42365 (9D)+ 5 bogies on 12.10pm London Road - Buxton.
42423 + 5 bogies on 2.25pm Buxton - London Road.

20.9.56 42344 + 4 bogies on 8.36am (SX) Whaley Bridge - London Road.
42814 on Up goods (Class K NJ) from Davenport 9.15am
42365 + 3 on 8.34am Buxton - London Road.
42366 + 6 on 9.0am London Road - Buxton.

29.9.56 43207 on Down goods at Whaley Bridge.
42366 on 2.25pm Mayfield - Buxton (3.0)
48720 on Down goods at Furness Vale.

1.10.56 42365 + 3 on 5.40pm Buxton - London Road.
42353 + 3 on 10.36 London Road - Buxton.

13.10.56 42306 + on 12.1(SO) London Road - Buxton.
48554 on Down mixed goods passing Davenport (*see above*).

25.10.56 42772 on Up goods passing Davenport.

16.2.57 42399 on 12.10pm (SO) London Road - Buxton.

17.4.57 New three-car unit (Birmingham Carriage & Wagon Co.,) first noted on Buxton line on 7.55 am Hazel Grove - London Road train near Davenport 17.4.57; The new Metro Cammell units also noted on the Buxton line a few days later.

29.4.57 56039 + 50137 (Metro Cammell) on 7.35am Hazel Grove - London Road.

4.5.57 50425+59133+50421 Birmingham Carriage & Wagon Co., noted at London Road.

4.5.57 42370 pulled 5 total 12.30(SO) Mayfield - Buxton train.

8.5.57 50420+59132+50424 BRC&W.

9.5.57 50421+59132+50424 BRC&W

23.5.57 50427+59135+50423 BRC&W

30.5.57 50425+59133+50421 BRC&W

1.6.57 2.54pm Buxton - Manchester train consisted of SC56095/SC50341+ SC50340/SC56096 - Gloucester RC&W; Lot 30278.

1.6.57 5.20pm London Road - Buxton on some days consisted of 56093+ 50135+56091 Metro Cammel.

Dec 1957 Hazel Grove and Middlewood Stations are being repainted.

11.12.57 42942+5 on 12.10pm ex-London Road and 42925+4 on 12.50pm ex-London Road. In the morning 42786+4 on 7.50am from Buxton. Diesel M50512 (BRC&W) noted in London Road. 42961, with 48636 banking in rear, were on Up goods passing Woodsmoor in the afternoon and 48709 on a Down goods. The 12.30 diesel from Mayfield consisted of M50504+ M59160+M50452.

11.1.58 Waiting for the 8.26am departure from Davenport (Buxton 7.50am) running late, I saw 48152 on an Up mixed goods, including cement wagons and many other fitted wagons, followed by 42930 on other goods, including mineral empties. 42923 (9A) + 4 was on our train. The 10.20am London Road - Buxton train consisted of 50432+59140+50484, 50433+ 59149+50441 (all BRC&W of course). 42942 +4 on 12.10 London Road - Buxton train. 42923 + 4 on 12.50 London Road - Buxton train. About 1.07pm, 44748 passed Woodsmoor on a Down special. It was running tender first with 'W560' chalked on. I heard from the Woodsmoor signalman (Mr Bailton?) that this was a Whaley Bridge - Belle Vue Special, perhaps for the circus. The 1.20 London Road - Buxton train was a triple unit including M50799. This was presumably a Craven set and was the first Craven I had seen on this line. This morning, the same set which also included M59321 was in London Road on a Crewe service. In fact this was the first time I had seen a Craven set in this area though I saw an earlier one on a Derby train at Crewe on 1.1.58.

14.1.58 Was told tonight at MLS by Bob Hunter that Crewe 3-car units have been running into London Road for about 3 weeks. Noted BRC&W No 50518 at London Road.

1.2.58 (Sat) The 12.10pm London Road - Buxton was hauled by 42943 (5 coaches). The 12noon (SO) express before it had consisted of a 2-car Metro Cammell set. Later came 48465 (9D) on a Down Class J train (all or partially all) coal. The 12.05 Buxton - London Road consisted of 3-car trains, set 50761+ 59316+50794 (Cravens). This was followed by 42923 (9A) on a 10 total football special to Rochdale. Didn't notice where it had started from but probably Hazel Grove. The 12.30 (SO) Mayfield - Buxton train consisted of 50134+56090 (Metro Cammell). The 12.50 (SO) London Road - Buxton (*See opposite*) consisted of 4 coaches hauled by 44935 (6G - Llandudno Junction). I have not seen many Class 5 engines on this line but understood that they were regularly used on some trains prior to dieselisation and probably still on week day steam trains. 49451 followed this train with a trainload of empties. I went into Manchester on the 3.05 Buxton - London Road train which consisted of Birmingham set 50422 + 59134 + 50426. At Longsight there were no less than five 3-car Birmingham sets in line on a road just beyond the carriage sheds. This, probably, and the general lack of Birmingham sets in use today was due to a defect being found in some of the cars (rumoured to be a king pin). This has affected the new timetable for London Road services due to have started on 3rd Feb.

8.2.58 (Sat) Went into Manchester on the 2.42 departure from Davenport (but I caught it at Edgeley). It consisted of 3-car Metro-Cammell set (1958 on builders plate and the set certainly looked new) M50306+M59117 +M50324. The 9.20pm from London Road consisted of Cravens; M50757+M59312 +M5079. The row of Birmingham sets noted last week was no longer at Longsight. Saw two Birmingham sets in service, one on the 9.05pm Buxton - London Road.

5.2.58 (Wed) On the previous Wednesday, had noted new train set No's M50802+M59324+ M50679 (Cravens) on the 7.59am departure from Davenport to London Road.

14.2.58 (Friday) I travelled into London Road from Davenport on the 8.21 departure (8.16am from Hazel Grove)................***continued across***

Davenport, 1st June 1957 (Saturday). Although the diesel railcars had arrived, there was still plenty of life left in the 'old guard', on this occasion **42365** of Buxton depot. Saturday mornings were still part and parcel of the working week and although a little early for 'shoppers', there was plenty of custom for this morning train, the 7.30am ex-Buxton which called all stations on the branch (except Chapel-en-le-Frith South) on its northbound journey to Manchester. Interestingly, Davenport was its last call before a fifteen minute run to London Road, the fare being 1/- (5p) Single or 1/7 (7½p) Return. ***J W Sutherland***

Davenport, 1st February 1958. The atmosphere of a cold and frosty.......afternoon is brought to life by a carriage heating system which is being worked overtime in the compartments of the 12.50pm (SO) London Road to Buxton train. This was one of the services according to the timetable that was still being worked by 'Steam train', taking slightly longer than its diesel counterparts. Despite not having to stop between Manchester and Stockport, the journey time was ten minutes over the hour. All the timings were overshadowed however by the 12 noon (SO) London Road departure for Buxton which ran non-stop to Disley (dep 12.20) before making its only other call, at Whaley Bridge (dep 12.27). Arrival at Buxton was scheduled for 12.46, ending no doubt what was an exhilarating trip! The locomotive incidentally is a clean looking Class 5MT No **44935,** allocated at the time to Llandudno Junction (6G), although for many years Longsight had been its home. ***J W Sutherland***

.....Although shown in the timetable leaflet as a diesel I understand this SX train is in fact usually if not always steam. It was right through to Oxford Road. On this day it consisted of 5 coaches (1 a corridor) hauled by 42391 which the driver said was a Longsight engine (I could not get round to the front to look, at No. 10 platform, London Road. At London Road I saw the 7.50am Buxton - London Road train of 6 non-corridor coaches arrive behind 44686 (Caprotti valve gear and double chimney).

1.3.58 (Sat) Last Saturday of regular steam passenger trains on Saturdays as new timetable comes into force on Monday. Last two Up trains were : 12.10pm London Road - Buxton; 42942 (9D Buxton) + 5 non-corridors; 12.50pm London Road-Buxton; 42887 (9A Longsight) + 4 non-corridors; Noted last train contained one BR recent suburban coach as well as older LMS types. Between the trains I noted 48462 (8A-Edge Hill) on a Down mixed goods.

8.3.58 (Sat) Reg Dean told me that Class 5's were often used on the 5.5pm London Road - Buxton trains (Longsight engines) while he has often seen Jubilee's on the 7.25am (or 7.27) London Road - Buxton train returning from Buxton about 10.30am.

15.3.58 (Sat) At about 1.35pm noted 48516 (9A) passing Davenport on a Down goods (coal only - Class J ?). The 1.20pm London Road - Buxton consisted of Birmingham RC&W No's M50464+M59172+M50516, M50486+M59142+M50434. The 1.15pm Buxton - Manchester consisted of a 3-car Birmingham set working in multiple with a 3-car Craven set.

19.3.58 (Wed) 45567 *South Australia* (8A-Edge Hill) was on the 8.26am departure from Davenport (7.50am from Buxton) this being the first time I have seen a 'Jubilee' on this line.

21.3.58 (Friday) 45527 *Southport* + 6 formed the 7.50am Buxton - London Road, the first Patriot I have seen on the line. Actually 45527 is a rebuilt engine (Class 7P).

27.5.58 (Tuesday) 42938 + 4 was on the 5.40pm London Road - Buxton train and 42887 (9A) on the 5.50pm train (5 bogies). 48175 (8D?) Was on an Up train of mineral empties which followed the latter train.The 5.45 train to Hazel Grove comprised a 3-car Birmingham RC&W set coupled to a 2-car Metro-Cammell set including car No 56091.

28.5.58 (Wed) The 5.40 train was again 42887 + 4

29.5.58 (Thurs) 48500 (9A) on Class H Up train passed Davenport at 9am.

31.5.58 (Sat) 48753 (8D Widnes) was on a Down goods (coal, etc) passing Davenport at 4.25pm.

1.6.58 (Sunday) Trinity Weekend. Sunday at Davenport; 42896 (17B - Buxton on 10 total excursion to Fleetwood; 73091 (26F-Lees) running up light, presumably for a late excursion, perhaps to Southport; 45300 (5B-Crewe South) on 10 total excursion to Llandudno;

5.6.58 (Thurs) 42934 (9A) was on the 5.40pm London Road - Buxton train.

11.6.58 (Wed) 42889 was on the 5.40pm London Road - Buxton.

14.6.58 (Sat) 48268 (9D) was on the Up train, Class K due to leave Davenport Junction about 9.5am, after shunting the Co-op siding; 48166 (9D) was on the Class H train, Longsight - Buxton Sidings. At the same time, about 8am, a 'Crab' came down light and parked in the Davenport coal yard siding........................***continued on page 134***

Davenport, 5th July 1958. (Saturday) One of the Stockport Edgeley MPD 'workhorses', Class G1 0-8-0 No **49010** (9B) gingerly passes between the platforms of Davenport station on its return journey after working the New Mills 'shunt'. Sometime known as the 'Stockport' or 'divi-shunt', the working commenced from Stockport (dep 5.43am) and en-route was allowed twenty-two minutes at Hazel Grove (arr 5.58am) before moving on to New Mills Newtown (arr 6.40) for a stint of up to almost three hours. Leaving Newtown at 9.32, having enabled the passenger train 'peak' period to pass, some fourteen minutes were subsequently allowed for shunting Disley Goods (dep 9.53) prior to what can only be described as a 'cautious' descent to Davenport Junction, the $5\frac{3}{4}$ miles taking some fifty-four minutes! The rate of progress, or perceived lack of it, would enable the 10.09 Hazel Grove to London Road passenger train to clear the branch in time for the 'shunt' to venture out on to the Slow Line at Edgeley Junction to allow a clear run for the 10.15 ex-Buxton passenger.

J W Sutherland

continued from page 133........It had taken the 'mail' up to Buxton and on such days comes down with one of the passenger trains In the afternoon, with Graham, went up to New Mills and had a look around the yard, talking to the Station Master and 'Beryl', the lady signal woman. Since I came back from New Zealand on 12.5.58, have noticed only Birmingham RC&W diesel units on Buxton line trains. Shed codes are now painted on the buffer beams, those noted being 9A, 9D and 5D.

15.6.58 (Sun) Went to ***Middlewood*** and had a wander round. Was able to get a photo of a J11 (64036) on a Macclesfield - London Road train on the upper line.

21.6.58 (Sat) Saw 46252 *City of Leicester* at ***Davenport Junction***, where it was being turned round the 'triangle' owing to the old London Road turntable having been removed and the Longsight turntable being too small for LMS Pacifics. This happens on Fridays and Saturdays, the engine returning on the 'Comet' On Saturdays it comes off the 3.43 arrival at London Road.

5.7.58 (Sat) Went up to ***Whaley Bridge*** in the morning. 48421 (9D) was on a Down goods (class J) probably to Hooton. Class 5 went up on a set of empty coaches from Macclesfield to form an excursion to Southport. 42886 (9D) brought nine coaches down (2 week-day sets combined?) For the usual Edgeley to Morecambe Summer SO services.

5.7.58 (Sat) 49010 was on the Edgeley - New Mills 'shunt'. Later at Davenport saw 45369 (5A) on 5 total excursion to Southport (presumably the set I had seen earlier at Whaley Bridge.) Noticed that the signalman, etc., talked of the LNW 0-8-0's as 'Wessy D's.

9.7.58 (Wed) 5.40pm London Road - Buxton train was hauled by 42416+4 coaches. The 5.50pm London Road - Buxton (5 coaches) was pulled by 48465 (8F). In between, 49210 (9D with tender cab) came down the line on a goods.

10.7.58 (Thurs) 5.50pm London Road - Buxton train was hauled by 42814 (9A).

23.7.58 (Wed) 42936 was on the 5.40 London Road - Buxton Train.

24.7.58 (Thurs) 49395 (with tender cab-9D) went through Davenport on a Down goods at 6.30pm. I went up to a historical exhibition at Disley (St Mary's School). Old 1905 postcards showed the station at that time did not have any shelter canopies and the present buildings would appear to be completely new since then.

30.7.58 (Wed) 42360 was on the 5.40pm London Road - Buxton train and 48744 on the 5.50pm.

2.8.58 (Sat) Visited Mr Platt, signalman at ***Davenport Junction***. He told me that for some days recently Edgeley turntable was out of order and all engines were being turned round the Edgeley - Davenport Junction - Cheadle Village Junction triangle.

3.8.58 (Sunday) We all went to Buxton by diesel. The hourly service was being provided by three Birmingham 3-car sets. Later we walked past the sheds where I noted 49132,

49395 (with tender cab) and 43300; Also in store three 0-4-4T's. The Millers Dale service was being worked by Gloucester twin set M56113 and M50358 (with notice saying it couldn't be attached to any other set without Derby permission, presumably because it is fitted with automatic gear change-which the driver said he found quite satisfactory. There is also a twin Metro Cammell set available, but on weekdays one twin set is used and the additional trips are worked by London Road triplets released from the latter service until the rush hours. The Millers Dale set carried the sign B7, London Road - Buxton is B3. Also at Buxton was an 8-car Metro Cammell set on an excursion from Birmingham and a Birmingham set on an excursion from Kidsgrove Central. On the return run we touched 60 mph between Chapel and Whaley Bridge. On this Bank Holiday weekend were stored on the Woodsmoor goods loop: 2 - 3 corridor trains on the Down loop, 10 corridor Bogies and another 10 corridor bogies on the Up loop. Some if not all of these corridors are for special weekend services from London and were not used on day excursions either on Sunday or Monday.

4.8.58 Bank Holiday Monday. 42938 was on the 8.32am departure from Davenport to London Road (from Buxton), normally departs 8.26.

7.8.58 (Thurs) 42848 (9A) was on the 5.40pm London Road - Buxton and 48744 on the 5.50.

9.8.58 (Sat) First day of Stockport Holidays (Wakes), I saw the following three trains at Davenport; 8.50am Hazel Grove - Scarborough, 44949 and 10 corridors (W613 reporting number on engine) depart Davenport approx. 8.55am; 8.25am Whaley Bridge - Blackpool Central, 42963 (Stanier Crab) + 9 non corridors. (W561) Davenport depart about 9.7; 8.40 am Whaley Bridge - Morecambe, 42923 (9A) (W563) + 10 corridors. Davenport depart about 9.34.

10.8.58 (Sun) The hourly service was being worked by two 6-car Birmingham sets and one 5-car consisting of a Birmingham triple and a Metro-Cammell twin. One of the cars of the latter was 50137. The inward facing destination sign read 'Millers Dale' so it may have been the Buxton Metro-Cammell unit. This morning, an Austerity 2-8-0 was on a work train at Davenport, from which 109lb Flat Bottom rails, sleepers etc., were being unloaded prior to relaying eighteen lengths of the down line through the station.

21.8.58 (Thurs) 48428 was on the 5.50 pm London Road - Buxton train.

30.8.58 (Sat) Went up to Disley and spent a little time at Disley Goods. Traffic is cardboard drums despatched from Bowater's factory and rolls of card. Also some coal, sugar beet pulp and manure and a little smalls traffic. They seemed quite busy this morning. 42886 passed on the nine- coach empty stock. Down train (to form Edgeley - Southport service). And 44271 was on the returning New Mills 'shunt'.

14.9.58 (Sun) Visit to ***Buxton*** Shed. Locos seen : 44061 (9A); 41905 (9D); 44339 (no plate); 41906 (9D); 44565 (17C); 41908 (9A); 45104 (26A); 42306 (9D); 48166 (9D); 42370 (9D); 48175 (8D); 42371 (9D); 48268 (9D); 42772 (9A); 48278 (9D); 42923 (9A); 48322 (9D); 42924 (9A); 48451 (9D); 42938 (9A); 48502 (8D); 43268 (9D); 48519 (9D); 43278 (9D); 48769 (9D); 43300 (9D); 48712 (9D); 43329 (9D); 48740 (9D); 43429 (17C); 48932 (9D); 43715 (41B); 49210 (9D); 43836 (9D); 49315 (9D); 43842 (9D) Stored; 49348 (9D); 43988 (??); 49395 (9D); 9A = *Longsight*, 9E = *Trafford Park, 8D = Widnes, 17C = Rowsley, 26A = Newton Heath, 41B = Grimesthorpe.*
Buxton loco facilities include vacuum operated turntable, skip hoist for ashes, coaling plant, incorporating wagon raising and tipping hoist and skip hoist under bunker. Just outside the shed are the................***continued on page 136***

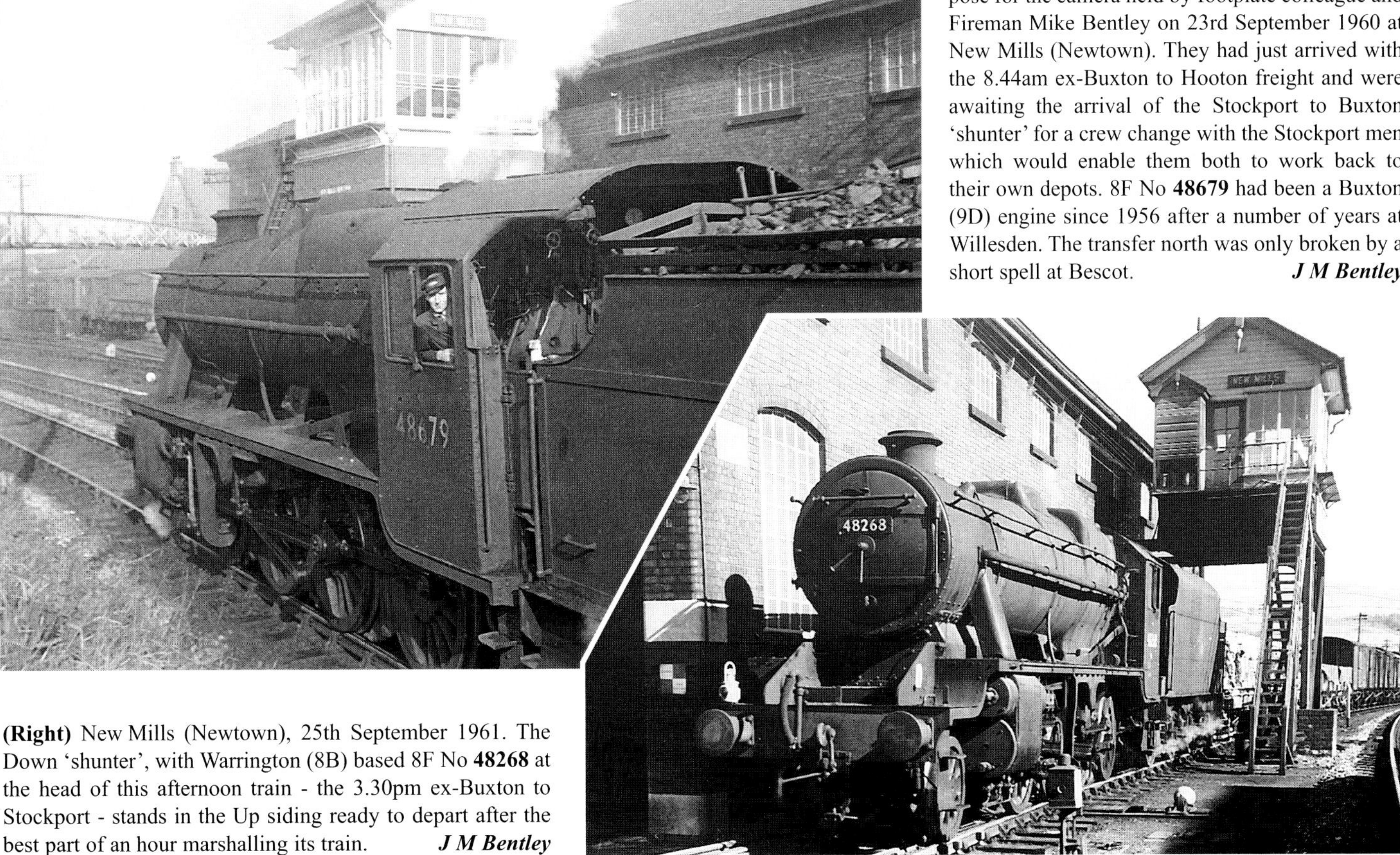

(Left) Buxton Driver Frank Martin finds time to pose for the camera held by footplate colleague and Fireman Mike Bentley on 23rd September 1960 at New Mills (Newtown). They had just arrived with the 8.44am ex-Buxton to Hooton freight and were awaiting the arrival of the Stockport to Buxton 'shunter' for a crew change with the Stockport men which would enable them both to work back to their own depots. 8F No **48679** had been a Buxton (9D) engine since 1956 after a number of years at Willesden. The transfer north was only broken by a short spell at Bescot. ***J M Bentley***

(Right) New Mills (Newtown), 25th September 1961. The Down 'shunter', with Warrington (8B) based 8F No **48268** at the head of this afternoon train - the 3.30pm ex-Buxton to Stockport - stands in the Up siding ready to depart after the best part of an hour marshalling its train. ***J M Bentley***

.... non-mobile snow ploughs, the larger complete with a '9D' plate. Among the locos outside the shed were a converted 'CLC' coach marked 'MP Buxton', old G&SWR van DM 191430 (6 wheel) and marked 'MP Dept. Bedford' built 1903 and complete with Maunsell wheels. Also L&Y bogie van DM 395143M built at Newton Heath. Near the coaling plant is a large water tank apparently in the roof of a former manual type coaling shed. There is a fitters shop at the shed, complete with lathe, etc., At the diesel depot, Millers Dale 2-car set M50358 and M56113 was noted working todays service and noted in the Midland platform 2-car set 50137 and 56093.

2.10.58 42416 was on the 5.40pm express from London Road and 42934 on the 5.50.

5.10.58 (Sun) An excursion to Ashbourne and other stations between there and Hartington, but from Manchester Exchange and Edgeley only, consisted of 9 corridors double headed by 42357 and 42468. *(See page opposite)*

7.10.58 (Tues) The 5.40pm express was hauled by 42369 (4 coaches as usual).

GENERAL NOTE. I have noticed in recent weeks that over 150 passengers get off the 5.45 pm London Road - Hazel Grove train at Davenport and another 50 or more off the 5.50 train.

9.10.58 (Thurs) 42318 was on the 5.40pm express.

15.10.58 (Wed) 45521 *Rhyl* was on the 8.26am departure from Davenport (+ 6 bogies).

18.10.58 (Sat) Went to ***Whaley Bridge*** on 8.39 am departure from Davenport (3-car set). 42859 was at New Mills on the short service from Edgeley. 43428 came through Whaley Bridge on what the driver said was a regular Longsight - Rowsley (probably Longsight - Buxton (arrived Whaley Bridge about 9.25 am). I went down to look on Shallcross Sidings. A lot of vans there, apparently stored. Traffic seems to be mainly confined to coal and coke, largely for the local Co-op, scrap iron for a local foundry and incoming fertiliser. The vans are apparently stored largely for Bowater's traffic and in fact the latter sometimes work their lorries as far as here from the Disley factory. I visited a Works near the line but gathered all their coal comes by road also nearly all their other traffic goes by road. The goods shed is let to a local corn merchant who has little more than a token wagon load of rail traffic per week. The siding is shunted daily about 11 am mid-day and sometimes on Saturdays about the same time. Before I left Whaley Bridge, 48740 (9D) arrived on an Up goods and appeared as if it was probably going to shunt Shallcross. The Furness Vale Siding has been lifted and I gathered the main line points are to be lifted tomorrow (Sunday).

25.10.58 (Sat) Went down to ***Davenport*** station to see the London Road - Buxton parcels train (due to depart Davenport 7.7am) It came in about 9.15am behind 42942 (9D) and consisted of two wooden vans, one LMR six wheeler the other a dirty green Southern van (6 wheel or long wheelbase 4 wheel). 48714 was on Down goods near Davenport 12.25 pm.

1.11.58 (Sat) Went up to ***Dove Holes*** to take some photos. Found that only the points at the up end of the Furness Vale siding (connecting to the Up line) had been removed. The composition of the diesel trains seen and travelled on as follows: 9.09am up from Buxton (3-car); 10.15am up from Buxton (3-car); 12.15pm up from Buxton (3-car); 9.20am up from London Road (6-car); 10.20am up from London Road (3-car); While at Dove Holes I saw the following as well as the diesel trains:- 48348 on Buxton - Arpley train; 48403 (16C-Kirkby in 1954) on special train to Whaley Bridge (bogie flats for collecting old rails during relaying south of Whaley Bridge tomorrow; 48326 (9D) on Stockport - Buxton shunting goods train; 90588 (55C-Farnley Junction) on train from Birkenhead. The signalman, Mr Milner, told me that there is one train of empties and one full train per day of tank wagons to or from the fuel sidings at the north end of the station. I don't think they run on Saturdays and they work via Stockport to and from Guide Bridge or somewhere beyond there. The Government depot is leased to Shell. His impression is that they will run fuel into the tanks for a month then out for a month. He also told me that the main goods traffic is coke, outwards, the coke being brought by road from Buxton gasworks from which a private siding was removed.

27.11.58 (Thurs) The 10.50pm London Road - Buxton service was worked by Birmingham set 50448+59156+50500 (9D), 'flashes' have apparently been added to the ends.

13.12.58 (Sat) Noted another Birmingham set with end flashes. Travelled home from Manchester (9.20pm train) in 5D set M50462+ M59170+ M50514.

27.12.58 (Sat) Visit to ***Chapel-en-le-Frith*** 48458 (6B-Mold Junction) passed through Davenport at 1.40pm on a Down mixed goods. As we went through Disley at about 1.55, 90217 was standing in the short bay of the Down platform. It should be recorded that BR 2-10-0's have occasionally run on the Buxton line though I have not as yet seen one myself.

17.1.59 (Sat) Went up to ***Buxton*** on the 9.39 am departure from Davenport. The 6-car train consisted of a Longsight (9A) set coupled to a Stoke (5D) set. On the way up noticed a LNW 0-8-0 (with tender tank cab) on the New Mills 'shunt' (passed at Disley Goods) while some Cadbury's vans were noticed on a Down mixed goods at New Mills. An 8F was on another Down mixed goods at Whaley Bridge. 48519 was noted at Buxton near the sheds and the 0-4-4T's were still in store near the shed. The return was on the 1.15 departure which was again of 6-cars, being a Stoke set coupled to a Buxton set, the latter comprising car No's M50432+M59140+M50484 with lined ends. 44426 was shunting in the Down yard. At Furness Vale, it was noticed that the Down main line connection (the siding) was still in place though much of the siding itself appears to have been removed together with the Up main line connection last year.

24.1.59 (Sat) Visited ***Norbury Crossing*** but apart from a pleasant morning with Mr J. Wood, one of the two crossing keepers and the one who, with his wife, lives in the crossing house. The line has to be kept clear normally and the gates shut. The latter are opened with the aid of a 'key' which is locked in the signal frame when the signals are in the 'off' position. While there I saw in succession:- 44379 (9F Heaton Mersey) on an up mixed goods; 42932 on the Down New Mills shunt; 90606 on a down mixed goods; 49391 on a down mixed goods; 48448 (6C-Birkenhead) on an up mixed goods, banked in rear by 90723 (56D-Mirfield); 44340 pushing two brake vans up the Up line and the usual diesels of course. Was there from about 9am till 11.35am; Mr Wood pointed out that the job was a 'compensation' one. In his case he had been on the civil engineer's side till he fell from a station roof eighteen months or so ago.

7.2.59 (Sat) Went up to ***Dove Holes*** on diesel. In spite of fog and heavy white frost walked back along main road, part of Peak Forest Tramway right of way and road across hill to Chapel South station. Stone sleepers are still in place in parts of right of way, also, at bridge, over both tramway and main rail line, apparently an old trough for towing horses. It being still foggy at Chapel I returned to Whaley Bridge on 10.25 departure. Here I found 49391 (9D) on the Edgeley - Buxton pick up goods (Edgeley depart, I believe 7.55am). They shunted the goods yard then went down to Shallcross, Mr E. Wilson, the driver kindly giving me a ride there and back. One wagon was taken down and another brought back. Mr Wilson, who said he was a 'North Western'

Davenport, 5th October 1958 (Sunday). The Peak District was, and remains, a magnet to the masses of north-west England, stations on the (by now) freight only Ashbourne line being popular destinations. British Railways worked hard to utilise their stock at weekends to provide access to these locations with excursions throughout the spring, summer and autumn from all manner of starting points, including East Lancashire, the Potteries and Birmingham. The District Passenger Manager, Manchester, was also keen to tap this market and provided the usual excursion trains for Ramblers and visitors to the annual Whitsuntide 'Well Dressing' celebrations. The view above shows one of the double-headed specials, originating from Manchester Exchange - reporting number C798 - piloted by Fowler 2-6-4T No **42357** (9B-Stockport). The train engine is Patricroft (26F) based Stanier Class 4MT 2-6-4T No **42468**. Details of the excursion are shown below in the handbill produced for the occasion.

J W Sutherland

PLEASE RETAIN THIS BILL FOR REFERENCE

Organised Rambles

FROM

HARTINGTON

ALSOP-EN-LE-DALE

and THORPE CLOUD

(FOR ROUTES SEE OVER)

RAMBLES AVAILABLE FOR INDIVIDUALS AS WELL AS ORGANISED PARTIES

LEADERS PROVIDED

Special Excursion

HARTINGTON ALSOP-EN-LE-DALE

TISSINGTON THORPE CLOUD

ASHBOURNE

SUNDAY 5th OCTOBER 1958

FROM	Departure Times	RETURN FARES—SECOND CLASS					Return Arrival Times
		Hartington	Alsop-en-le-Dale	Tissington	Thorpe Cloud	Ashbourne	
	am	s d	s d	s d	s d	s d	pm
MANCHESTER Exchange	9 35	6/–	6/6	6/9	7/–	7/6	9 0
STOCKPORT Edgeley	10 4	5/–	5/9	6/–	6/3	6/9	8 30
ARRIVAL TIMES		am 11 18	am 11 27	am 11 34	am 11 38	am 11 43	
RETURN TIMES		pm 7 15	pm 7 8	pm 6 58	pm 6 53	pm 6 45	

PLEASE SEE OVER FOR DETAILS OF RAMBLES

Children under three years of age, free; three years and under fourteen, half-fare.

CONDITIONS OF ISSUE

These tickets are issued subject to the British Transport Commission's Published Regulations and Conditions applicable to British Railways exhibited at their Stations or obtainable free of charge at Station Booking Offices.

TICKETS CAN BE OBTAINED IN ADVANCE AT THE STATIONS AND OFFICIAL RAILWAY AGENTS

Further information will be supplied on application to the Stations, Official Railway Agents, or to Mr. T. W. POLDING, District Passenger Manager, L.M.R., Hunts Bank, Manchester, 3. Telephone: BLA 3456, Ext. 382.

LONDON MIDLAND

E 1120/HD

CONDUCTED RAMBLES

FROM

HARTINGTON ALSOP-EN-LE-DALE

and THORPE CLOUD

Any person travelling on the Special Excursion may take part in the Organised Rambles but those Not accustomed to long walks are asked to refrain from joining the STRENUOUS Party. The Rambles are led by Official Guides of the Ramblers' Association (Manchester Area) by the following routes:—

A Party
Strenuous
15 miles
approx.

Book Thorpe Cloud—Alight at Alsopledale.

Alstonfield Manifold Valley Hamps Bridge—Musden Grange Ilam—Dovedale.

B1 Party
Moderate
12 miles
approx.

Book Alsopledale—Alight at Alsopledale.

Milldale—Thors Cave Priests Way—Sugar Loaf Barrack Farm to Hartington.

B2 Party
Moderate
13 miles
approx

Book Thorpe Cloud—Alight at Hartington.

Beresford Dale—Wolfscote Dale Mill Dale—Thorpe Cloud.

C Party
Easy
8 miles
approx.

Book Thorpe Cloud—Alight at Thorpe Cloud.

Thorpe Circular, via Coldwall Blore—Ilam.

The organisers reserve the right to adjust the numbers in the parties to suit the capacity of the catering facilities, etc.

Routes will be altered at the discretion of the leaders to suit prevailing conditions.

Passengers intending to join one of the parties should carry some food; it is also advisable to have suitable strong footwear and to carry a light waterproof.

Guides and their assistants will give every help and information possible to passengers, but no responsibility is undertaken for accident or loss.

Passengers taking dogs on the Rambles are requested to keep them under control.

man, classed the D's as good engines and would do the job as an 8F 2-8-0 on half as much coal (to which the fireman nodded his head in agreement). Apparently 49391 is one of four 0-8-0's recently allocated to Buxton. It is from Preston I believe and the others may be also. After the train went on, I went into Whaley Bridge and looked at the remnants of the C&HP tracks. There are still a lot of rails in position on the Incline and on the sidings to the wharf and the mills. On the way home noticed an Austerity hauled Up goods standing in the loop at New Mills with 90370 banking at the rear. 49391 was built as LNW No.1894 (Crewe No.4188) a Class B 4 cylinder compound.

28.2.59 The 12.30pm London Road - Buxton train consisted of 56093+50137 (Metro Cammell - no shed code) and M50484+ M59140 +M50432 (BRC&W - 9D).

27.3.59 (Good Friday) Visit to ***Middlewood.*** Found the signal box and all the signals at Middlewood Higher (High Level Junction) had been removed, two months ago according to the station assistant. The crossover at the south end was still in place, but all rodding etc., to move the switches had gone. 'Car Stop' signs have been installed at various if not all stations on the line within the last week or two. Those at Davenport read 'CAR 5 STOP' (Down) and 'CAR 6 STOP' (Up). At Middlewood both signs read 'CAR 3 STOP'.

28.3.59 (Easter Saturday) Visit with Graham to ***Buxton*** Shed. Engines actually in the shed:- 42306 (9D); 46500 (17A); 42370 (9D); 48247 (8B); 42469 (9E); 48322 (9D); 42942 (9D); 48448 (6C); 43329(9D); 90664 (55C); Outside the shed in use:- 41905; 48740 (9D); 41906; 48741 (9E); 41908; 48744 (9A); 42357; 48932 (9D); 43287 (9D-stored); 49210 (9D Tender Cab); 43538 (9D); 49348 (9D Tender Cab. Stored); 43562 (9D); 49391 (9D); 43836 (9D); 43842 (9D); 48278 (9D); 48712 (9D); *9D-Buxton; 9E-Trafford Park; 17A-Derby, 8B-Warrington, 6C-Birkenhead, 55C-Leeds (Farnley).* 49281 (9D) came in while we were there, probably from Hindlow; 43961 was in the goods yard adjacent to the shed and 48421 was shunting in the yard beyond the Down line. I was told that 46500 was on a Derby roster working a morning passenger run from Derby and returning on the 5.5pm Buxton - Derby passenger (though in fact the latter is shown in the timetable as SX). 48712 was fitted with plate reading 'LNER Built 1944 SR'.

30.3.59 (Easter Monday) Visit to ***Furness Vale.*** Was told the siding (now taken out, though some old rails remain) belonged to a Brick company, not BR. On return to Davenport, the train consisted of a Birmingham 3-car set plus a 2-car Metro Cammell (I think) set M51192+M56350. Outward trains from Manchester in the morning are well patronised and at least two unadvertised workings were run (one at least was to Whaley Bridge only....***continued next column***

Dove Holes, 3rd October 1959 (Sat). October services for 1959 on British Railways London Midland Region came under the category of *or until further notice.* The summer time table for 1959 was due to cease from the 13th September but in the event was not subsequently replaced until 2nd November due to 'important changes in the (regional) passenger services timetable to allow for the large amount of engineering work in connection with the modernisation and electrification of the west coast lines out of Euston. How did this affect the Buxton line? Not a lot, the 10.20am departure from London Road, seen here passing the site of the long abandoned Dove Holes Brickworks and the erstwhile Peak Forest Tramway, still being allowed sixty-five minutes for the all-stations journey to Buxton. Clean ballast and a freshly painted semaphore signal give a tidy appearance to the railway although full tanks of diesel fuel on the downhill journey, allied to extensive rail cant, caused spillage which accelerated discolouration to the stone. ***J W Sutherland***

Dove Holes, 2nd May 1959 (Saturday). Occupying the Down loop at Dove Holes with the 8.44am ex-Buxton to Hooton freight is Austerity 2-8-0 No **90254**, a long way from its Farnley Junction (55C) base. The Saturdays Only scheduling of this mixed formation train allowed an extra thirty or so minutes for the nineteen and a half mile journey to Cheadle Village Junction, the pause here enabling the 9.09am ex-Buxton to Manchester London Road passenger train to pass. The loops at Dove Holes were opened in February 1932 and provided greatly increased operational flexibility in and around Buxton. Details of the morning activity at Dove Holes can be read below. ***J W Sutherland***

.............On the return run, according to the stationmaster, we reached about 69 mph when nearing Hazel Grove.

28.4.59 (Tues) 45624 *St Helena* was on the 5.40pm express .from London Road, most unusual for a Jubilee to be on an evening train.

2.5.59 (Saturday) Visit to ***Dove Holes*** area in morning. On way up (on 8.20am diesel from Manchester), 49191 was at New Mills on the 'shunt service'. The relaying which took place last week-end was in the neighbourhood of Hazel Grove while today I noticed a lot of new rails and sleepers south of Whaley Bridge (apparently for the Down line on the curve round Combes reservoir). Noted there were at least two track miles for the Up line on the long curve south of Chapel also at least one at the opposite end of the curve for the Down line. Davenport has now got a '2/3 CAR STOP' sign on the Up platform. 48254 left Dove Holes on a Down goods (partly tankers) about 9.20; A further 8F hauled Down goods went down about 9.30; 48094 passed the short tunnel on the Up goods about 10.34 (probably train for Longsight) while 48715 went past on a Down train at about 10.45; The Up train from Birkenhead was double-headed by 48274 and 42978 passing at 11.50.

10.5.59 (Sunday) Excursion to Ashbourne etc., The train, 10 bogies from Manchester Exchange was headed by 45133 and 42379 (9B), the latter from Stockport only. Passing Buxton shed noted another excursion apparently just arrived from Millers Dale line and headed by a 'Crab' for Ashbourne, whilst 42370 and 42371 were near the coaling plant, presumably about to take over when we got out of the way. At Alsop-en-le-Dale, where we alighted, we found another excursion, probably from Nottingham and double-headed. A return excursion to Nottingham in the evening was headed by 42668 and 44472 (these numbers not guaranteed to be exactly correct. We joined the train back (same engines) at Thorpe Cloud (single track station - no loop). Noticed passing track adjacent to Up platform had been lifted at Tissington.

14.5.59 (Thursday) The 5.40pm from London Road was headed by 42936 and the 5.50pm by 42416.

16.5.59 (Sat) Visit to Chapel-en-le-Frith South, going up on the 8.39am departure from Davenport. I noticed a 4F on the 'shunt' from Stockport at New Mills. A Down goods train passed through Chapel at about 9.27am consisting mainly of mineral and tank wagons and headed by 73039 and 42943. This, I gathered from the signalman was the train to Hooton. The train to Ince and Elton headed by 48451 and containing coal and mixed goods followed at 9.50am; 11.40, 48274 passed on the Rowsley to Edgeley train while at 11.45am, the train from Birkenhead pounded through at a good pace, headed by 42977 with 90642 pushing in the rear. The signalman said It had only taken 10 minutes for the 3¾ miles (longest at 1 in 58) from Whaley Bridge. Later 42943 (9D) came through, running light engine; 48519 (9D) was on the Up train , probably the 'shunter' from Stockport at New Mills. The young clerk (Mr J. Roe) at Chapel kindly lent me some old timetables (80's) and invoices out of the station loft for me. He said they still have some wagon load goods traffic there, e.g., cotton and cattle food. They also get a lot of parcels traffic from Ferodo, a letter service to North Wales from Central Station. Stone sets used to be shipped away from the siding on the Down side of the line at Chapel. Some of the sets were for use at Euston station.

18.5.59 (Whit Monday) 45560 *Prince Edward Island* was on the 7.50am from Buxton, mainly as a stopping train to an altered holiday timing.

19.5.59 (Tues) Visit to ***Whaley Bridge***. Up on the 5.18pm from Davenport and back on the 6.47pm from Whaley Bridge. Going up we passed 48500 (9A) shunting a Down train (no doubt the afternoon Buxton - Stockport train). Coming back we passed 42977 on a long train of mixed empties at Middlewood. The 5.40pm train from London Road was hauled by 42925

(9A). The 5.50pm train from London Road was hauled by 42848.

21.5.59 (Thursday) 42943 (9D) was on the 7.30am Buxton - Manchester and 45678 *De Robeck* was on the 6 total 7.50am Buxton - Manchester. I was at Hazel Grove in the evening and saw 42854 (9B) come past on the Down line at 5.45pm with a short load of vans. 42786 (9A) was on the 5.40pm from Manchester and 42889 (9A) on the 5.50pm.

22.5.59 (Friday) 45539 *E C Trench* was on the 8.32am from Davenport to Manchester (7.50 am ex-Buxton with extra stops) and in the evening, 42582 was on the 5 total 5.50pm from Manchester.

23.5.59 (Sat) 42886 (9D) was noted on the morning Up parcels train which consisted of one bogie parcels van and a four-wheel 'white' Insulated Fish van. Visit to ***Bibbingtons***. Went up on the 7.53am from Davenport, 49191 (9B) was on the 'shunt' at New Mills. At Bibbingtons, 48246 came through on the train to Hooton and 48505 (9D) was on the one to Ince and Elton. Both were banked up to Bibbingtons by 43562 (9D). 49392 (8A) was on the Rowsley- Edgeley train, which was banked up to Bibbingtons by 43429 (17C). 48684 (6C) was on the train from Birkenhead which was light today so did not have the usual banker. Going back from Dove Holes on the 11.15am diesel from Buxton, I saw 42910 in the sidings at Middlewood.

24.5.59 (Sunday) Our outing to Millers Dale Relaying on the Up line necessitated single track working between Whaley Bridge and Chapel. 48451 (9D) was working the ballast train. At Buxton 45088 (16A) came in, probably on an excursion from Nottingham.

28.5.59 (Thursday) 42772 (9A) was on the 5.50pm Manchester to Buxton train. 48439 (9A) came through Davenport with a Down goods.

30.5.59 (Sat) Visit to ***Middlewood***. A 4F was on the Down New Mills 'shunt' (came through at 10.12 am). At 10.35 a 4F came through on a train from Hooton. 42856 was on the train from Birkenhead (no banker). The train to Ince & Elton was headed by an 8F 2-8-0.

13.6.59 42390 was on short goods which passed Davenport Junction at 3.27pm (probably empties from Longsight.

18.6.59 42936 (9A) was on 4 total 5.40 train. 42924 (9A) was on 5 total 5.50 train.

20.6.59 Visit to ***Dove Holes*** and ***Buxton***. 49191 was at New Mills on the 'shunt'. The only Down goods seen all morning was the ore to Hooton which passed a point south of Bibbingtons at 8.50 hauled by 48247 (8B Warrington) and banked by 43305 (9B). It totalled 40 vehicles. 42856 (6C-Birkenhead) headed the train from Birkenhead banked by an 8F 2-8-0 (LMS type). 42786 (9A) took the coaches (9) down to Stockport for the (SO) Morecambe service. Near Buxton shed we noted 48932, 49008, 48691, 48683, (and stored) 49348, 43842; 48679 (9D) was shunting at one stage and 43268 came in about 12 on a train from the Ashbourne line. 42306 was Also seen arriving at the sheds at this time, while on the return home I noted 48519 (9D) shunting at Dove Holes on the goods from Stockport. I visited Higher Buxton Goods Depot. Noted petrol, or fuel oil tank wagons,

Bibbingtons Siding, 5th March 1960 (Saturday). Making a vigorous effort during the last stages of its journey to Buxton, Warrington (8B) based Class 5MT No **45276** passes Bibbingtons Sidings signal box - Signalman Bowyer presiding over the event - with the morning freight from Birkenhead. A few yards ahead marks the summit of the line after a severe seven mile climb from Whaley Bridge, peaking at 1 in 70 before the two mile descent at 1 in 68 into Buxton. The photograph opposite continues the story. ***J W Sutherland***

Bibbingtons Sidings, 5th March 1960. The crescendo of the exhaust from the Class 5 will have momentarily given way to the clatter of wagon wheels. However, with a heavy train still requiring assistance, Stanier 8F N0 **48326** of Widnes (8E) brings up the rear, its work almost done as it too approaches the summit of the line. 48326 was on familiar territory, having been a Buxton engine for many years. The visit by Wallace Sutherland to Dove Holes is chronicled in volume 2. The sheeted wagon typified the way in which unit loads of limestone were handled. ***J W Sutherland***

also their depot is used by several coal merchants. Just missed seeing the shunt there, it was worked by 48673.

21.6.59 (Sunday) 45689 *Ajax* took an 11 total excursion to Rhyl had started at Hazel Grove having been organised by Avro's though run as a further excursion.

30.6.59 48613 (9F-Heaton Mersey) ran through Davenport at about 9.3pm on an Up Class J goods consisting mainly of wagons of sand (perhaps from Congleton Wharf) and the small grey bulk containers, which are totally enclosed and have top and bottom doors. It was probably the train from Adswood Sidings to Buxton. The Down parcels train included a goods brake and goods vans and was hauled by 48500. It did not stop and passed there about 9.20pm.

7.7.59 42886 was on the 5.40pm train. 48744 (9A) was on the 5.50 train.

18.7.59 Visit to ***New Mills***. 49453 (9B) was on the 'shunt' service from Stockport. Because Bowater's was on holiday there was less than usual traffic and no vans to be dropped off at Disley Goods. 48106 (8B) was on the Stockport - Buxton goods which crossed 48531 (8B) on the Hooton goods here, the engine crews changing over. The loads in the Hooton comprised oil tankers, empty oil drums, coal and ore wagons and one wagon load of small bulk containers. 42778 was at the head of the train from Birkenhead (no banker).
3.8.59 Bank Holiday. 42848 (9A) + 6 was on the 8.32am departure from Davenport to London Road. (7.50am from Buxton, re-timed).

7.8.59 (Friday) A Patriot (unrebuilt) was noted banking the Birkenhead - Buxton train from Cheadle Village Junction.

26.8.59 (Wed) 42854 (9B) + 4 on the 5.40pm Manchester- Buxton train. 42848 (9A) + 5 on the 5.50pm.

27.8.59 (Thur) 42773 + 4 was on the 5.40 train 48465 + 5 was on the 5.50 train.

Note: Chronicles for the periods 1960 and 1961 appear in the corresponding locations on the line in both volumes 1 and 2.

19.8.59 (Sat) 45182 was on a 9 total (non corridor) special to Buxton Illuminations

2.9.59 (Wed) 42886 was on the 5.40pm express.

7.3.62 *Cheadle Village Jcn - Davenport Jcn.* (Weds) 42775 noted passing Davenport on the "Khyber Pass Line" at Bakery Bridge with a load of vans and class F headlamps at 5.30 pm.

17.3.62 *Dove Holes* (Sat). A sunny day, then rather murky until 10.30am. Went up to Dove Holes on the 7.51am departure from Davenport. Would be a 2-car Birmingham R C&W set which we passed in the down siding. Walked to beyond Bibbingtons.

28.4.62 (Sat) Went up to ***Whaley Bridge*** on the 7.51am from Davenport, then walked up to the rocky cutting just beyond the Chapel road underbridge, about 1 mile from the station. On the way up noted 42848 (9B) on the 'shunter'. At New Mills 42813 (9G-Gorton) headed the Birkenhead - Buxton train, with 49293 (oozing steam at every pore in typical 'D' fashion) banking; 48165 on train to Hooton.

2.6.62 (Sat) Up to ***Middlewood*** for photos in the morning on the High Level line. The first train was 76048 (9F) running towards Macclesfield with a mixed collection, mostly, I think, coal wagons at 10.20am. Another train followed it at 10.45, 48094 heading a train of fitted mineral and low sided wagons, many labelled *'Sand-return to Oakamoor'* or some such. Then at 11.53, 76048 returned with a short train of full sand wagons (from Oakamoor). At 12.20 noted 48322 on the other line, probably the Rowsley-Adswood train. In the sidings was the frame and bogies of a burnt out coach, coupled to a six wheeled end door van (Wolverton 1932) marked *'Return to Longbridge - M35367'.* At the end of the track was a coaching wagon M41670M painted red, steam piped and vacuum fitted. Plate 'LMS Wolverton 1914' - 21ft long body. Low skeleton sides, swinging down, and plates on the buffers. Perhaps a wagon for carrying road vehicles. Noted LNWR NSR and LMS chairs in sidings, some of the latter as recent as 1945.

23.6.62 (Sat) 44042 seen at ***Stockport Edgeley*** this morning on morning parcels to Buxton. Travelled from Stalybridge to Edgeley in train set M50358 + M56113. This is, or was normally, a Buxton - Millers Dale set.

21.7.62 (Sat) To ***Cheadle Village Junction*** in the morning. No trains seen to or from the Buxton line. 44284 (9G) was on a local goods from Broadheath, 45182 (26F) on a Widnes - Leeds goods, 45204 and 44687 on the two Saturdays Only trains to North Wales and 45694 on the Llandudno - Leeds train (due to cross at 11.50).

11.8.62 Next went to ***Whaley Bridge***, noting on the way that a new Up distant is being installed at Disley, about 300 yards nearer Middlewood than the present one, which is upper quadrant on an old wooden post. The Blackpool train (from Whaley Bridge) was better patronised, 45291 (9B) - running backwards but early + 44948 (24B Rose Grove) + 8 bogies. Then back to Hazel Grove where there was a fair custom for the Scarborough, etc., train. 45564 (55A-Holbeck) + 9 bogies (the end ones being articulated, ex LMS twins). 48062 (9D) was on the Birkenhead-no banker. 48278 (9D) was on the 'Shunter'. 42921 (9B) was at Hazel Grove at the same time as the Scarborough train (in the Up siding at the Woodsmoor end of the station) though why I do not know. As the train set had been in the Down siding when I went up to Whaley Bridge so no shunting had been required ?

11.8.62 There was no sign of the usual shunting engine at ***New Mills***, though I was told later that a load of vans had, required taking up from Stockport late in the morning. At ***Stockport Edgeley*** in the afternoon 44990 was noted on a Scarborough - Hazel Grove. 45101 (26A) was on 1Z47 a similar train - non-corridor to Whaley Bridge, probably from Blackpool, or perhaps Liverpool. 42343, which had been standing in the Up bay went on the front as a pilot from Edgeley.

18.9.62 (Tues) Went up to ***Buxton*** on 8.14 train from Davenport. Long rows of coaches on both Woodsmoor loop sidings - Southern Region green. 45632 (9A) at *New Mills* on the 'shunt'. 42941 was standing on the Shallcross line with a long Up train of vans. (Class E headlamps). Had passed a tank engine (class not noticed) running down bunker first just after leaving New Mills. 48159 was in Buxton Down yard. 44315 and 46430 were standing in the Up yard and I think both went out with the 9am combined Uttoxeter - Friden goods, at least I noted 44315 on the rear end. 46143 *South Staffordshire Regiment* was in the Midland station and the driver said it had brought in a...........***continued on next page***

Buxton, 28th May 1960 (Saturday). Leaving Buxton with a freight for Arpley (Warrington) is Class 8F No **48322**, a Buxton (9D) engine. This morning train would be allowed ten minutes at Bibbingtons to pin down the wagon brakes for the descent to Whaley Bridge, just under seven miles away for which thirty-seven minutes was scheduled. A thirty-two minute stop at Whaley allowed for wagon brakes, as appicable, to be 'picked-up' and also allow for the 10.15 ex-Buxton passenger train (DMU) to pass on its way to Manchester. Further allowances for the adjustment of wagon brakes was again provided for at Disley (10 mins) and Woodsmoor (10 mins). If the water stop at Cheadle Village Junction was taken into account, a journey time from Buxton approaching 2 1/2 hours would be encountered. the concrete posted signal to the left is Buxton Junction No 1 outer distant and would be the last signal of LNWR vintage to remain on the branch. The houses with the commanding view to the right are on Brown Edge Road. ***J W Sutherland***

Davenport, 7th June 1960 (Tuesday). Commuters and holiday-makers alike crowd Davenport's Down platform on a sunny spring morning for the 7.47am ex-Buxton train, due to depart at 8.26 for Manchester (arr 8.49) with only one more call (at Stockport) scheduled for the remainder of the journey. 'Crab' 2-6-0 No **42892** (9B-Stockport) had been a Speke Junction engine for many years before being transferred east. For the passenger, the last three years had seen a progressive increase in the return (to Manchester) fare at the rate if 1d per year. It now cost 1s/10d (approx 9p) for the return journey! ***J W Sutherland***

.................passenger from Manchester via Millers Dale - presumably the 6.5am from Central. A very dirty 42940 (9D) took out the 9.15am to Central, 75063 coming in at the same time with some empty stock. The following 'D's were all standing at the sheds: 49262, 49281, 49350, 49406, 43425, 49439, 49446, also 43514, 43185, and other 3F's etc., 90317 was on the Birkenhead which was banked by 44247. Went down to Barmoor Clough to take photos but the sunny weather turned to cloud and rain so didn't take many more. However, noted 48451 (9D) was on the up 'shunter'; 48275 (9D) on the 1.30 for Buxton, 44748 (9A) was on the Longsight goods; 48106 went down on a short goods at about 3.45; Not sure whether this was the new 3.30 from Buxton or the 3.40 train running early as we passed it at Whaley Bridge (it was in the station on the Up line; went down with 4 pm from Buxton. A string of vans was on the Shallcross line no doubt waiting to be taken down to Disley Goods. On the way up noted the make up of Down trains as follows: Birmingham RC&W except 8.13 train; 7.35am from Buxton, 3-car; 8.13am from Hazel Grove, 2-car Metro-Cammell; 7.50am from Buxton 5-car; 8.20am from New Mills, 3- car; 8.5am from Buxton, 3-car; 8.20am from Buxton, 3-car (express); 8.42am from Whaley Bridge, 3-car; 8.35am from Buxton, 3-car; At New Mills, found that 42848 (9B) had finished shunting and was going up to Whaley Bridge - Shallcross side with two or three wagons, to collect vans for Disley Goods. Later, at Furness Vale, 48558 (9D) came up on the 'shunter'. The returning 42848 passed through Furness Vale en-route. Around mid-day, a 4F came through on the Rowsley-Adswood and a few minutes afterwards 44760 (6G- Llandudno Junction) pulled out, and 42815 (9B) banked the train from Birkenhead. Left on the 12.51 diesel for Chapel South. Passing Whaley Bridge found the 'shunter' was waiting to follow us up. There was also a string of vans on the Shallcross line near the junction. Walked back down the track to get a photo of the 'shunter'. Forgot to mention that just as we left Furness Vale, 48519 (9D) came down with a loaded ballast train. The next 'train' was a track tamper which came down under its own power. 48465 was on the 1.30 from Buxton; 42815 (the Birkenhead banker) came down light at about 2.40; 48338 (9F) was on the goods from Longsight; 48428 was on the 3.40 from Buxton; 48437 (9B) came up on the empties passing Chapel about 4.30; Noted 48428 again at New Mills on way home (on the 4.48 departure from Chapel a 6-car train). The engine crew came up in the box with the lady signalman!

19.9.62 (Weds) Our outing to Chatsworth. 45429 was at New Mills on the 'shunter'. D53 was on the 9.15am Buxton to Manchester Central. 75067 was in the Midland Station at Buxton.

29.9.62 (Sat) 90268 (8F) was on the 'shunter'. 42892 was on the New Mills 'shunter'.

6.10.62 (Sat) 45632 ***Tonga*** was on the New Mills shunt.

1.11.62 (Thurs) 42813 was on the Birkenhead train with 44588 banking.

3.11.62 (Sat) Class 5 on New Mills 'shunt'.

Continued in Volume Two

(Above) Buxton, 17th March 1962. Making a very photographic, and no doubt audible, departure from Buxton, 8F No **48679** toils up the 1 in 66 gradient with the morning train to Hooton in the direction of its first port of call, Bibbingtons Sidings, to enable the pinning down of brakes. Once the operation has been completed, the whole train will move forward into Dove Holes Goods Loop, allowing the 9.5am ex-Buxton passenger train a free run on its thirty-eight minute journey to Manchester Piccadilly. A similar privilege was granted at Whaley Bridge for the 9.20 ex-Buxton to Piccadilly train and again at Woodsmoor (Goods Loop) for the 10.20 ex-Buxton to Piccadilly.

(Right) Assisting at the rear of the above is another Buxton engine, this time in the form of Class G2 0-8-0 No 49403. After clearing the summit at Bibbingtons Siding, she will cease her banking operation before reversing to the Up line for the gentle trip back to Buxton. Blake Edge Farm, seen in the upper picture to the right of the engine, will witness many more stirring moments.

Both; ***J W Sutherland***